Law School

Without Fear

Strategies for Success

THIRD EDITION

Helene Shapo and Marshall Shapo

FOUNDATION PRESS

2009

THOMSON REUTERS

© 1996, 2002 FOUNDATION PRESS

© 2009 By THOMSON REUTERS/FOUNDATION PRESS

    195 Broadway, 9th Floor
    New York, NY 10007
    Phone Toll Free 1–877–888–1330
    Fax (212) 367–6799
    foundation–press.com

Printed in the United States of America

ISBN 978–1–59941–419–5

 TEXT IS PRINTED ON 10% POST CONSUMER RECYCLED PAPER

For Nat and Ben

Our Children
and
Our Teachers

*

Preface

This book began when one of our children decided to go to law school. It wasn't originally planned as a book. It just grew, out of conversations between us. The subject was what we ought to tell our son about ways to overcome the toughest hurdles that confront law students. Year after year, with every new group of first year students, we see the same patterns of intellectual confusion and emotional tensions. As we talked about how to advise our own child about how to deal with both sets of problems, we began to put our thoughts into writing.

In introducing those thoughts, we want to tell you up front that at times you may feel that all you can do is to cope. You will think that the title of this book promises more than it can deliver. And in one sense you will be right. For many students, fear is part of the experience. When we were deciding on a title for this book, we asked several students for their reactions to the title we selected as well as several others. One mature and able student confessed that she was indeed fearful at the beginning and admitted, late in the spring semester, "I'm still scared."

Our message, however, is that you not only can cope with your fear and your stress, but you can overcome them. What we really try to tell you, beyond how to survive, is how to get the most out of your legal education. Besides being expensive, studying at an American law school is a privilege—and it is an opportunity.

Law professors ask a lot of questions, but they also at least suggest a lot of answers. As a famous professor once said, "Sometimes I asks 'em and sometimes I tells 'em." In this book, we mostly tell you.

How do you "tell" people how to capitalize this valuable opportunity? One of our fondest memories as parents comes from a long telephone discussion we had with one of our children in which we were making a forceful argument about how he should deal with a personal matter. He resisted everything we had to say. Finally, one of us said, wearily, "You're grown up now, a college graduate. All we can give you is our advice." Without hesitation, he responded, "Well, I value your advice."

We don't remember whether he took that piece of advice or not. We don't even remember what the specific issue was. That is not the point where this book is concerned. We hope only that after reading this book, you will value our advice.

Acknowledgments

This book has benefitted from the teaching of many people, but we must single out two. Those are our sons Nat, now a law graduate, and Ben, a research scientist. We learned from them even when they were children, we have learned more from them as adults, and they are a joy. During the final rewriting of the initial edition of this book, we were especially informed by Nat's experiences as a first year law student. Those experiences emphasized to us, even after all our years in teaching, just how much law school asks first year students to do.

The lessons of our own teachers since elementary school have enriched our understanding about how teachers impart knowledge and understanding. Our teachers when we were law students—at the University of Miami, at Harvard, at Texas and at Virginia—have focused that knowledge on the law. And our faculty colleagues—for both of us at Northwestern and for one of us at Texas and Virginia, have added immeasurably to our understanding of what makes a legal education. Our gratitude to them is itself immeasurable. We are grateful particularly to some sympathetic critics of parts of the manuscript: Larry Marshall, Linda Rubinowitz, Len Rubinowitz, and David Haddock.

We express our special thanks to our faculty assistant Michael Sobczak for his tireless work on this edition, to Derek Gundersen for his work on the second edition, and to Christy Bailey, for her labors on the first edition. We greatly appreciate the thoughtful comments of Matthew Burke and also the contributions of Ericka Johnson.

Contents

Preface		**v**
Acknowledgments		**vi**
Introduction: How to Approach Law Study		**xiii**
1	**Law: Constitutions, Legislation, and Courts**	**1**
	Overview	1
	Sources of Law	1
	1. Constitutions	1
	2. Legislatures	3
	3. Administrative Agencies	4
	4. Judicial Decisions and the Common Law	4
	The Court System	5
	1. Trial and Appellate Courts	5
	2. State and Federal Courts	6
	Jurisdiction	8
	1. Generally	8
	2. Federal Diversity Jurisdiction	10
	Different Kinds of Law	11
	1. Civil and Criminal Law	11
	2. Private Law and Public Law	12
	Private Institutions as Lawmakers; Uniform Laws	14
	1. Generally	14
	2. The Restatements	14
	3. Uniform Laws, Including the Uniform Commercial Code	15
2	**Briefing a Case**	**17**
	The Facts	18
	The Procedural Context	20
	The Issue	21
	The Holding and the Rule	23
	Applying the Rule	25
	The Reasoning for the Decision	27
	The Procedural Result	28
	Postscript	28
3	**Classes**	**29**
	The Class Itself	29
	It's the Question	31

Preparing for Class	33
Taking Notes	34
Laptops	35
Surfing	35
Commercial Outlines	37
Talk to the Professor	37

4 Precedent and How to Use It: Holding, Dicta, and Rules **39**

The Concept of Precedent	39
Holding and Dicta	41
1. Holding: Broad and Narrow Interpretations	41
2. Dicta	42
The Tension Between Broad and Narrow Rules	44
Rules and Standards	45
Stability, Room for Argument, and the Psychology of Law Study	46

5 Expanding On Procedure **49**

The Complaint	50
The Motion to Dismiss	51
The Answer	52
Motion for Summary Judgment	52
The Motion for Judgment as a Matter of Law (Motion for Directed Verdict)	54
Renewed Motion for Judgment as a Matter of Law (Motion for Judgment Notwithstanding the Verdict) (Judgment n.o.v.) (j.n.o.v.)	55
Motion for New Trial	57
The Distinction Between "Substance" and "Procedure"	57

6 Roles of Judge and Jury; Facts and Law **59**

Judges Rule on the Law	59
Juries Decide Facts	60
Distinguishing Issues of Law and Fact	60
Questions About Who Decides	61

7 Legal Reasoning **63**

Inductive Reasoning	63
Synthesizing Cases	65
Exceptions to Rules (or New Rules)	67
Applying General Rules: Deduction	68
Reasoning By Analogy	70
Distinguishing Cases	72

Alternative Arguments   73
Being Relevant   74
The Use of Hypotheticals   75

8 Interpreting Language   77
The Same Word May Mean Different Things   78
Pouring Meaning into Phrases   79
Stretching Words   80
Using Policies to Define Words and Phrases   82
Interpreting Statutes   83
    1. Read the Statute   83
    2. Plain Meaning   84
    3. Legislative History   85
    4. Ambiguous or Vague Language   86
    5. Canons of Statutory Construction   86
        Expressio Unius   87
        Ejusdem Generis   88
        Narrow Construction of Statutes in
            Derogation of the Common Law   88
        Broad Construction of Remedial Statutes   89
Illustrations   90
    Case 1   90
    Case 2   92
    Case 3   93

**9 Balancing Competing Interests and
Factors   95**
Law as Influencing Behavior   95
Balancing of Interests   97
The Concept of Factor Analysis   99

10 Policy Foundations   103
Some Basic Jurisprudential Concepts   104
    1. The Descriptive and the Normative   104
    2. Is the Law Neutral?   105
    3. Reason and Arbitrariness   106
    4. Clarity and Notice   106
    5. Predictability and Stability   107
    6. Treating Like Cases Alike   107
    7. Flexibility in the Law   108
    8. Responsiveness to Social Change   108
    9. Policies and Balancing   109
    10. The General vs. the Specific   109
    11. Different Kinds of Rationality   111
Approaches to Justice: Different Lenses   112
    1. Corrective Justice   112

2. Instrumentalism 113
3. Distributive Justice 114
Courts and Legislatures Compared 115
Concepts of Judicial Administration 117
1. Requirement That There Be a Dispute 117
2. Discouraging Frivolous and Fraudulent
Litigation 117
3. Administrative Efficiency 118
4. Promoting Settlement 119
5. Open Courts 120
Limiting the Judge's Role: Self-Restraint and
Activism 120

11 Choices Among Policies **123**
The Struggle Over the Goals of the Law 123
Justice-Oriented Concepts 124
Some Basic Economic Ideas 128
1. Scarcity, Prices and Demand; The "Free
Lunch" 128
2. Free Markets 129
3. Efficiency 131
4. Property Rights 132
5. Incentives and Disincentives 134
6. Externalities 135
7. The Moral Hazard 136
8. The Coase Theorem 137
9. Transaction Costs 138
10. Fairness, Overreaching, and Coercion 139
11. Free Riders 141
12. The Tragedy of the Commons 142
13. The Prisoner's Dilemma 143
14. Public Choice Theory 144
15. A Note on Selfishness 145
Empirical Questions 147
A Concluding Word on the Value of Argument 147

12 Remedies **149**
Legal and Equitable Remedies 149
Damages 150
Equitable Remedies and Related Categories 150
1. Injunctions 151
2. Specific Performance 152
3. Constructive Trusts 152
Alternative Dispute Resolution 153

13 Legal Writing   155

Having a Purpose and Audience In Mind   156
Organize Your Thoughts   156
Logical Flow of Ideas; Transitions;
  The Problem of Jerky Sentences   158
Active Voice   159
Nominalization: Natural Verbs as Weak Nouns 162
Short Words, Short Sentences   163
Practice, Practice, Practice   165
Citation Form   166
Just a Word on Research Techniques   167
Appendix: Common Problems in Writing That
  Can Be Fixed   168
    Subject-Verb Agreement   168
    Referents   168
    The Dangling Modifier   169
    Apostrophes   170

14 Studying and Reviewing   173

How To Study, Generally   173
The Study Group Question   174
Reviewing   175
  1. The Outline   176
  2. Illustrations of Outlines   179
    a. Battery   179
    b. Wills   180
  3. The Strategy of Reviewing   181

15 Exams   185

Two Introductory Tips and Some Preliminary
  Disclaimers   186
Key Word Outlines; Open Book Exams   187
Time Limits   188
Read the Question   188
Analysis and Application   189
Organize Your Answer   190
Answering Specific Questions Specifically and
  Providing Discussion   191
Do Not Repeat, or Invent, Facts   192
Be Relevant   193
Get to the Point   195
Some Pitfalls to Avoid   196
Summing Up   197
Sample Exam   198

**16 It's a Mind Game: Psychological Tips for
   the Study of Law**   **205**
   There Is Pressure in Law School   206
   Preserving Your Humanity   208
   Echoes of the Paper Chase: The Socratic
     Method And Feeling Put Down by the
     Professor   209
   What Does the Professor Want?   211
   The Professor Can Be Wrong   211
   The Awesome Other Student   212
   Resentment and Alienation   213
   A Conclusion   214

17   Lawyers Reflect on Law School   **217**
   General Advice on Law School   217
   A Critical Perspective   219
   Use of Socratic Method   219
   Legal Reasoning   221
   Argument   222
   Defining the Issue/Maintaining a Sense of
     Relevancy   222
   Professional Traits   223
   Personal Growth   224

Glossary   **227**

Introduction: How to Approach Law Study

The study of law is a fascinating pursuit. Along with your teachers, we welcome you to it. We are sensitive to the fact that many of our readers will be incurring substantial levels of debt to pursue a legal education. Knowing that, we want to emphasize our belief that you will find that your law school experience repays your personal effort as well as your financial expenditure. Besides being preparation for a variety of interesting careers, law study ought to be a stimulating experience. You will find downs as well as ups in the process. But we urge that when you get discouraged, you keep in mind the benefits you are seeking: not only professional preparation, but a considerable broadening of your general ability to analyze problems and a sharpening of your mind.

We have devoted more than a combined half century of our lives to the teaching of law, and in particular to the teaching of first-year law students. We have sought in writing this book to guide students as they begin the study of law. We aim to provide a framework for dealing with fundamental elements of law study that, on the basis of our experience, appear to be the ones that have proved most difficult for students to grasp. Many things we say in this book are, in one way or another, what your professors will say. In that sense, we are trying to reinforce their instruction.

Because law school involves learning both a new vocabulary and new forms of analysis, we provide what are sometimes simplified explanations of terminology, concepts, and analytical techniques. We hope these will help you to understand some foundational ideas and to go on to comprehend the more complex ideas that build upon them. We also seek, however, to help you make sense of an experience that at the beginning is frustrating for many, but should be fascinating if you approach it correctly. Thus, we set these ideas in the context of the psychological environment of law school—from which, you will see, it is difficult at times to separate the ideas and intellectual approaches of law itself. Besides focusing on the psychology of law study in an entire chapter—the last chapter of the book—we refer to it in several places throughout the book in ways that we hope will prove helpful.

Some of the ideas and techniques we identify can be learned only by constant exposure and repetition. Moreover, there is no substitute for mastering the details. We use many examples from courses found in most first-year curriculums—civil procedure, constitutional law, contracts, criminal law, property, legal writing, and torts. However, even as a reference, this book will not take the place of more detailed treatments of those subjects. We try here to do no more than give you a general framework that will aid your grasp of the law school curriculum.

We do believe that you will find it useful to consult this book for concise descriptions of ideas that recur throughout the first year of law school. Beyond that, we think that even in your exalted status as second and third year students, you occasionally will turn back to this little book as a refresher. As teachers and scholars, we hope that you will probe deeply into the concepts briefly presented here. Yet, we are mindful that sometimes students desire a highly directed catalog of the principles and ideas they are asked to learn. With that reality in mind, we have arranged the sub-headings in the book so that you may consult them quickly, perhaps sometimes even use them as checklists.

Our principal goals, however, go far beyond checklists. We are trying to present enough of an overview of law—at least the law that law schools present to their students—that when you get stuck in the trees of law school, re-reading this book may help you to see the forest. We also hope that on certain mornings during your first year of law study—mornings unpredictable in advance—you will wake up and suddenly understand what we meant when we explained something that you now have *learned.*

We want to emphasize here a point that appears in several ways later in the book. This is that studying law will teach you to ask questions and to analyze problems, but will not always provide clear answers. Many of your law school professors will not spend much time communicating clear legal rules, except to question them. The law student's lot is to live with uncertainty, and that can be unsettling. However, everyone goes through this experience. If you begin to feel troubled as you explore this new educational world, you are reacting normally.

A related observation is that there are a lot of lessons to be learned from law school that go far beyond book learning. The pressures of law school will reveal inner resources that you may not have known you had. Eventually, they will help you to put things in a more mature perspective. For many, law school will enhance a sense of community in a society where that sense is diminishing.

There are, moreover, some basic human truths that it is well to remember. Many students come to feel isolated in law school because of the pressures of time and the intellectual demands. Most first year students remark that their assignments—for classroom preparation and written work—usually take far longer than they would have imagined. If you understand that you are not alone in matters like these, it will bring at least two benefits. You will be able to reach out to others—for simple companionship as well as for academic help. But that understanding will also enable you to give help to others, which is a pretty good beginning for someone who is entering what is, after all, a helping profession.

Finally, you should not neglect your friends and your family. Try to explain to them the experience you are going through and the time pressures and emotional stresses it involves. Test out on them some of the problems that your professors put to you. Doing this even with those who are not lawyers—perhaps especially those who are not lawyers—will help them to understand your new environment. Their common sense often will help you to see approaches to legal questions you may have ignored. Moreover, you will maintain your connections to your life outside the law school environment, which will help maintain a balanced perspective about law school.

Aristotle told Alexander the Great that there is "no royal road to mathematics." There is no royal road to learning law, either. This book tries to help smooth some of the bumps.

*

1

Law: Constitutions, Legislation, and Courts

Overview

Legal philosophers spend a lot of their time trying to define "law," but most of the first year of law school consists of trying to understand some very basic practical aspects of the legal system. The principal elements of that study, which will occupy the bulk of your time, are the decisions of courts, which are an important part of our "law." But courts themselves operate in a broader framework of law, which includes constitutions and the laws enacted by legislatures—called statutes or legislation. This chapter briefly summarizes these three forms of law, as well as mentioning a fourth kind of lawmaking body, the administrative agency.

Sources of Law

1. Constitutions

Constitutions represent the fundamental law of the United States. Where the United States Constitution applies, it outranks all other laws in the country, including state constitutions, statutes passed by Congress and state legislatures, and court decisions. Within each state, the state constitution outranks laws passed by the state legislature and the decisions of the state courts.

An important practical consequence of the superiority of constitutions is that legislatures and judges must always try to insure that their statutes and decisions do not violate an applicable constitutional provision. For example, in 1938 Congress passed a law that, among other things, established a nation-wide minimum wage and barred the shipment in interstate commerce of goods made by workers paid less than that wage. Opponents of the law argued that only a state, and not Congress, had the power to impose a minimum wage because that power is not given to Congress in the Constitution. As you may remember from undergraduate political science or government classes, Congress can make law only if the Constitution grants it the power to do so. The question was whether the minimum wage law came within the constitutional power of Congress to regulate interstate commerce. The Supreme Court concluded that the law did not exceed that power.[1] If Congress had exceeded its constitutional power to regulate interstate commerce, the Court would have declared the statute unconstitutional and refused to enforce it.

The courts also test laws enacted by state and local governments for their constitutionality. A well-known example is *Brown v. Board of Education*,[2] a case consolidated from cases in four states in which the Supreme Court decided that provisions of state constitutions and statutes that required or permitted segregation of public schools by race were unconstitutional. The Court concluded that these state laws denied African–American students the equal protection of the laws in violation of the Fourteenth Amendment to the United States Constitution.

The point of both these examples is that courts sometimes must consult the "law" of the United States Constitution, or of state constitutions, to determine whether a disputed action of state or federal officials—executives, legislators, or judges—is "lawful."

---

1. United States v. Darby, 312 U.S. 100 (1941).

[This reference to the *Darby* case is a "citation," which tells you the name of the case, where to find it in a publication that reprints Supreme Court decisions, and its date. This case is reprinted in volume 312 of the United States Reports, starting at page 100. The case was decided in 1941.]

2. 347 U.S. 483 (1954).

[This case is reported at volume 347 of the United States Reports beginning on page 483. The case was decided in 1954.]

2. Legislatures

Legislatures—for our purposes, the Congress of the United States, the legislatures of the 50 states, and the legislative bodies of municipalities and counties—enact law in the form of statutes. Other names for this kind of law are "legislation" or legislative "acts." Legislation passed by city and county bodies often is called ordinances. Judicial decisions sometimes will refer to a single statute, for example, the Occupational Safety and Health Act, as "the Act." A comprehensive statute on a single broad subject may be called a "code." A familiar example, the Internal Revenue Code, is itself a substantial book.

Legislation, generally speaking, is superior to judicial decisions. This means that courts must enforce legislation even if they do not agree with its provisions, subject to their own judgment of whether it is constitutional. Legislatures may create rights that courts have not created, or expand on judicially created rights, or limit or abolish those rights.

An example of legislative limitation of judicially created rights is the enactment of statutes that impose dollar maximums on the amount of damages that people suing for personal injury can recover for pain and suffering. Legislative limitations of this sort are in turn subject to challenges as being unconstitutional. For example, injured patients who bring actions for medical malpractice might claim that a "cap," or limit, on pain and suffering damages in legislation that restricts remedies for malpractice is invalid. They would argue that the legislation violates the provisions of federal and state constitutions that forbid denial of equal protection of the laws because the medical malpractice statute treats them differently from other personal injury claimants. A court faced with such a challenge would have to interpret the equal protection clause of the state or federal constitution and decide whether, by treating medical malpractice claimants differently from other claimants, the legislative "cap" violates the right of medical malpractice claimants to equal protection. If the court decides the cap is constitutional, it must enforce it, even if the judges on the court disagree with the statute as a matter of policy—even if they find it downright distasteful.

3. Administrative Agencies

Administrative agencies are an important component of state and federal governments; they run much of the government's business, and perform a number of functions. Most agencies are part of the executive branch of government and administer the area of government for which the agency was created. Agencies also serve a type of legislative function, making law when they issue rules and regulations, for example industrial safety regulations or drug testing regulations. The Occupational Safety and Health Administration (OSHA) creates rules about subjects as specific as how high workplace guardrails must be.

Some agencies also perform quasi-judicial functions through hearing officers and administrative law judges. The judicial arm of the National Labor Relations Board, for example, will initially determine whether an employer has committed an unfair labor practice.

Agency rule-making and adjudication are subject to review by the courts. Frequently the courts decide whether a regulation is an appropriate way to implement an agency's statutory authority, or whether an administrative law judge correctly decided a dispute.

4. Judicial Decisions and the Common Law

An important feature of judicial decisionmaking in this country is that it is part of a common law system. The common law, as we use the term here, is judge-made law: the body of law that emerges from decisions by courts—principally appellate courts—in specific cases.[3] The decision of a court on a specific case not only decides that particular case, but may have consequences for later cases. The decision will exert a governing effect on other cases that present the same type of legal problem. That is, it becomes a legal precedent that courts in that system of courts must follow. Courts will then enforce this law that they have themselves made—known as the common law—just as they would enforce legislation.

In the United States, we have become so used to the concept of a common law system that we lose sight of the fact that in

---

3. The common law originated in England, and a more specific use of the term "common law" refers to a particular system of courts in England, the common law courts.

many countries only the legislature and constitutions are the sources of law. These countries have what are known as civil law systems. The courts in those nations enforce the rules of their legislative codes, but they do not create new rules. In the United States, the courts also enforce legislation, and their decisions in those cases constitute binding case law, but not common law.

Many times, courts will develop a series of decisions on a particular set of legal problems. They will extend, modify and otherwise elaborate on the principle that they established in the earlier cases in the series. This method of step-by-step development—a favorite word of law teachers that describes this method is "incremental"—is a principal feature of the common law.

The Court System

1. Trial and Appellate Courts

The United States has a well-developed, sometimes complicated, system of courts. This section provides an overview of the structure of that judicial system. We use the terms "case," "litigation," and "dispute" more or less interchangeably, just as courts and lawyers tend to use them. All these terms refer to a controversy between two or more parties that requires a court to make decisions on the facts and the law.

The usual first stop for litigants—and for most litigants, the last stop—is the trial court.[4] This court performs a lot of sorting and screening tasks. It decides, as we shall explain, whether litigants are properly before it—that is, whether it has jurisdiction.[5] In a trial, the litigants introduce evidence by examining witnesses and submitting documents. The judge, in conjunction with a jury if the case is argued to a jury, decides the case.

The next level of courts is the appellate courts, which exist principally to review the decisions of trial courts when losing parties appeal those decisions. If an appellate court decides that a trial court made an error, it will reverse that decision, often sending the case back to the trial court for further proceedings. If, however, the appellate court finds that the trial court's decision was correct, it will affirm that decision.

---

4. Some parties litigate in small claims courts, which we do not include in this discussion.

5. See pages 8–10 below.

In reviewing trial court decisions, appellate courts employ many tools. Their most characteristic function is to decide whether the trial court properly applied "the law." This law may include the common law—that is, the law developed through judicial decisions as we explained above. It may also include statutes and state or federal constitutional law, when the litigation involves those bodies of law—and it also will include judicial decisions interpreting statutes and constitutions.

Appellate courts hear the lawyers' arguments as to whether the trial court should be reversed or not and they read the transcripts and see the documents introduced at trial. They do not hear witnesses or introduce new evidence. However, appellate courts do exercise some review over the judgments that trial courts make about "facts," that is, determinations about what "happened" or "occurred" that serve as the basis for the application of the legal rules we call the "law." Generally, however, appellate courts defer to the decisions of trial judges and of juries about the facts unless the trial court or jury clearly erred. This is especially so concerning such matters as the credibility of witnesses. The theory is that the trial judge or jury actually observed the witnesses and can make better judgments about their truthfulness than can an appellate judge who is only reading a transcript.

2. State and Federal Courts

Your course work will include a substantial dose of the work of both state and federal courts. Both systems have well-defined levels of trial and appellate courts.

State court systems feature at least one level of trial courts, most of which are courts of general jurisdiction—that is, they will hear all kinds of cases. Some state systems also include specialized trial courts for such classes of cases as criminal cases and family disputes.

Most states have intermediate appellate courts. These courts serve as the first place where litigants bring appeals. Each state also has a "court of last resort," which is the highest court and which exercises supreme judicial power on matters of state law. Most states call that court their supreme court, although a few give it another designation. For example, in New York the highest court is the Court of Appeals, and the term "supreme court" refers to various lower courts. In states with intermediate appellate courts, litigants disappointed in those tribunals may be able to appeal further to the state's highest court. Frequently, the highest court in a state has substantial discretion about which cases to hear on appeal, unless a case is of a particular type that the court is required to consider, for example, a death penalty case. If the court decides to deny the appeal, which means it will not hear the case, then that litigation comes to an end. However, if federal law is involved, the losing party may appeal to a federal court.

The courts of the *federal* judicial system hear cases that involve "federal questions," that is, issues involving federal statutes and the U.S. Constitution, and cases in which the United States is a party. Federal courts also hear cases between citizens of different states—called "diversity jurisdiction," explained at page 10 of this chapter.

Federal trial courts are called district courts. Appeals from their decisions go to twelve geographically defined federal courts of appeals, known as circuit courts. These courts have numbers from 1 to 11 (for example, the United States Court of Appeals for the First Circuit, usually simply called "the First Circuit") plus the United States Court of Appeals for the District of Columbia Circuit ("the D.C. Circuit"). The highest court, of course, is the Supreme Court of the United States, which exercises appellate review of decisions of federal courts of appeals as well as of state appellate courts on federal issues. Although there are a few types of cases that the Supreme Court must review, that court generally imposes a severe limit on its jurisdiction.

The federal judicial system also includes some courts that specialize in particular subject matter, like the Tax Court, the Court of International Trade, and a court called the Federal Circuit. At least during the first year of law school, you are likely to encounter decisions of these courts very seldom.

The court system hierarchy dictates which judicial decisions other courts must follow. The lower courts in each system of courts must comply with the decisions of the higher courts in that jurisdiction. So for example, a state intermediate appellate court is "bound by" the decisions of the state's supreme court and also by its own prior decisions. These decisions are called "mandatory" or "binding" precedents. "Precedents" means the prior case law and "mandatory" and "binding" mean that the court must follow these decisions. A federal district court (the trial court) is bound by its own prior decisions, by decisions of the Circuit

Court of Appeals to which its decisions go on appeal, and by the decisions of the Supreme Court of the United States.[6] Courts defer to the authority of the courts above them in this vertical pattern. We discuss this important concept further in Chapter 4.

This is a simple verbal chart of the court system. We want to emphasize that the jump from trial to appellate court is a big leap. Courts at all levels engage in sorting and screening functions. Among other tasks, judges are trying to do two different things at once that often conflict—for example they are attempting to do justice to individual litigants, and they are trying to protect their courts' resources. Those resources become scarcer as one moves up the chain to appellate courts. For that reason, where appellate courts have discretion to choose cases to hear, they tend to be rather guarded concerning the number of cases they accept for review, and concerning the amount of review they will give the cases they do take or are required to take. As much as they are able, they will try to interest themselves in questions of "law" rather than questions of "fact," and in the classification of emerging patterns of facts that allow them to state general "rules of law."

An important practical byproduct of the effort of courts to guard their resources—at all levels—is that most parties who bring cases to court will eventually settle them. They will work out compromises, frequently expressed in money, about their disputes. Settlements save resources all around—not only the resources of the court, but also the time and money of the litigants. In a particular effort to protect judicial time, some courts require that certain cases first be heard by means other than judicial trials, known as alternative dispute resolution, such as mediation.

Jurisdiction

1. Generally

The law of jurisdiction is extremely complicated. We simply wish to make a few basic points. The simplest observation is that one does not just come to any court and get into that court. The court must have jurisdiction to hear the case.

---

6. Federal courts are also bound by a state's highest court's decisions on matters of state law if the case is heard in federal court. See the section on "diversity jurisdiction" on page 10.

For our present purposes, jurisdiction refers to the power, that is, the authority, of a court to adjudicate a dispute. A court's jurisdiction first is limited geographically to the area in which it can enforce its decisions. A state supreme court, for example, can enforce its decisions only within that state. So, for example, you will often see the expression "The courts in this jurisdiction," as in, "The courts in this jurisdiction do not enforce oral promises." That use of the term jurisdiction refers to the courts within a particular system, such as the state courts of a particular state or the federal courts of a particular circuit.

Other fundamental forms of jurisdiction are jurisdiction over the subject matter and jurisdiction over a person or thing. To establish jurisdiction over subject matter in both state and federal courts, a party generally must show that the court has power to hear and decide a controversy under an applicable constitutional provision, or statute, or a judge-made (common law) rule. In many cases it may be relatively easy to establish this subject matter jurisdiction. For example, a few lines in a complaint that identify an alleged breach of contract, a subject covered by common law and statutory rules in each state, will show the court that it has jurisdiction to hear the case. Other cases may present knotty problems as to whether there is a basis in legal rules for the court to consider the case, for example, whether a state court has jurisdiction over a case involving certain federal statutes if the statutes say nothing about state court jurisdiction.

Courts must also have personal jurisdiction over the parties to the dispute. This means that the court must be able to subject the party to the power of the court. For example, a court may not have jurisdiction over out-of-state parties—including individuals and corporations—whose links with the court in which suit is brought are arguably tenuous. Illustratively, a court may have to decide whether it has jurisdiction over a company whose allegedly defective product caused injury in that state even though the company had no office or factory there and did not actively market the product there.

Sometimes courts exert jurisdiction over things rather than persons—called "in rem" jurisdiction. This often happens when a governmental agency seizes an object, or group of objects. One of our favorite examples is the case, *United States v. 1,500 Cases More or Less, Tomato Paste*,[7] in which the government alleged

---

7. 236 F.2d 208 (7th Cir.1956). [What does this citation mean? The to-   mato paste case is reprinted in volume 236 of a reporter known as the Federal Re-

that the product was adulterated under the definitions in the Food, Drug and Cosmetic Act. Of course, the cases of tomato paste are not the operational defendant. They need a lawyer, and it will be their owner who provides one. Yet the owner is not the defendant in the eyes of the law. The outcome of the litigation will not be, for example, to send the owner of the tomato paste to jail, but it may well be to transfer title from the owner to the government, which will confiscate the adulterated products.

2. Federal Diversity Jurisdiction

An important jurisdictional power of federal courts involves cases between citizens of different states. This is known as "diversity jurisdiction"—the "diversity" being the difference in the state citizenship of the litigants—and involves a rather technical body of law that you will study in your civil procedure class. Diversity cases involve litigation over issues of state law, yet the federal courts must hear these cases because Article III of the U.S. Constitution requires that they do. There are various limitations on this jurisdiction, including dollar minimums for the value of cases, and some other refinements; there are also frequent proposals to do away with it or to limit it severely. Under present law, if the parties to a dispute come from different states, the attorneys may consider the "diversity" route into federal court. The existence of diverse citizenship does not mean that a controversy will automatically wind up in federal court—only that it may. Whether a dispute winds up in federal or state court often depends on strategic choices made by lawyers.

A significant consequence of the diversity jurisdiction, which will be an assumed part of many cases you will read in various classes, is that in diversity suits, the federal courts will apply certain state legal rules. Specifically, this is so with respect to rules of "substantive" law—for example, the rules of tort and contract—although not with respect to rules of procedure, which are governed in all federal cases by the Federal Rules of Civil Procedure.

porter, second series, starting at page 208, and the case was decided by the Court of Appeals for the Seventh Circuit in 1956. The Federal Reporter reports only cases from the United States Courts of Appeals.]

Different Kinds of Law

1. Civil and Criminal Law

A fundamental distinction between types of cases is that between civil litigation and criminal prosecutions. The parties in civil cases most frequently will both be private parties, either individuals or corporations, although sometimes one party in a civil case will be the government. The plaintiff in a civil case is the party who initiates the action by filing a complaint with the trial court. The complaint will explain the plaintiff's grievance and seek a remedy. It will ask the court to force the party complained against, called the defendant, to pay money to the plaintiff, or, in some cases, to do or stop doing something. Even if the government is a party to a civil case, it may be treated as if it were a private person. If, for example, a government driver has a traffic accident, the government as the driver's employer will be treated like any private employer and will be judged by a standard of conduct that makes it stand in the shoes of its driver.

By contrast, in a criminal case there is no plaintiff. The government always initiates the litigation; it is the prosecutor. It acts on behalf of the state or the commonwealth, or the United States. The victim of a crime obviously is a party to a criminal proceeding in a moral sense, and frequently will testify as a witness; yet the government does not sue on behalf of the victim, but rather on behalf of "the People." The victim is not a party to the prosecution.

Moreover, the government as criminal prosecutor acts with consequences that are often different in kind from normal civil litigation. A striking difference is that many crimes involve the possibility of imprisonment. It is true that some successful criminal prosecutions will lead only to money payments made to the state, commonly called "fines," rather than to a jail sentence. It is also true that some regulatory actions involve civil fines, and thus the categories are not airtight in either direction. An important point, however, is that usually there is a stigma of guilt associated with a criminal conviction, whether it leads to imprisonment or only to a fine.

This distinction explains why the term guilt is not technically appropriate for civil litigation. Of course, in ordinary conversation, we may casually use that terminology in the context of civil cases ("she was guilty of negligence"). As a matter of careful usage, however, it is probably better to reserve the idea of guilt for crime rather than for the civil wrongs called torts or for breaches of contracts. Defendants in those cases will be "liable" if they lose the litigation, but not "guilty."

It is very possible for a particular kind of conduct to render an actor vulnerable to both criminal prosecution and civil litigation. Thus, someone who physically assaults another might be prosecuted by the state as a defendant before Judge X in a criminal case for the crime of aggravated assault. And the same person might be a defendant before Judge Y in a civil suit by his victim, asking money damages for battery—a suit tried in another courtroom in the same courthouse. Accusations that O.J. Simpson killed his ex-wife and another man provide the most celebrated recent example. Simpson was acquitted of murder charges, but later faced and lost civil liability suits for "wrongful death," a tort action.

2. Private Law and Public Law

Your teachers sometimes will refer to "private law" and "public law" as relatively distinct categories. These classifications are not air-tight, but lawyers, especially academic lawyers, perceive a distinction between them.

The classic "private law" subjects for first-year students are torts, contracts, and property. These subjects encompass law that principally emerges from disputes between private individuals. The focus, typically, is on resolving a particular controversy within a set of rules evolved for the purpose of dealing with private disputes. The basis for these rules often is the common law, although there are now many statutes that supply the governing law—for example the Uniform Commercial Code applies to many contract cases.

Public law subjects typically found in the first-year curriculum are criminal law and constitutional law. Other public law topics, which invariably involve governmental bodies, are subjects like administrative law and such specialized branches of law as securities regulation and labor law. The public law subjects usually find their roots in legislation or constitutions. Court decisions in the public law area represent judicial efforts to resolve disputes about such questions as the meaning of statutes, and whether regulations promulgated by administrative agencies fit within the purpose of the statutes under which they were issued.

Courts dealing with public law issues do not start with rules that they have developed themselves—that is, common law. They begin, instead, with enacted law—which law professors sometimes call "positive law"—such as legislation and constitutions. When questions arise about the interpretation of legislation, the main issue usually is what the legislature, acting on behalf of the political community as a whole, should be taken to mean by the language in a statute. In the public law arena, courts often resort to procedural devices and to rules of statutory interpretation, discussed below,[8] which may tilt a hard-fought dispute one way or another. When courts fulfill this role, they generally are not supposed to act as the guardians of the community's political or moral views—only as interpreters.

When you study public law and statutes generally, you should keep in mind how powerfully some legislation manifests the deeply held views of the electorate. Consider legislation as technical as the Internal Revenue Code. The rates of taxation it sets, the exemptions it creates, the deductions it allows—all these represent highly political declarations of preference about such matters as the distribution of wealth in society and the desirability of particular activities. The tax rules of the Code affect individuals' incentives to create new businesses, to accumulate wealth, even to enter into marriage or buy a home.

Other kinds of legislation do not mask their social purposes at all: statutes prohibiting discrimination on the basis of race and gender, laws restricting the conduct of both employers and workers in labor disputes, legislation requiring notification of the parents of minors seeking abortions. When you deal with the rules embodied in statutes of this kind, you know you are dealing with "public law."

It has been observed that even "private law" has "public law" aspects.[9] Once courts employ notions of public policy in judging private disputes, explicitly taking into account the broader consequences of their decisions, they are importing "public" characteristics into private law. Nevertheless, most people would still maintain the broad distinction.

---

8. See Chapter 8.

9. *See, e.g.*, Leon Green, Tort Law Public Law in Disguise, 38 Tex. L. Rev. 1 (1959); 38 Tex. L. Rev. 257 (1960).

[This is a citation to two articles written by Leon Green, published in volume 38 of the Texas Law Review. The first article starts at page 1 and was published in 1959. The second article was published in 1960 and begins at page 257 of volume 38.]

All law schools publish law reviews, which are journals run by student board members.

Private Institutions as Lawmakers; Uniform Laws

1. Generally

This chapter about "the law" has devoted itself principally to rules that come from constitutions, legislatures, courts, and agencies—rules that have some sort of binding effect on people who make decisions about how to conduct their activities or who bring disputes to court.

There are, however, various private organizations that contribute to the making of legal rules—sometimes with great influence. For example, industry trade associations and other institutions publish standards to guide, or even dictate, the conduct of their members. Such organizations may articulate requirements that apply to various kinds of activities, ranging from professional behavior to standards for the design of buildings or products. Thus, a private medical or hospital organization may set standards for the behavior of medical personnel in particular situations involving hospital patients. Or an association of swimming pool manufacturers may declare that all swimming pools must display pictographs that warn of various hazards that swimmers face.

Law students will become familiar with at least two collections of rules that have exerted particular influence on judicial and legislative lawmaking. These are the Restatements of the Law and the legislative proposals of the National Commissioners on Uniform State Laws.

2. The Restatements

Some comprehensive compilations of common law legal rules that you will come across in your first year are known as Restatements of the Law, or just Restatements. The organization that publishes the Restatements is the American Law Institute (ALI), a private organization made up of approximately 3,000 lawyers, including judges, practicing lawyers, and law professors. As their names suggest, the Restatements originally sought to "restate"—that is, sum up the pre-existing common law on a given subject, as derived from the law of various jurisdictions. The goal of Restatements is to provide guides for judges when they deal with questions on which their jurisdictions have not yet ruled or concerning which they are in doubt, or rules they may want to change. A Restatement itself is not "law." It becomes binding law only if a court adopts particular sections.

The Restatements you are most likely to meet in the first year of law school are the Restatements of Torts, Contracts, and Property. All of these are multi-volume works. It would be useful to pick up one of them in the reference section of the library and skim through it.

The usual style of Restatements is to present a bold-faced rule—called the "blackletter"—that covers a recurrent pattern of situations, followed by comments and illustrations that justify and explain the rule. Thus, the sections of the Restatement of Torts that deal with the law of false imprisonment define this tort by setting out its basic elements—for example, the requirement that a plaintiff claiming false imprisonment must show that the defendant completely confined her and acted intentionally to do so. The blackletter sections also spell out various ways in which a defendant may effect a confinement, including physical barriers, threats, and other forms of duress. The illustrations provide fact-based examples that spell out the meaning of the blackletter—for example, explaining that a threat to shoot a person's child if the person leaves the room is a form of duress that effectively creates an imprisonment.

Although most Restatement rules represent consensus views about the law, some may represent choices made by members of the ALI on rather controversial matters. In this regard, it is important to understand that the force of the Restatements principally comes from their power to persuade. Since the ALI is a private organization, it has no lawmaking power. As we have noted, a Restatement section becomes binding law in a jurisdiction only if its courts adopt it. Thus, a court's acceptance of a Restatement rule on a novel question represents, at least in theory, its acceptance of a reasoning process. That is why the comments and the illustrations to Restatements are important; they help to give flesh to the bare rule of the blackletter and to convince the reader that that rule is the best one.

3. Uniform Laws, Including the Uniform Commercial Code

Another private organization, the National Commissioners on Uniform State Laws, publishes statutory codes. These codes have a different goal than the Restatements. Rather than providing a restatement of principles drawn from the common law to guide judges, uniform codes and acts seek to present comprehensive legislation for adoption by state legislatures.

The uniform law that you will encounter most regularly in your first year will probably be the Uniform Commercial Code (UCC). The UCC deals with a wide range of commercial transactions, from lending transactions involving the use of personal property for security on loans to everyday banking business. The sections you will most likely confront in the first-year Contracts course are those dealing with sales—Article 2 of the UCC. The many sections of that article provide rules on such subjects as when an offer may be considered to have lapsed, when oral agreements become contracts, and what rules should be applied when a contractual term is left open.

The hope of the drafters of uniform laws is that they will in fact be uniform: that all states will adopt them. Indeed, this is what has happened with the UCC, although some states have created exceptions to certain provisions and, with respect to a few particularly controversial subjects, the commissioners have provided state legislators a set of alternative provisions to consider for adoption.

A uniform law or code is not a law until a legislature enacts it. Despite its name, it represents a draft offer of a statute, made to legislatures by the Commissioners. Like the Restatements, it depends on its power to persuade. That persuasive force comes from the reasoning that supports the many provisions in the uniform law as well as from its comprehensiveness, and the hope that it will be truly uniform across the country. Thus, uniform laws depend in part on a political argument—that legislators who may be opposed to specific provisions in a uniform law should swallow their opposition in order to serve the greater goal of uniformity.

2

Briefing a Case

The assigned reading for most first-year courses is in what is known as a casebook. Casebooks—or, more broadly, coursebooks—are mostly compilations of reports of judicial decisions about the subject matter of the course, like torts, property and contracts. The author of the book has usually edited the cases and added notes, questions, and problems, as well as excerpts from other materials such as statutes, books, and articles.

Most teachers of first-year courses will ask you to "brief" the assigned cases, that is, to write a summary and evaluation of the judicial decisions you read for class. There is nothing mysterious about this process. It breaks down into a few categories that, with practice, will become understandable. Various instructors will use slightly different terms to label these categories. Your first rule in that regard is, follow the particular instructor's preferences. The categories we employ, however, are in fairly widespread use and should give you a starting point for briefing cases.

The process is one that is basic to lawyers' work. It requires the person doing the brief to take apart a case—to analyze its facts and the law that the court applied in a procedural context, and to explain the reasons for the decision. At a minimum, case briefs will help you prepare for class, and many first-year students use them for that purpose. Beyond that, the repeated practice of briefing will give you a feel for the legal profile of cases.

The first and perhaps most helpful advice we can give you about briefing is to read through the entire decision before you write anything, except perhaps the case name, in order to see what the case is about. Because the several segments of the case brief that we explain below are all interrelated, you also will get an early idea of what the relationships of those segments are. Another benefit of reading the entire case first is to see if there are words or phrases that you are not familiar with. In your first year of law school, you will run across many terms you don't know yet. For example, a property case may include the term "words of limitation and not of purchase." Very few students will know what that means. (In fact, many lawyers don't know what that means). If you read the case first, you will see if the court explains the term. If it doesn't, and if the notes after the case also don't explain the phrase, then go to a legal dictionary. That's what legal dictionaries are for. Look up the words you don't know before you go on to brief the case.

Another benefit of reading through the case first is learning whether more than one judge has written an opinion. One or more judges may disagree with the majority and write their own dissenting opinions. Or a judge may agree with the majority but have different reasons for his conclusion and may want to write his own opinion; this is known as a concurring opinion, because the judge concurs with the result reached by the majority. Your case brief should summarize these other opinions. Concurring and dissenting opinions may help you better understand a majority opinion and help you evaluate its reasoning. A casebook author's decision to include concurring and dissenting opinions is significant: it indicates that the author believes that those opinions have something to teach about the law.

The Facts

The first segment of a brief usually is the facts. The appellate cases that form the basis of many first-year coursebooks usually squeeze into a few paragraphs what the appellate court thinks are the relevant facts. Students who have worked in law offices know that these capsules of the "facts" sit atop what may be rooms full of documents and stacks of testimony. But for the purposes of assignments based on appellate decisions, concentrate on the facts as the appellate court sets them out. First-year students tend to lose sight of the importance of the facts of a particular case, probably because they are so busy learning rules. But cases often are won or lost on the facts.

Moreover, because an appellate court decision typically shortens and summarizes the facts, the writer of an appellate opinion will have selected those facts that she considers important, interpreted them, and—whether consciously or unconsciously—characterized them to construct a story that supports the outcome of the decision. It is often interesting and helpful to see how differently from the majority decision a dissenting judge or concurring judge narrates the facts.

The best way to learn how to summarize the facts of cases is to do it several dozen times, if not several hundred times. We will provide a few examples and hints, but perhaps the most important part of stating the facts—as it is an important requirement in the law generally—is to be relevant. The quest for relevance, as it applies here, means that after reading and re-reading a case, you identify the facts the court found important for the ruling it made about the law.

One example of facts that may differ in their relevance in particular cases concerns matters related to the personal characteristics of the parties. Thus, the age of a plaintiff suing for personal injury—even if the court mentions it—may not be at all important to the applicable law. The crucial legal questions on appeals of personal injury cases typically involve how the defendant behaved and the manner in which the plaintiff suffered injury. However, in some cases, the age of the plaintiff may be crucial. For example, some states have a doctrine (sometimes called the "child trespasser" doctrine and sometimes called "attractive nuisance") that changes the level of care that landowners owe to young visitors to their land. In a case of that sort, obviously the plaintiff's age would be relevant. The age of a plaintiff would also be relevant to a court's determination of the amount of damages; a disabled plaintiff's life expectancy is a key factor in the question of how much earnings she has lost because of an injury.

Another example of a fact that may or may not be relevant is the race of a party. To identify a party by race in an ordinary contract action, for example, is not relevant. But in a civil rights case that turned on a business establishment's refusal to serve a potential customer, the fact of race is crucial.

One practical hint for both your routine preparation and any recitation you may give in class is, don't be wooden. That is, do not just write out the "facts" by using the exact words the court used (unless there appears to be a particular reason to do that). Do the brief in your own words. This will force you to understand what the case is about. It may even impress your teacher.

The Procedural Context

The procedural framework of a case is important because the procedural context in which the court decides the case often can determine the meaning of the court's decision. Different instructors may ask for the procedural context in different ways. We give some brief explanations of main procedural checkpoints in Chapter 5.

Cases have histories when they arrive at appellate courts, and indeed even when they come to trial. Those histories are not only the human stories of the case, although that is very important. They include the legal packaging in which the case came to the court. You will be reading appellate decisions in the context of the trial court's decision, including its procedural framework. Did the case get to a jury? If it did, then the plaintiff overcame the defendant's earlier motions to dismiss the case before a trial and also probably survived other motions during the trial. You probably will not understand that kind of procedural terminology at first, but you will come to see its importance to the eventual disposition of the case.

There are a few terms that usually will signal the trial court context from which a case came to the appellate court. This list is not exhaustive, but appeals from decisions on these motions probably cover nine cases out of ten that you will read:

- The motion to dismiss (or Rule 12(b)(6) motion in federal cases) (or demurrer in some state courts) (or nonsuit)
- The motion for summary judgment (or Rule 56 motion in federal cases)

Appeals from favorable decisions on motions to dismiss or summary judgments mean that the case did not go to trial.

- Motion for judgment as a matter of law (formerly the motion for directed verdict)
- Renewed motion for judgment as a matter of law (formerly the motion for judgment notwithstanding the verdict (judgment n.o.v.) (j. n.o.v.))
- The motion for a new trial

You also will encounter the concept of appeal, and mechanisms such as the petition for a writ of certiorari and "certified questions," which, besides direct appeal, are other principal ways to get into appellate courts.

In your brief, you will have to straighten out the labels that decisions give to parties at different times in opinions. In a civil case, the plaintiff is the party who initiated the lawsuit, and the defendant is the party against whom the lawsuit was brought. Either may become the appellant, who appeals against the decision in the lower court. The appellee is the party who defends the lower court's decision on appeal.

When a defendant initially sued by a plaintiff turns around at the trial level and sues the plaintiff for something related to the occurrence on which the plaintiff sued, the defendant's suit is a counterclaim. If the original defendant brings in another defendant, claiming that the other defendant is liable in whole or in part for the injury on which the plaintiff initially sued, the original defendant is labeled a "third party plaintiff," and the added defendant is a "third party defendant."

The Issue

The issue is the point that the litigants are disputing. Different people will suggest varied ways to state an issue. We suggest that you think of an issue as a question, a *legal* question that relates to the facts of the case that the court must answer. Your statement of the issue should explain the question in one sentence understandable to someone who has not read the case.

Here is an example of an issue. Assume that the law attaches certain consequences to calling an act a battery. Assume that within a particular state the courts define battery as an unconsented act, done with the intent of bringing about a harmful or offensive contact with the person of another, that causes such a contact. Assume that Jones walks up to Smith as Smith is waiting in line, holding a tray, at a buffet at a business meeting lunch. Jones snatches the tray from Smith's hands, but does not touch Smith, and yells at him that he wasn't invited to the meeting or the lunch. Smith is humiliated. He sues Jones for a battery.

Here is one way to state the issue (which we would ordinarily not prefer): "Did Jones commit a battery when, without touching Smith, he pulled a tray from Smith's hands and insulted him?"

This question is specific to the case. It names the two parties and specifically describes what Jones did (the tray, Smith's hands, etc.) It is one sentence and written as a question. It begins by identifying the legal claim involved (a battery) and then moves to the facts, and it will help you remember what the case is about.

However, there is another way to construct the issue that also is an interrogative sentence and that identifies the claim up front and then moves to the facts. But in this version, you identify the facts more broadly than by using the specific names of the parties. For example, you could write the issue, "Does a person commit a battery when he pulls an object from another person's hands and insults him, but does not touch the other person's body?" This question also lays bare the legal problem in the case—that the defendant didn't come into contact with Smith—that the court will have to decide. Contrast these two examples of issues with the issue, "Was the defendant's action a battery?" That question is a poor one. It does not include any facts of the case and does not isolate the particular issue of contact. Moreover, identifying a party as the defendant does not help either. There is always a "the defendant," and that designation does not help solve the legal issue. Further, the actual names of parties are almost invariably irrelevant, and too specific.

You will have to decide which way to write the issue–for a case brief, the first two both are "correct." The second example, however, is written in a way that will include a broader array of facts, by using more general language, like "an object" instead of "a tray." General language creates broader descriptions. "Flower" is a more general term than "tulip." The more general language could cover the situation if Jones had pulled on a dog leash that Smith was holding while Smith walked his dog. It is important that you understand the difference between these different ways of stating the issue, and the difference between general and specific language. It is also important to understand how and when to move between the specific and the general. You will be doing that in class and in your other writing, and we will discuss this skill and its use in legal analysis in the rest of the chapter and later in the book. The ability to move from the specific to the general and back is an important skill of a lawyer.

We want to elaborate a little more on this distinction between the general and the specific. A general term refers to a group or a class of people or objects. A specific term refers to a particular member of the general group. Usually, an issue should tend towards general terms. In the battery example "a tray" is specific; "an object from another person's hands" is more general, and is a broader description of the facts because it encompasses more items than does the specific noun "tray."

To take another example, assume that a case involves a store alleged to have advertised products at a very low price when it did not have any in stock, simply to lure customers. For your case brief, you might specifically cast the issue by using the name of the defendant and what it did: "Must Payless Stores provide the product at its advertised price to a customer who did not find it in stock?" One defect of this statement of the issue is that the reader has insufficient information about its factual background. Tied in with that is the problem that this issue really does not identify the legal principle involved. It might be legally more helpful to identify the defendant more generally by its relationship to the claim, for example, as a store that advertises. Note how this statement of the issue defines it better: "Has a store that advertises a product at a particular price made an enforceable offer at that price to a customer who did not find the product in stock?" This statement has two advantages: it identifies the defendant by its relationship to the claim (a store that advertises) and it identifies the legal issue more specifically (was the ad an offer?).

It is often difficult to decide just how general or specific to be in stating an issue. That decision often depends on the purpose for which you are analyzing a case. For case briefs you may prefer to be specific. For class discussion, however, you probably will find that your teachers will move towards generalization. In class, your teachers will probe to see how far they can move the case beyond its specific details. Even so, do not write an issue that goes so far beyond the facts that you lose the relationship with the case. Be as plain as you can about what happened when you state an issue.

The Holding and the Rule

Your case brief should now progress from the question of law—the issue—to the court's answer to that question—the holding, and ultimately, the rule. Your teachers will differ about just how general a holding should be. Again your sense of this will come more easily with experience. To start you on the path of experience, we will continue with the case of Jones pulling the tray out of Smith's hands, introduced on page 21.

One rather specific way to state a court's holding in that case would be to turn around the question that is the issue and make it a declarative sentence. To answer our first example of an issue, you could write, "Jones committed a battery by pulling the tray from Smith's hands and insulting Smith." Another type of holding would answer the second example of the issue: "A person who pulls an object from another's hands in an insulting way is liable for a battery even though he did not touch the other person's body." This is a valid statement of a holding. It answers the question in terms of the facts of the case that raised the issue. It sends a signal to future possible litigants about what "the law" is concerning the consequences of indirect contact in the law of torts. This holding is fairly specific to the facts and does not bite off more facts of future cases than it can chew. It does not invite unnecessary argument by being too broad. A broader holding, a more general one, might identify a larger category. For example, it might use the phrase "an object closely connected to the person of another" instead of "an object from another's hands." The "closely connected" terminology encompasses more events than contacts with items held in someone's hand, for example, pulling on a dog leash held by the plaintiff. The most narrow holding would describe the object as a tray and repeat the defendant's insulting words.

The holding is not necessarily the same as a rule; it is not a definition of what a battery is. A holding is a statement of the court's decision in the case, in terms of the legal claim made in that case and the important facts of that case. It is the authoritative source of law from that case and it establishes a common law precedent. By comparison, a rule is a general statement of the law that may prescribe, prohibit, or permit particular conduct. A common law rule typically results from a synthesis of several decisions on the same issue. Not all the elements of a rule may be at issue in any one case. In our battery hypothetical concerning the tray, the definition of battery is the rule about what a battery is, but only the contact element of the definition of battery was at issue and would be the holding of the case.

There are at least two reasons why a court might wish to make a rule relatively broad. First, the court might want to signal attorneys dealing with cases that involve insulting contacts with things connected with others whether it would be prudent to litigate that behavior under the battery category. If those signals were clear, they would keep some cases out of court that might otherwise be litigated. Second, the court might want to indicate to people just how far they can go in venting their anger against others, at least with respect to certain legal consequences. The court's message might eventually reach beyond lawyers to the public, and thus help to keep the amount of antisocial conduct within tolerable limits.

The line between holding and rule sometimes becomes indistinct. Many of your teachers, and many judges, will use the holding for more general principles of law in order to test how the particular case may be used as a precedent for later cases. Your teachers will engage you in this process by using hypothetical questions—for example, strings of hypotheticals that involve increasingly indirect contacts. We explain this method in the next chapter. Those hypotheticals might lead you to a more general statement of the contact element, for example, "An intentional harmful or offensive act that results in an indirect contact with the body of another is a battery." This would make clear that the definition of battery does not limit itself to direct physical contacts, but also covers indirect ones. This broader definition would cover the case of someone who, while yelling vulgarities at the plaintiff, kicks a dog the plaintiff is holding on a leash. If we stated the rule in the broader way, no future defendant could argue, "I never touched the plaintiff's body and thus never directly offended his dignity in a way that justifies calling my act a battery."

A question that lies behind the formulation of a rule on battery is whether the rule advances the interests of society. A proper answer to that question would require us to determine the basic rationale for the law of battery. We briefly discuss that very important inquiry at pages 27–28 below, and give it fuller treatment later, especially in Chapters 10 and 11. That material will summarize some important tools of "policy" that help you to decide whether rules are good rules or bad rules. Our limited purpose in this section is to help you to state an operationally useful and fairly precise rule.

Applying the Rule

A court reaches its holding by applying a rule to the facts. In our *Smith v. Jones* hypothetical about the tray, the court will apply its definition of the contact element to the facts. This kind of application is at the heart of law study and of "thinking like a lawyer," and it indicates why facts are so important. In the hypothetical, those facts that the court analyzed to determine whether the plaintiff satisfied the requirements of the rule are the relevant facts.

It is useful, at least initially, to concentrate on applying rules in syllogistic fashion. For those purposes, the rule is the major premise, the facts present the minor premise, and the application of the major premise to the minor premise leads to a conclusion. The rule that the court used that is relevant to the case of the tray in the hand—the major premise—is the definition of a battery as an intentional act that directly or indirectly causes an offensive contact with the person of another. Our facts—the minor premise—present a case in which one party intentionally caused an indirect contact by touching an object held by the other person although the first person did not directly touch the body of the other. To derive its conclusion, a court applies the rule to the facts: that is, it decides that Jones indirectly committed an offensive contact on Smith when he pulled the tray.

The conclusion that Jones committed a battery on Smith is not a mechanical exercise. First the court has to decide the proper rule to apply to the question of whether the battery requirement of contact with the person of another includes indirect as well as direct contact. In our hypothetical, we assumed that issue had not arisen in that jurisdiction before. Then the court analyzes whether under these facts the plaintiff proved the requirements of a battery. So the decision required another level of definition: a contact with the person of another includes contact with an object that the other person holds. Only after this process of reasoning does the court reach its decision. It will be left for future courts, dealing with other fact situations, to decide how indirect a contact may be and still be a battery.

Another example, from property law, concerns a situation where the basic rule has already been decided, but in which there is a fact that requires a specialized application of the rule. A rule of property is that a mortgage lender (X) can foreclose on mortgaged property and takes priority over a prior mortgage lender (Y) if X had no notice of Y's loan. If Y had recorded its loan with the county clerk's office, but the clerk had misspelled the name of the owner of the mortgaged property, so that X's search of the records did not retrieve Y's loan, did X have notice of Y's mortgage loan? The court has before it a rule and the facts of a particular case. It must determine then whether under those facts X had notice of Y's loan.

The Reasoning for the Decision

An important section in the traditional case brief includes the "reasoning," or rationale for a decision. The reasoning usually appears where the court explains the outcome of the case. Even simple rules depend for their persuasive power on reasons. As we will explain further in Chapters 10 and 11, American courts, especially appellate courts, tend to reason their way to legal conclusions at least partly on the basis of policy considerations. Those chapters will elaborate a little on some of the policies to which judges commonly refer in deciding difficult cases. However, even in your initial stage of learning to brief, you will begin to understand that competing policies may underlie such simple issues as whether a deliberate act that causes humiliation but does not result in a direct contact should be held to be a battery, with the overtones of wrongdoing that term carries.

In the case of Jones and Smith, Smith might argue that to label conduct like Jones's a battery will have good social results. Smith would contend that such liability for indirect contacts would deter people from violating the same dignitary interests clearly protected by the law of battery in the case of direct contacts.

By contrast, Jones would argue that the requirement of a direct contact serves as a rough kind of guarantee that plaintiffs whose bodies are in fact directly touched are likely to suffer significant injury, and that a more flexible rule might encourage people to bring frivolous litigation based on no more than insulting words and boorish behavior. More generally, Jones would contend that society needs precise rules because they are easier for busy courts to administer than rules that lack sharply defined contours. A court's decision for either party would reflect one of these competing rationales.

Law professors will urge students to dig out the policy arguments that underlie judicial decisions. You may think, at least sometimes, that your professors push awfully far this idea of searching for the policy roots of rules, even simple rules. Indeed, our illustrative use of policy in the simple case of the tray in the hand may be somewhat exaggerated. But you should get used to this policy-based form of analysis, because it is a useful tool in many legal situations.

Let your common sense remind you: somewhere there is a reason for every rule. In some of the opinions you will read, the court may make you a gift; it may clearly state the reasons for its decision. But if it did not, your professor will push you to think about a reason—a rationale—for the rule.

The Procedural Result

A good brief should make clear the procedural result of the case. For example, the appellate court may affirm the lower court's dismissal of the case. Or it may affirm or reverse the grant of a motion for judgment as a matter of law or a motion for a new trial. Decisions on these motions have different consequences, which is why you should include them in your brief.

Postscript

We know that first-year students are strapped for time, but, if you can, read the case again after you write your brief. The more times you read a case, the more new insights you will discover.

3

Classes

Class time and class preparation will be the central focus of your time in law school, certainly of your first year in law school. Classroom teaching, especially in first-year classes, typically involves what is called the case method. The focus of this method of study is cases, mainly appellate cases, that are reproduced in your coursebook, and other cases that your professor adds to your reading.

The Class Itself

Many teachers employ a style of teaching known as the Socratic method.[1] Most students have heard rumors about what classes are like before they even arrive at law school—perhaps they have even seen a movie about it—and they already fear what they consider the dreaded Socratic method to which they will be subjected. Indeed, most teachers of first-year classes do conduct their classes in that style. Even teachers who do not use the Socratic method will usually ask questions in class, sometimes calling on particular students for responses rather than waiting for a volunteer.

The Socratic method itself is not a rigid classroom technique and has many variations. Generally, however, teachers who use it

---

1. This teaching style is named after Socrates, the Athenian philosopher who died in 399 B.C.

will ask questions designed to elicit a discussion of the cases assigned for the day's class. You will have to know various details in each case. Specifically, you should be able to discuss which facts are relevant and why, which arguments the judge accepted and why, and in general what the judge's reasoning was. The need to answer these questions is an important practical reason to be prepared for class, and the method of case briefing described in Chapter 2 will enable you to deal with those questions.

The professor will probably go on to explore the implications of a decision, often asking you a series of questions involving hypothetical situations based on the case under discussion. What students often consider the most difficult, and even irritating, part of class is that the professor will rarely answer questions or tell the student if her answer was right or wrong. Instead, in the classic version of the "method," the professor will reply to a student's answer by posing yet another hypothetical, often based on the student's response.

Students often criticize this aspect of classes as confusing, wasting time, and hiding the ball. The Socratic method has been targeted as one cause of law student stress. You may get tired of "hypos." You may say to yourself, "Why doesn't she explain this instead of making us jump through hoops?" Or as one of us heard a student say to the professor in a first-year contracts class she took as a student, "You can answer that; it's just 'yes' or 'no.' "

However, the purpose of class is not just to impart information, but to expose the uncertainties in the law, even in what appear to be pretty straightforward rules. A lot of the law is unsettled. You will see that yourself when you take a holding from a case you read for class and thought you understood when you briefed the case the night before, and you try to apply that holding—that is, you try to see how it works—in the situations that the professor poses in class. Does the holding, and the rule you have developed from it, apply to the hypothesized new case? Are there limits to the rule that the facts of the hypothetical reveal? Must you create an exception to the rule? Can you reconcile what appear to be conflicting decisions? These questions will often demonstrate that the nice clean rule you thought you had mastered has a lot of ambiguity in it.

It's the Question

What we have just said emphasizes a truth that is often difficult for students to accept: the questions are frequently more important than the answers. If you ask, "Why doesn't she give us the answer? She knows the answer. Let her give it to us," you are missing the point. Especially in the first year of law school, the law is not Einsteinian physics. However, it is not easy, either, and it is the process of formulating questions about the rules that poses the greatest challenge. Law school tends to concentrate on imparting a method for putting the questions—stating the issue, as we have discussed in Chapter 2.

Although the questions truly are often more important than the answers, where professors use the Socratic method, some students complain about what they consider its unfair aspects. A few years ago, one student sued his law school and started a hunger strike, attributing his depression and anxiety to the law school teaching method. He described the school's teaching practices as "humiliating and embarrassing."[2] Most students' reactions are not that extreme, but many students do criticize the Socratic classroom as creating a competitive environment in which they are subjected to harassing criticism. Some view it as an enterprise that rewards speed rather than depth, and the quick-witted student rather than the thoughtful one.[3]

Women students especially have criticized the Socratically-conducted classroom as intimidating and adversarial; many women view it as an environment in which they are disadvantaged because it does not suit their communication style. Although the days are gone when faculty members would never call on women, some students say that women today still are not encouraged to participate in class as much as men students are, and are not taken as seriously.

Others believe that the classroom is equally tough on everyone, male and female, and that women students adapt as well to a teacher's classroom style as do men students. However, as women have become half or more of the law school student population and more women are hired as faculty, and as minority enrollment and faculty numbers increase, a change may be

2. Former Law Student Stages Hunger Strike, Chronicle of Higher Education, Jan. 23, 1998, at A–8.

3. Emily Bernstein, Law School Women Question the Teaching, N.Y. Times, June 5, 1996, at B10.

coming. Many people think that these trends will contribute to classes becoming less abrasive and less focused on the abstract analysis often involved in the Socratic method. Classes may become more concerned with lawyers' need to communicate with their clients and to understand their clients' problems and priorities, as well as to understand the ethical implications of their work. Those who see changes coming also believe that new styles of teaching respond to the different perceptions and traditions that women and minority students bring to the classroom and the study of law.

Still others emphasize that the positive side of the Socratic method is to encourage students to construct arguments, to think through problems, and to explain their views. To gain these benefits, it is a good idea to formulate an answer to the professor's question, even if you are not called on. If a class goes well, you should hear a variety of views from your classmates and some creative thinking, and you may even participate yourself. Thinking on your feet in class prepares you to think on your feet in court, in business negotiations, at agency hearings, or wherever else you may be representing a client. And the fact is that Socratic teaching often provides a good way to learn. If you know any young children you may have discovered already that, at least sometimes, the best way to get a child to the right answer is to pose questions that lead her there rather than to tell the answer straight out. People of all ages often learn better when they have thought through a problem rather than memorized an answer.

We won't belabor the real advantages of the Socratic method. We know that for many students the most positive thing about upper-year classes is that they usually are not conducted Socratically. In any event, you may be somewhat relieved to know that for most courses, your class participation will not count towards your grade. For better or for worse, most grades are determined solely, or almost entirely, by the final examination. Thus, even if you commit a blunder in class, or what you think is a blunder, it won't affect your grade. So you may as well participate in class. You may learn more from class exchanges than from passive listening. As one of our students told us, "It is better to speak up and be wrong, than not to speak up at all."

You can also take comfort from a memory of the actress Meryl Streep concerning something that a psychiatrist told her at the Yale Drama School, which she described as "a pressure cooker . . . with everybody competing." The psychiatrist told her,

"You know what? You're going to graduate in 11 weeks and you'll never be in competition with five women again. You'll be competing with 5,000 women and it will be a relief. It will be better or worse, but it won't be this."[4]

As to class atmospherics generally, students who dislike traditional law school teaching will find some relief in the use of technology that has brought changes to the classroom. More professors now use visual presentations such as power point outlines of the day's topic. Some professors put case briefs on power point or on the blackboard, and some distribute the outlines and briefs to the class, sometimes before class by e-mail. You may have a professor who makes other use of technology, using chat rooms or other electronic visuals.

Preparing for Class

It is important that you be prepared for class. We probably cannot emphasize this enough. The more you have read the cases and have thought through them, the less intimidating the classroom experience will be. One of our students has suggested these reasons why being prepared for class is so important:

- The more you prepare, the more you will learn and understand generally, and the more you will understand what is going on in class, specifically.

- The more you understand, the more you can engage in and maybe even come to enjoy the learning experience that is law school. Law school is not only a time-consuming experience, it is also an enterprise that can consume your life. You may as well participate and enjoy it.

- As in everything else, practice can make perfect.

- Exercising the mind provides discipline and conditions your mental muscles for the work that lawyers do all their lives.[5]

To prepare for class, you should brief the cases and review them just before class. And, depending on how much time you have, and what you have figured out as your professor's classroom style and interests, there is more that you can do. If your learning style is not well suited to the classroom styles of your

---

4. Getting Personal About Yale's Drama School, N.Y. Times, Nov. 12, 2000, Arts & Leisure 7, 26.

5. This list draws heavily on comments by Matthew Burke, Northwestern Law 2003.

professors, such as Socratic discussions, but is more visually oriented, you may benefit from preplanning charts, decision trees, and other aids.

One important way in which you can spend precious time beyond case briefing is to focus on the Notes and Questions in most casebooks after each case or topic. Casebook authors usually spend a lot of time preparing notes and questions to focus on the important issues involved in the cases. Some professors go through notes and questions in detail in class; some select one or two notes to discuss; some don't refer to them at all. Unless you've decided that your professor does not use these notes at all, you should at least read through them and think about the questions.

Notes also mention other cases and articles. We know that most students will not have much time to look at these sources. But we suggest that if you do have the time in your schedule, you should do some of that outside reading to give you an idea of important concepts and issues. Extra reading may give you more of a feel for the "buzz words," the vocabulary that is used to analyze the topic. And you may want to make sure that you read articles and relevant portions of books written by your professor. You will be more prepared for class and, ultimately, you will be able to use the information to study for exams.

While we are on the topic of your casebooks, we should mention the question of new books versus second-hand ones. New law casebooks are expensive, and obviously you will save money if you buy used books. The downside of used books is that the prior owner has probably underlined the text and has written marginal notes, so that you're influenced by someone else's thought processes and conclusions when you ought to make your own original judgments. Thus, some students think that the money for new books is well spent.

Taking Notes

By the time you become a law student, you will have your own style of taking notes in class. You may find, however, that taking notes in your first-year law classes requires you to alter that style because few classes are strictly lectures and most are conducted in some version of the "Socratic" style we have been explaining.

As we teach, we have noticed that many students seem to pick up their pens or put their fingers to the keyboard only when the professor announces some clear rule. But that may be the least important time to take notes. The clear rule is readily available in the case, or in the casebook notes, or in texts or even commercial outlines. Instead of focusing only on rules, you should pay more attention to the questions your professor asks, the criticisms she offers of the decisions, and the hypotheticals she poses. It is wise to include these in your notes. If your notes sometimes look more like a series of questions than a group of rules, that's good. Learning involves asking—and trying to answer—hard questions. You also should listen to the responses of your classmates, especially those who offer ideas different from your own. If you jot down those ideas that at least at first blush sound interesting, you can evaluate them later for their strengths and weaknesses. In addition, when the professor asks questions, think about how you would answer them and about why you agree or disagree with your classmates' responses. You may want to include your silent responses in your notes.

Laptops

Most of you probably have been using a laptop in class to take notes for years now. You may not be able to conceive of the idea of not having your laptop in class. Many universities and law schools require their students to have a laptop and more schools strongly suggest that students have a laptop. So it may surprise you to learn that laptops in class have become controversial. At least one major law school has banned the use of the Internet in class, and several professors at other law schools have banned laptops. They do so for different reasons. They worry that students spend their time in class surfing, or playing video games, or sending messages to each other; and even if most students are taking notes on laptops, many professors believe the very use of laptops to do so changes the dynamics of a law school class.

Surfing

The computer makes it very easy to send messages, check the weather, play video games, and keep up with sports scores. Observers have noted large numbers of students who surf the Internet, even in classes of dynamic, charismatic professors.

Here are some arguments against surfing in class:

- Surfing unavoidably reduces your attention to what's being said in class, and your ability to reflect on class discussion.

You diminish your opportunity to gain from a most important part of law school learning.

- Surfing distracts those sitting behind and next to you. Many of them complain that the distraction diminishes their learning experience.

- Your messages distract the students to whom you are sending messages.

- Your surfing is rude to your teacher. Moreover, when she sees a silly smile on your face at an inappropriate time, she knows what's going on. She may come to associate you with a lack of attention.

- Surfing wastes your tuition money.

Although, along with many people, we believe that there are no positives associated with surfing in class, we understand that there are good reasons to use a laptop in class for taking notes. There are also some disadvantages, however.

By the time you are in law school, most of you will be dedicated to using a laptop in class. And there are advantages over handwritten notes: You may type faster than you write, your handwriting may be illegible, and it's easier to e-mail your notes to a friend who wasn't in class than to photocopy and deliver them. You can also organize your notes more easily. For example, you can add notes to an earlier topic if the professor goes back and forth among topics during one class. And, you can use the wonderful fonts and colors to organize your notes.

Many professors, however, note a change in the classroom with the advent of laptops. They feel as if they're conducting a class of stenographers, that is, of students who are intent mainly on getting down everything that is said in class rather than thinking and participating in the give and take of classroom learning. In fact, when we think back on our recent classes, we realize that many of the students who participated fully in class discussion did not use a laptop. They also did well on their exams. These students often jotted down important points during class, and then after class reviewed the class discussion and filled out their notes—on their laptops.

You may want to try that for two or three classes and see if it makes a difference.

Commercial Outlines

Many students rely on commercial outlines to prepare for class and also to study for exams. There are now several series of study aids that outline most subjects of law school courses and explain cases and concepts. Some of these publications even brief cases for you. One of the first questions some law students ask is which outlines to buy. We know some students who use them exclusively, and some of them do rather well in law school. Some students use commercial outlines only if they just don't understand what's going on in a particular class, or don't understand a particular case. Probably the most valuable published outlines are those by one of your own professors, but you won't find that very often. The best alternative when you want to clarify something that confused you in class is to talk to your professor.

In any event, it is important to understand that most faculty members have never read commercial outlines and do not use them as a source of their class preparation. Some faculty advise you that if you read the casebook, including the notes, and you come to class—and even participate—you will have everything you need for the course. We tend to think that, too, but we know that most students don't agree. And we recognize that for some classes you may need—or perceive that you need—more help than that. The professor may be opaque, the subject matter may be daunting, or you may think that everyone else is using outlines and that they will have an advantage over you. Then you may want to use an outline, but you should be sure to fit it into the professor's "take" on the class material rather than using it as your sole source of information. And we advise that even if you use commercial outlines, you create your own outlines also. As we will explain in Chapter 14, the value of an outline is in making it yourself.

Talk to the Professor

We advised above that you talk to your professor if you are confused about a particular case or issue. We think that is important; however, that's not the only reason to make an appointment to see the professor or to e-mail her. If you have questions or comments about class or you want to discuss a particular topic in the course, make an appointment and talk to your professor. It is good that the professor gets to know you. It might help in the future if you are interested in working as her research assistant, or if you may want her to write a recommendation for you. Many faculty members answer questions by e-mail, although some may not. For questions that require complicated answers, it's best to make an appointment for an office visit.

4

Precedent and How to Use It: Holding, Dicta, and Rules

The Concept of Precedent

Courts put great stock in precedent. If a court has established a rule on a subject, it ordinarily will follow that rule. The governing Latin phrase is *stare decisis*, which means to adhere to decided cases. Occasionally, a court will decide not to continue following one of its precedents and will overrule a prior decision, explicitly saying that the old decision no longer responds to social and economic realities, or perhaps even that the court was wrong the first time. Sometimes a court will implicitly overrule a prior decision, or will narrow it or create exceptions. However, when there is a clear rule in a particular jurisdiction, for example, a state or a federal appellate circuit, judges in that jurisdiction will follow it as the law. Precedent and the power to make rules for a particular jurisdiction are important concepts in our legal system.

Precedent plays an especially significant role for lower courts, because a lower court is always bound by the decisions of higher courts in that jurisdiction on that issue. For example, not only state trial courts but state intermediate appellate courts will adhere to the decisions of a state's highest court on state law issues.[1]

Besides learning about the governing power of rules within particular jurisdictions, that is, about binding precedents, you will become familiar with the concept of *persuasive authority* from other jurisdictions. If one state or federal court has not ruled on a particular question, its judges will often consult the decisions of other states or federal courts that have dealt with that issue. Thus, decisions from those other courts may be persuasive on a question, although they do not have the mandatory authority of precedent from that jurisdiction. Because your course work often treats cases and issues across jurisdictions, you may find that you lose sight of the significance of the law of a specific jurisdiction. The law school process may encourage you to look at a general body of American law, although, in actual practice, courts will require you to focus much more closely on the law of their particular jurisdictions.

Law school will expose you to differing perspectives about how courts view, and treat, cases as authorities. A rather cynical view is that judicial rulings depend on "what the judge ate for breakfast." A more sophisticated but also critical opinion suggests that judges are "result oriented"—they decide the outcome that they want to achieve on the basis of their personal philosophy, or their heart, or their gut, and then use intellectual hook or crook to achieve it.

We will not attempt here to argue with these views, which rest on some realistic insights about the human aspects of judging. However, it would be imprudent for you as a student to assume that judges do not take case law seriously, and it would be downright dangerous for you to act on that assumption when you are in practice. Moreover, depending on how cynical—or result-oriented—a particular professor is, it might not be wise for you to proceed, even in the classroom setting, on the belief that cases do not count.

---

1. One illustration of the very infrequent situation in which a lower court announces a contrary rule would be when a rule fixed by the highest court of a jurisdiction is very old, and most other jurisdictions have changed it. On a very few occasions an intermediate appellate court will change such a rule, and its decision will most likely be quickly appealed to the state's highest court for a binding determination.

Holding and Dicta

The idea of precedent is not one that courts apply mechanically. Indeed, judges possess several tools for defining the law within the framework of precedent, and these tools provide lawyers with a lot of scope for creative argument. These include the concepts of holding, dicta, rules, and standards.

1. Holding: Broad and Narrow Interpretations

We explained in Chapter Two that courts frequently must decide how broadly to cast the holding in a case. In the technical sense, the holding represents a description of how the court answered the issue. The holding is the decision in a case consisting of the rule of law applied to the particular facts. Technically, only the holding is the binding law that emerges from that case.

The challenge for future litigants and courts is to define the holdings of prior cases in the context of a new case. When it considers that new case, a court will look to precedents to determine the law that applies to the issue in that case. In that situation, the court must decide how to interpret a precedent. Later courts can restate the holding of a previous case as they interpret it. Many times a court will state the holding of the precedent broadly so that it is binding on the case at issue. The broader the statement, the more cases to which it will apply. If a court does not want to be bound by a precedent, it will describe the precedent narrowly so that it does not apply to the current case. Lawyers often call this technique "limiting the previous case to its facts."

For example, the law of gifts requires a delivery of the item being given. Suppose that in Case 1, the court held that an uncle's delivery to his niece of the key to his safe deposit box at a bank was effective to make a gift of the contents of the box. In Case 2, decided by the same court, an uncle buried gold coins in his backyard. He drew and gave to his niece a diagram showing where the coins were buried in order to make a gift of the coins to her. The court in Case 2 could interpret Case 1 as holding only that delivery of a key to a safe deposit box effects a gift of the contents of the box. However, the court could also interpret Case 1 as deciding that delivery of the means of access to an intended item of gift is sufficient delivery of the item of gift. This holding is broader and applies to the facts of Case 2 as well as of

Case 1 because in Case 2 the uncle's diagram gave his niece access to the buried coins.

Now suppose that the uncles in both Cases 1 and 2 were ill, so that the uncle in Case 1 could not get to the bank to retrieve the contents of the box and the uncle in Case 2 could not dig up the gold in the backyard for presentation to their nieces. In Case 3, however, a mother who is healthy gives her daughter the key to her office drawer, an act that the daughter claims made a gift of the stock certificates in the drawer. The court may decide that this is the same situation as the previous cases (access to the locked-up or hidden item of gift). However, by contrast, it might decide that an important fact in the prior cases was that the uncle could not retrieve the items in order to deliver them himself. If it adopted that view, the court would then add the fact of the uncles' illnesses to its interpretation of the rule that came out of Cases 1 and 2, and conclude that because the mother could personally have gotten the stock certificate for delivery, her presentation of the drawer key was not a gift to her daughter of the certificates. (The difference in relationship between the parties—uncle and niece and mother and daughter—should be irrelevant; that is, it should make no difference to the outcome.) Lawyers, and law professors, use the term synthesis to describe the process of piecing together the elements of a rule from a series of cases. The two interpretations we have presented show how they may arrange those elements in different ways.

2. Dicta

Language in a precedent case that is not necessary for its decision is not binding and is called dicta (the singular is dictum). One way to describe dicta is as pronouncements in which a court goes beyond the bounds of the kind of statement that is necessary to produce the decision that governs a particular case. Law-trained people make a rather sharp distinction between holding and dicta. Because dicta are non-authoritative statements in a court's decision, they function only as persuasive authority, and courts in future cases are free to disregard them. However, judges frequently use dicta for various reasons. For example, they may discern other legal problems on the horizon that are analogous to the one in the case before them, and they may want to send signals to lawyers and litigants about how they are likely to decide those future cases.

For an illustration of dicta, suppose that in Case 2 of the gift example, the court had said, "But, if the uncle had just told his niece to dig in the backyard and look for the coins, that would not have been a delivery of the coins for purposes of gift law." That statement would have been dictum. These were not the facts of the case.

Now suppose that a court with a strong "free speech" majority has before it a prosecution for statements that offended a particular group, such as members of a religion. The court decides that to allow prosecution for such remarks would violate the First Amendment. But a majority of the justices, feeling as strongly as they do about liberating all kinds of speech, decide that they want to send prosecutors a more general message. Their opinion declares, "The First Amendment is so broad that its prohibition on government interference with speech applies across the board to offensive and even repulsive uses of language, including not only speech that is hateful to religions, but even pornography."

The court's declaration about pornography would be dictum, for it is not necessary to decide the case at issue, which deals only with "hate speech." It represents the appellate court's effort to advise lawyers, potential litigants—and lower courts—about its views on a general set of legal issues related to free speech. Such broad statements can provide useful signals for future litigation, as well as being persuasive to the court itself in future cases. However, many lawyers would prefer that courts limit their inclinations to issue dicta and would say that judges should stick to the case at hand.

An example of a more difficult holding/dictum question would be this: The case before a court deals with a hateful anti-gay statement, and the court concludes that it would violate the First Amendment to prosecute the maker of the statement. But instead of confining itself to the issue of anti-gay declarations, the court says, "It is unconstitutional to regulate hate speech that offends any societal group—homosexuals, racial minorities and religious groups—because the First Amendment informs us that the antidote for bad speech is good speech and, in any event, more speech." This judicial statement presents a closer question than the reference to pornography discussed above, because this one deals only with hate speech, although it refers to groups other than gays. Yet, although many people would say that the reference to groups other than gays is the holding of the case, others would argue that it is only dictum and would not govern a case involving members of another group mentioned in the court's statement.

There is thus room for a serious difference of opinion on this issue of holding/dictum, and we do not have to resolve that question here. Rather, our point is simply that you should recognize that the issue exists. In the second hate speech case discussed above, the practical problem is how a court in that jurisdiction should view the broader statement, embracing several groups, when it is considering a future case involving hate speech directed against a group other than gays, for example, a racial minority. The court in the later case might say that the broader statement was the holding of the earlier case, and thus binding on its decision in the later case, or it might say that it is not bound by the broader statement in the earlier case because it was dictum. Quite possibly, the court will acknowledge that the statement was dictum, but it will agree with the substance of the statement and will rule accordingly—that is, it will not penalize the remarks at issue.

The Tension Between Broad and Narrow Rules

We have suggested that courts in particular cases often face a tension between resolving a single dispute and fashioning a broader rule of law. There are competing truths here. Courts exist to resolve disputes, individual controversies that arise between parties who are in court at particular times. But courts, especially appellate courts, also have a lawgiving—even lawmaking—function. In connection with that function, they are supposed to provide some explanation to the community about why they have decided for Smith and not for Jones. The statement of a rule contributes to that explanation. The rule tells the community the major premise from which the court derived its particularized conclusion—that is, its decision.

This technique of rulemaking helps to bring efficiency to the administration of justice. If the court states a relatively broad rule in one case, and does so effectively, it may avoid five more disputes that might otherwise come to it. This is because the rule will advise claimants' lawyers, "Don't bother—here's the rule, and it tells you that your case won't have a chance," or, it will tell defendants' attorneys, "You had better settle this one without fighting it; it's a clear loser."

There are opposing arguments, however. If a court states a rule too broadly, it will invite a lot of wrangling in the future about what it meant. It will create more need for interpretation, and resultant uncertainty, than if it stuck to a relatively narrow rule that is just enough to decide the case before it. People who take this position will emphasize the constraining idea that courts exist to resolve disputes. They will say something to this effect: "Instead of trying to set out broad rules for future disputes— which is a legislative task rather than a judicial one—judges should confine themselves to solving the problem before them. If other cases are going to arise that are analogous to the instant case (the one before the court) it will be time enough to deal with them when they come. When they do appear, the court can then formulate a concrete rule that solves them." Critics of relatively broad rules identify another disadvantage. They point out that if a court states an overly broad rule, future courts may apply the rule in ways that the first court did not intend and does not agree with.

Rules and Standards

We have been using the terms "rule" and "rules" to mean a general statement of the law that applies to a particular legal context. For example, the "rule" about battery, discussed in Chapter Two, was the definition of battery that the courts in that jurisdiction had adopted (an unconsented, intentional contact with the person of another that is harmful or offensive). This rule tells people in advance what type of activity will subject them to the claim that they committed a battery. When a specific dispute presents the issue, a court will determine whether the facts come within that rule. As we have pointed out, this inquiry is not always simple. For example, the court may have to interpret what the rule means (does "contact" mean direct bodily contact only or also indirect contact?) or whether an exception to the rule applies (did the defendant act in self-defense?).

Some general statements of the law give the court even more room for interpretation than do rules. Such statements, which may use vague or relatively general language, are often called "standards." Standards give judges more discretion to evaluate facts and determine what is important to the outcome.

Of course, there is not always a clear line between rules and standards. So, for example, in gift law, a requirement that a donor deliver an item of gift to an intended recipient would be a rule (subject to interpretation of the concept "deliver"). A standard would say that a donor must do everything possible in her situation to transfer an item to an intended recipient.

An example of a rule that is like a standard and that gives a good deal of leeway to a court is a concept used in family law, that the court must act in the best interests of the child. So, in a child custody dispute where the court must determine to which parent it will award custody, the court will evaluate the parents in terms of the child's best interests. To do that, they will look to guidelines provided by statutes or precedents, such as which parent has provided more child care, or which parent will enable the child to continue in the same school, or to have maximum contact with friends and relatives.

Stability, Room for Argument, and the Psychology of Law Study

The subjects of holding and dictum and rules and standards lead to a practical point that will trouble many students, but is one with which you should get comfortable. This is simply that law is always subject to argument. You will rarely be working with unassailable ideas. There are few clear "yes's" or "no's" in law school.

People complain that lawyers are argumentative. That is a trait that arises partly out of the nature of law. It is true, of course, that law is a stabilizing force in our society. There are thousands of rules and standards that we accept as relatively fixed to govern the way we live. But the law also is a vital and growing thing, and it deals constantly with specific facts. That means that on any legal subject that is worth discussion—which means the kinds of questions that often get presented in law school courses—there will be a lot of room for disagreement, even disagreement over what a prior decision means.

This is not welcome news to many law students, who want the security of well-defined answers. A subject that engenders constant argument introduces uncertainty into your life, and you probably will find unsettling the fact that the law is full of uncertainties. You should try to get used to this feature of law study, however. At least, you may take some comfort from the fact that all your classmates face the same uncertainties. Moreover, you should understand that this mode of operation represents practical training. Lawyers, for example, lawyers dealing with litigation or efforts to avoid litigation, always have to think about what an opponent will say, including how the opponent will interpret precedents or statutory language. Lawyers drafting a contract for a client may have to argue with the other party to include or change terms in a draft of the contract. Judges always have to consider whether other judges on their court will read language, or assess the strength of arguments, differently than they do. The more practice you get in reflexively considering possible arguments against the position you represent, the more secure you will feel with this technique.

If you are someone who does not relish argument, law school is a place to learn to tolerate it, and even to appreciate it. A story about Justice Oliver Wendell Holmes is that when he was practicing law, he would come to his office in the morning and tell a junior associate in the firm, "Mr. Evans, I am ready to contradict any statement you will make."[2] That attitude may not endear you to others, but it does sharpen your mind.

It may be helpful to conclude with a point of personal psychology. The argumentative style of law school may spill over into your personal life. You could find yourself trying to score adversary points with a non-lawyer spouse, roommate, or parent. After a while, you will understand, consciously, that this is just part of lawyers' play. It would be useful if you become aware of this tendency early. You might even want to show this section to your spouse, or friend, or parent, to help him or her understand.

2. Louis Menard, Bet-Tabilitarianism, Book Review, New Republic, 47, 48 (Nov. 11, 1996).

*

5

Expanding on Procedure

This chapter presents a brief overview of the procedural framework that courts apply to civil disputes—the system of "civil procedure." Most law schools will introduce you to this subject in your first year, primarily through the Federal Rules of Civil Procedure, a comprehensive code that embodies the basic principles of the subject. Besides governing procedure in all federal litigation, the Federal Rules provide a nice model for classroom discussion of basic procedural principles. Each state also has its own set of rules—some of which follow the Federal Rules—that govern procedure in civil disputes. Some instructors may employ these state procedural codes in their classes. This chapter, using terminology that is fairly basic to both federal and state procedural systems, approaches the subject primarily through the motions that parties most often make at crucial stages of litigation.

When you read a case and brief it, it usually is important to note its procedural history, often called the procedural posture or procedural context. You should specify, for example, any motion on which the case was decided. It may be difficult at first to understand the procedural context of a case and why it is important. But, the procedural context frames the questions the trial judge must decide and, if that decision is appealed, frames the issues to the appellate court.

The Complaint

Civil litigation usually begins when the plaintiff (or claimant) files a document called a complaint. The complaint must announce the jurisdictional basis for the court to take the case and identify the plaintiff's grievance. There is theoretical dispute, and there are differences among jurisdictions, about just how specific the complaint must be. Subject to the requirement that in some cases the plaintiff must swear to certain kinds of material, an important controversy turns on whether the complaint must be quite precise about the facts on which the plaintiff is relying (often called "fact" or "code" pleading) or whether it may allege just enough to put the defendant on notice of what the plaintiff will later try to prove (often called "notice" pleading). This dispute involves policy issues concerning both the fairness and the economics of the litigation process. On the one hand, on the plaintiff's initial trip to the courtroom, how far do we want to push her into the business of specifying facts, especially when critical facts may be within the control of the defendant? On the other hand, is it fair to the defendant to allow a relatively vague complaint that will force him at an early stage to expend resources to defend against a somewhat unspecified grievance?

Whether a jurisdiction requires fact or notice pleading, complaints offer allegations, not proof. The court considers a complaint on the assumption that the plaintiff will be able to prove what she alleges, but the complaint itself consists only of assertions.

At the least, the complaint should disclose a theory of liability or other basis in law for the lawsuit. To borrow an example from Chapter 2, a plaintiff might contend that someone committed a battery on him by pulling a tray out of his hand and insulting him. One way to present that theory would be simply to allege the fact that the defendant yanked the tray away and specify what the defendant said. It is helpful, however—and sometimes necessary—to specify a particular legal doctrine: in this case, that of battery. This would frame the theory that the defendant acted intentionally to bring about a harmful or offensive contact. The issue of whether it is a battery for someone to make contact with an object closely connected to the plaintiff, rather than making direct contact with the plaintiff's body, would present a question of law for the court. That issue could be resolved on one of the procedural motions discussed below.

The Motion to Dismiss

The first major checkpoint after the filing of a complaint appears with the defendant's opportunity to file a motion to dismiss; a synonym, still used in some states, is a demurrer. In federal court this motion is often identified as a Rule 12(b)(6) motion. The motion to dismiss is just what its name says. The defendant asks the court to dismiss the plaintiff's complaint—to say that the lawsuit is at an end because the complaint is legally deficient. The motion to dismiss is a way of testing complaints to see if they have legal merit. A decision to grant a motion to dismiss means that the complaint simply cannot succeed even if the plaintiff proves everything she says she can prove.

Initially, the theory behind this motion is hard for many students to grasp. You may have to wrestle with a substantial number of cases before the concept begins to take hold. An aspect of the motion to dismiss that puzzles many students is that the motion allows the court to assume, for the purposes of argument, that the plaintiff can prove all the facts that she alleges in her complaint. Given that assumption, the motion to dismiss asks, "So what?" In essence, the defendant says to the plaintiff, "Even if you can prove all your allegations, there is no legal basis to support your claim."

The motion to dismiss, then, challenges the plaintiff to show that there is law to support the theory of her complaint. It thus presents a "question of law." If the plaintiff cannot invoke a legal rule that supports her action, the court will dismiss the complaint and the suit will end there unless the plaintiff appeals.

Let us now return to our hypothetical case about the tray. The definition of the tort of battery requires the plaintiff to show that the defendant intentionally committed a harmful or offensive touching "with the person of another." In our hypothetical, the plaintiff alleged that the defendant intentionally and offensively touched a tray he was carrying, but did not claim that the defendant touched his body. Since the traditional definition of battery requires a contact with the person of another, the defendant would move to dismiss, and the court would have to decide whether the defendant's contact with a tray held by the plaintiff falls within that definition. Some courts would dismiss the case, reasoning that as a matter of law—the law of battery—there was no battery because the defendant did not make contact with the body of the plaintiff. The plaintiff could then appeal this decision on the motion to dismiss. Other courts would deny the motion, reasoning that contact with an object closely connected with someone falls within the practical meaning of the phrase "with the person of another." A court that ruled that way would then let the case continue. We make two points here: (1) a motion to dismiss requires the court to decide whether on assumed facts, there is a legal rule on which the plaintiff may rely; (2) different courts may respond in opposite ways to questions of law.

This relatively simple illustration highlights the distinction between allegations and proof. If a court decided that for the purposes of the law of battery, nastily touching the tray would be enough like touching the plaintiff's body to be a contact with "the person of another," then there might be a dispute about whether the defendant offensively touched the tray. If there was such a controversy, it would present a question of fact for the judge or the jury to decide. But at the motion to dismiss stage, the court does not concern itself with the factual truth of the plaintiff's allegations. Indeed, if the court denies the defendant's motion to dismiss, it does not decide at that point that the defendant is, or is not, liable to the plaintiff. Making the assumption that the plaintiff's allegations are true only for purposes of the motion, the court considers only whether there is a rule of law that would support recovery if the plaintiff proves those allegations at trial.

The Answer

If the defendant does not move to dismiss, or, if the motion to dismiss is unsuccessful, the defendant must file an answer to the complaint. This pleading may take several forms. The defendant may deny the plaintiff's allegations, or may allege facts that would refute the facts pleaded by the plaintiff. The focus of the answer is on the facts alleged by the plaintiff, rather than the legal theory presented in the complaint.

Motion for Summary Judgment

As litigation progresses, the parties will be collecting information and evidence about the case, through what is called the "discovery" process. They may, for example, collect information through depositions, which are oral examinations of parties or witnesses under oath, and interrogatories, which are questions propounded by counsel in writing to the other party.

The next principal checkpoint in litigation is the motion for summary judgment. Either party may make this motion. A party who moves for summary judgment asks the court to decide the case without a trial. She contends that she is entitled to judgment as a matter of law and that no material facts are in dispute. So summary judgment requires the party making the motion to present a combination of law and facts, but those facts will not include testimony by live witnesses at trial who are subject to cross-examination. Rather, summary judgment facts will be limited, typically, to documentary evidence, such as depositions or interrogatories. It also would include affidavits—sworn, written statements—of people who might later testify at a trial if one is held, as well as such documents as contracts or property deeds.

The party seeking summary judgment would argue that, given the applicable legal rule and the undisputed facts exhibited by the documents, a reasonable court would be compelled to rule in its favor. The effect of a summary judgment is to dispose of a case without a trial. For the court to hold that way, there must be a rule that is capable of concrete application to documentary evidence, although the rule may be a rather general one. Moreover, the fact evidence presented by the maker of the motion for summary judgment must be specific and convincing enough to persuade the court that a trial would add no facts necessary for decision. A court may grant summary judgment only if there is no dispute about any material facts—those essential to the determination of the legal issue. It is important to understand that the court cannot resolve disputes about facts and cannot make judgments about the credibility of witnesses at the summary judgment stage.

An example of summary judgment procedure would be a case in which a plaintiff claimed that a drug caused injury to her, but offered no expert testimony on causation. The defendant, by contrast, presented the affidavits of five qualified scientists who declared that two dozen studies on the clinical effects of the drug had demonstrated no statistical association between use of the drug and the kind of injury the plaintiff suffered. One applicable rule of law is a rule that a plaintiff in a personal injury case must show that it is more probable than not that the defendant's conduct or product caused the plaintiff's injury. Since all of the evidence before the court indicated that the probabilities were that the product at issue did not cause that injury, the court presumably would grant summary judgment for the defendant. The reason would be that under the law—that is, the requirement that personal injury plaintiffs show a probability of causation—the defendant's uncontradicted factual evidence that there was no such probability requires the conclusion that there is no reasonable basis to hold for the plaintiff. By contrast, if the parties' documents included conflicting evidence on causation, then the court would deny the motion and require a trial on the facts.

The Motion for Judgment as a Matter of Law (Motion for Directed Verdict)

If a case goes to trial, after the presentation of evidence either party may make what historically has been called a motion for directed verdict. Under a 1991 amendment to Rule 50(a) of the Federal Rules of Civil Procedure, this motion is now called a motion for judgment as a matter of law. That terminology now governs all federal court decisions, although many states still preserve the "directed verdict" label, as did the pre–1991 federal cases. The defendant typically initially makes this motion after the plaintiff presents his evidence, and the plaintiff typically makes this motion at the close of all the evidence.

There is a costly jump between the stage of the pre-trial motions to dismiss and for summary judgment, on the one hand, and the motion for judgment as a matter of law on the other hand. The jump occurs because in the interim a trial has begun, an event that involves a steep rise in expense. The judge must spend time presiding over the trial, at the cost of dealing with other matters on the court calendar. The trial ties up other officials, jurors if there is a jury trial, and a courtroom. In addition to those expenses borne by society, the costs to parties themselves will also escalate, with attorneys' fees being a substantial part of the toll.

Another important point is that a trial involves witnesses. It goes beyond not only the motion to dismiss, which involves arguments only about law, but also beyond the summary judgment stage, where the court considers documents along with the law. When there are live witnesses, the judge and the jury must both consider the demeanor of witnesses and make judgments about their credibility. In addition, they must weigh for its persuasiveness the testimony of witnesses who often will be in open conflict, including conflict about how an event occurred.

The motion for judgment as a matter of law represents an effort by the maker of the motion to persuade the court that in light of the applicable law and the facts that have been developed by the time the motion is offered, the party seeking the judgment *must* win. The theory is that given the facts presented at trial that are most favorable to the party who did not make the motion (the "nonmoving party"), that party could not succeed under the law. This is analogous to the motion to dismiss in this sense: The party making the motion for judgment as a matter of law in effect tells the court that she is willing to concede, for the sake of argument, the facts that the other party claims to have proved. Even so, the moving party insists, what the nonmoving party proved is not enough to make a case under the law. We have said this several different ways in order to give you a variety of opportunities to understand the function of this motion. However, the only way you will truly grasp the point is to read a lot of cases in which that motion is crucial.

Here is an exaggerated example involving an automobile accident. Cars driven by Mr. A and Ms. B collide. Mr. A suffers injuries and sues Ms. B for negligence. Mr. A cannot recall the accident. Ms. B and three eyewitnesses testify that the light was green in Ms. B's favor and two other eyewitnesses testify that the light was red against Mr. A. Ms. B moves for judgment as a matter of law. Given a legal rule that running a red light is a form of negligence that will bar recovery for injuries by a driver who does so, the court would grant Ms. B's motion. In the light of the evidence, as well as the legal rule, no reasonable person could find in favor of Mr. A, the nonmoving party.

Renewed Motion for Judgment as a Matter of Law (Motion for Judgment Notwithstanding the Verdict) (Judgment n.o.v.) (j.n.o.v.)

The motions we have discussed to this point occur either at the preliminary stages of litigation or during the trial. After a trial is over and the fact finder reaches a verdict, the losing party usually will make two motions. The first is what historically has been called the motion for judgment notwithstanding the verdict (judgment n.o.v. or just j.n.o.v.).[1] Rule 50(b) of the Federal Rules of Civil Procedure now calls this post-trial motion a renewed motion for judgment as a matter of law. For convenience, we refer to it as a renewed motion. We discuss the second motion, the motion for new trial, in the next section.

In making the renewed motion, the losing party in effect offers the court an opportunity to correct what the losing party perceives as a misjudgment during the trial. Your procedure teacher will discuss many technical refinements concerning this motion, but a very simplified way to look at it is to view it like an after-trial repetition of the motion for judgment as a matter of law. In a renewed motion, the losing party often will in effect be arguing to the trial judge that the judge made a mistake in not granting a motion for judgment as a matter of law during the trial. The maker of the renewed motion—who at the moment has lost the trial judgment—contends that under the law, and the best version of the facts from the prevailing party's point of view, the trial judgment was wrong and that indeed no reasonable person could have held for the prevailing party. "Please reconsider what you did on the prior motion now that you have the hindsight of the entire trial—and perhaps a less hurried look at the law." That is what the maker of a renewed motion respectfully tells the judge.

Let us briefly tie together the last several sections. When a court grants any of the motions discussed immediately above— (1) to dismiss (2) for summary judgment (3) for judgment as a matter of law or (4) the renewed motion for judgment as a matter of law—it is saying that reasonable persons could not disagree about the outcome. In the case of the motion to dismiss, it makes its ruling entirely on the law. In the case of the motion for summary judgment, it considers both law and the facts in documentary evidence. Finally, in granting either the motion for judgment as a matter of law or the renewed motion, it takes into account both the law and the facts as they have been developed in a trial. In each instance, a court that grants one of these motions concludes that the nonmoving party has no case under the law.

---

1. J.n.o.v. is an abbreviation for "judgment *non obstante veredicto*," the last three words being the Latin for "notwithstanding the verdict."

Motion for New Trial

The motion for a new trial represents the other major opportunity for the losing party to convince the court to reverse the results of a trial. This is a catch-all motion that asks the court to declare that there was some kind of legal error in the trial.

One frequent reason for seeking a new trial is that the court made an erroneous statement of law in its instructions to the jury. Suppose, for example, that the law of a state requires that the prosecution in a case for manslaughter prove that the defendant was guilty of "gross carelessness." A jury convicts a defendant after the judge gives instructions saying that he could be found guilty if he acted "negligently or carelessly." Since negligence is not as difficult to prove as gross negligence, the defendant could move for a new trial on the ground that the instruction misstated the law, and an appellate court would reverse the conviction if there was no proof that the defendant acted in a grossly negligent way or was indifferent to the consequences of his actions.

Another reason for seeking a new trial relates to the manner in which the trial was held. One example would be a personal injury case with high emotional content in the county where the injury occurred and the trial was held. The defendant claims that he could not get a fair trial in that county. In ruling on a motion for a new trial, the court would have to decide whether the psychological environment of the proceedings rendered the trial unfair.

A party may also move for a new trial on the grounds that the court erred in a ruling on the evidence. For example, a losing party might claim that the court admitted the testimony of an unqualified witness. Or, by contrast, that party might argue that the court improperly decided that a witness was unqualified when it should have allowed that person to testify. In that case, the losing party would contend that the evidence that was excluded would have made a difference in her favor.

The Distinction Between "Substance" and "Procedure"

It is useful, in this overview of procedure, to mention a distinction that courts routinely make between "substantive" and "procedural" rules. For simplifying purposes, we might think of procedure as a series of gateways and roads, through and on which litigants travel through the courts. By contrast, substantive rules would be measuring rods to guide the actual resolution of disputes. One place where the difference is especially important is federal court litigation involving diversity of citizenship. In diversity cases, the federal court must apply state substantive law (for example, the law of contracts), but must conduct its proceedings according to the Federal Rules of Civil Procedure.

In practice, the distinction is not always easy. Consider, for example, the matter of statutes of limitations. Every state has this type of legislation that sets time limits for the filing of lawsuits, usually attaching a specific time period to particular classes of litigation. For example, a contracts statute of limitations may impose a four-year limit on suits for breach of contract, measured from the time of the breach.

For various reasons, the question sometimes will arise whether a statute of limitations is procedural or substantive. Is it clear to you what the answer is? Some people argue that because the statute performs essentially a gatekeeping function for the remedial power of courts, it is procedural. Others would say that because a statute of limitations keeps someone from enforcing a legal right, it is substantive. We do not propose to settle the argument, about which you will learn in your civil procedure class—only to alert you to the distinction between substantive and procedural rules, which will confront you in many legal contexts.

6

Roles of Judge and Jury; Facts and Law

Our outline of main topics in procedure leads directly to two related subjects: the way the legal system divides litigation tasks between judges and juries, and the distinction between questions of "fact" and questions of "law." As is so with most important legal topics, most students will fully grasp these ideas only after exposure to many cases.

Judges Rule on the Law

A fundamental point is that judges, not juries, rule on the law. This makes good sense. Judges have legal educations. They, or their clerks, know how to use a law library. To take just one example, if the question arises as to whether a particular crime requires proof that the defendant had a purpose to injure the victim or whether the prosecution can succeed by showing only that the defendant acted recklessly in injuring the victim, it is the judge who must decide the question. This is a question of law, to be answered by professionals consulting statutes or judicial decisions, or deciding the question for the first time. It is not an issue for jury determination.

Juries Decide Facts

A second fundamental principle is that jurors, where there is a jury, decide facts. When a trial is to a judge alone without a jury (a "bench trial"), the judge acts as both a "fact finder" (often called the "trier of fact") and rules on the law. Sometimes the question of fact is a simple one. Did A hit B? Did C drive through the intersection while the light was red? Sometimes it is more subtle: Did A purposely hit B? With reference to any questions of fact, even relatively subtle ones, the practical premise is that the jury is making a decision, based on the evidence at the trial, with respect to what happened or what exists. That determination, it should be noted, does not necessarily dispose of the facts; jury determinations of fact are subject to judicial review. Although courts usually will not overturn a jury's findings, a court may decide, on combing through the evidence, that a jury could not reasonably have found the facts as it did.[1]

Distinguishing Issues of Law and Fact

Sometimes one has to work at telling the difference between a question of fact and one of law. One of us understood the distinction a little better during a ride on a state highway lined with signs warning about statutes that impose fines for littering. She wondered whether she would be guilty of littering if she threw out the car window the core of the apple she had just finished eating. Is an apple core "litter" if it is biodegradable and is nourishing to the grass on the shoulder? The question of who threw the core out the window would be a question of fact. The question of whether an apple core is litter is a question of law. The judge must use her professional training in statutory interpretation to analyze the term "litter" to decide whether that term includes biodegradable objects.

(Does this incident give you an idea of how you will start thinking once you're in law school? A former student once said that he had seen eleven different legal issues when he looked out the bus window coming to the law school.)

---

1. As we discussed in Chapter 5, a court that decides to grant a renewed mo-   tion for judgment as a matter of law would be making exactly this determination.

Questions About Who Decides

When a judge reviews a jury's verdict on the facts, she measures that verdict against a relatively objective standard—that of what a "reasonable person" could conclude given the facts submitted in evidence—concerning events as they took place or a state of the world that can be observed or verified.[2] Because of the difficulty in establishing objective tests for events where there is conflicting evidence, the question of what a "reasonable person" could conclude is often open to dispute. Let us assume that the issue is whether A had a purpose to hit B, and there are differing and believable accounts about A's relationship to B or possible motive for hitting B. In that case, we are no longer in territory where we can ask, with relative certainty, whether the light was red.

As courts tend to classify these issues, we are still in an area where judges ordinarily leave the question to the jury. Indeed, juries often decide on things that cannot be measured as well as things that can objectively be verified. That happens frequently in cases involving suits for allegedly negligent conduct. A judge will ask a jury whether a defendant acted "unreasonably" in not clearing his walk of ice and snow. Purists might desire a quantitative standard for such questions—rules like, one must clear snow down to the bare sidewalk no more than two hours after the end of a snowfall, or one must use so many tablespoons of salt on so many square feet of ice. But common sense tells us that, in a lot of cases of that sort, there is no numerical test. Despite the lack of a scientific gauge, courts often say that this kind of issue presents a question of fact for the jury about whether the defendant behaved reasonably.

Still, there will come a time when a court will say that a jury could not reasonably have reached the decision it did in deciding a question of fact, and will reverse the jury's verdict for that reason. Let us say that, in a busy supermarket, a customer reaching for something on a shelf knocks over a bottle of cooking oil that breaks and spills. The next person coming up the aisle slips on the oil within the next minute and a half. In a suit by the person who slipped, a sympathetic jury might say that the market was "unreasonable" in not cleaning up the oil and give a verdict

2. Students with training in such subjects as philosophy will recognize the over-simplified character of this definition, but we believe it will be of practical help.

for the plaintiff on the ground that the store was negligent. But a judge might grant a renewed motion for judgment as a matter of law to the store on the basis that it would be unreasonable to require anyone to clean up a spill of liquid in a supermarket aisle within 90 seconds.

One way to ease the tensions created by sharp distinctions between law and fact is to speak of "mixed questions of law and fact." Some of your teachers will take you through the complexities of these concepts, and you will learn to deal with these ideas reflexively after you read a lot of cases. For now, it is worth underlining a few simplified ideas: judges rule on the law, juries (or judges acting as fact finders) find facts, and sometimes judges control "unreasonable" jury verdicts by saying that, under the law, no one reasonably could have found the facts the way the jury did.

7

Legal Reasoning

This chapter discusses several types of thought processes typical of the work of law students, and indeed of lawyers. Some of these logical processes will be familiar to you from your previous academic work as well as from your prior experiences in life. Some of them were mentioned in earlier chapters, and are further explained here.

Inductive Reasoning

Lawyers engage in reasoning patterns that are sometimes inductive—that is, from the particular to the general—and sometimes deductive—working from the general to the particular—and they go back and forth between these patterns.

Inductive reasoning, which is a fair amount of the thinking that lawyers do, consists of reasoning from a chain of particular cases to a general rule. Assume that over time, the courts of one state decide a series of three cases in which one person tells a second person that the first person is willing to pay a named sum of money for a certain kind of activity or accomplishment. It might be mowing the first person's lawn, or giving information that leads to the apprehension of a criminal, or shooting a hole-in-one in golf. In each of these cases, a third person who did not previously hear about the first person's willingness to pay for the designated accomplishment actually achieves that result. In the first of these cases, the third person mows the first person's lawn;

in the second case, the third person provides information that helps catch a robber; in the third case, the third person shoots a hole-in-one. In each case, the third person hears later about the first person's offer, and asks that the first person pay for what he has done. In each case, the first person rebuffs the request for payment and the third person brings a contract lawsuit. The courts reject the third person's suit for the named sum in each of the three cases. Although it does not articulate a crisp rule that guides its decisions in the first two cases, and it describes their holdings very narrowly, by the time it decides the third case, the court begins to perceive a general rule that governs all three cases. In rejecting the claim of the person who shot the hole-in-one, it articulates that rule as being that no one may recover from another for performance of an act that the other requested if the person did not know of the request before performance.

This kind of development of a legal rule represents a form of induction—using several specific holdings to derive a more general rule. Professors may ask you to do this in class—that is, to formulate a rule from the assigned case and the hypos that the professors pose. This is often what happens in Socratic teaching.

You may discern that besides being a technique of legal reasoning, this is one way that people learn and run their lives generally. People learn by creating categories of information. They accumulate a group of specific experiences, and they generalize from them to fashion standards for guiding their responses to new situations.

This inductive mode of thought also captures an important feature of what many lawyers think of as the genius of the common law—that is, judge-made law. The common law proceeds by increments, building precedent on precedent. It then establishes general rules and, as new cases arise, broadens or narrows those rules or creates exceptions to them. In our basic example, the court synthesized three cases; it put them together to formulate the rule that governed them.

The conclusions you reach by inductive reasoning are not necessarily true, or valid in the sense used in formal logic. The cases you use as evidence to support your conclusion (your general rule) don't necessarily compel that conclusion. Consider the examples in Chapter 4, at pages 41–42, about delivery of a key to a safe deposit box and of a map of buried gold. In that chapter, we synthesized a rule from the two cases that delivery of the means of access to property is effective delivery for purposes of making a gift of that property if the donor (the person who gives the gift) is not able to gain access to the property himself. We also said there that the relationship between the donor and the donee (the recipient) as uncle and nephew, or mother and daughter, was not relevant to the rule, although the fact that the donor was ill and could not retrieve the property himself was relevant. We made these conclusions based on our judgment about the facts in these cases and the general principles pertinent to that area of the law. But those judgments may not be reliable statements of the law because they were based on only two cases,[1] and decisions in later cases may show that they are not reliable.

Induction is a matter of probabilities, not certainty. We were saying that in our judgment it is very likely that the relationship between the parties was not relevant to the rule we formulated, but that the donor's physical ability, or lack of ability, to retrieve the property was relevant. This was our personal forecast, based on inductive reasoning from precedent and our knowledge of the reason for the delivery requirement. However, by contrast with what is only our prediction of probabilities, when a court in a jurisdiction arrives at the same conclusion, it is the law, and if the court is the highest court, it is a mandatory precedent. So, assume that a state supreme court concludes that delivery of the means of access to property is effective delivery if the donor is ill and cannot retrieve the property, and does not refer to the relationship between donor and donee as relevant. Then the court has announced a rule that is certain for purposes of the law of that jurisdiction, subject to defining "means of access," until the court overrules that rule or qualifies it at some later date. That rule will then be applied deductively (see pages 68–70 below).

Synthesizing Cases

The ability to synthesize cases is an important tool in your kit of legal skills. Legal synthesis involves more than one precedent, and sometimes many. When you synthesize cases, you seek to put together two or more precedents involving a fairly specific topic. Typically, these decisions will not have announced really distinct rules, or perhaps the rules they do articulate are so

---

1. In logic, this can be the fallacy of hasty generalizations, that is, creating a rule based on an insufficient number of examples.

narrow that they cover only the case that was then before the court. The synthesizer will seek to use those precedents to establish a new, relatively comprehensive rule that embraces the prior cases as well as the case at issue.

An example comes from the subject of torts. Over a period of years, courts began to impose liability on people who had mishandled dead bodies, in suits brought by relatives of the dead person. In apparently very separate developments, courts also began to impose liability on bill collectors for deliberately harassing behavior, in suits by vexed debtors. Finally, in a third group of seemingly unrelated cases, some courts began to give recovery to persons who complained of what today would be called sexual harassment, although that term was not initially used.

A leading torts scholar synthesized these lines of cases by finding certain common threads among them. He saw those threads as including three specific elements: (1) the defendant had behaved intentionally (2) to cause the plaintiff severe emotional distress (3) and the defendant's conduct was so reprehensible—"outrageous"—as to be an offense against decency. He brought together this synthesis of seemingly unlike cases under the heading of a new tort action, the doctrine now called "intentional infliction of emotional distress."[2]

Besides synthesizing cases to form a rule that defines a claim, judges and lawyers also synthesize facts in an effort to identify the types of factors that courts consider persuasive as proving or disproving claims. Consider, for example, a case where a landlord denies a minority person's application for an apartment lease though several vacant apartments are available. The court must decide whether the landlord violated federal law by intentionally and discriminatorily denying that person a lease or, if instead, the landlord turned down the application because the applicant had significant drawbacks not related to race in her credit history or background check. Drawing on several cases, you might identify facts that were important to the decisions in those cases, which you then could group into categories. One category of facts may concern the credit history of the person who was denied a lease; another category could be whether the applicant played a musical instrument. Another category might be whether the landlord subsequently leased to other, nonminori-

---

2. William L. Prosser, Intentional Infliction of Mental Suffering: A New Tort, 37 Mich. L. Rev. 874 (1939).

ty applicants who also had credit problems, and one other category might be references from previous landlords. When you see similarities among sets of facts, you can construct the relevant categories—often called factors—and can relate the categories to the claims being litigated. For example, if the landlord denied the application of an African–American woman with no credit problems and subsequently approved the application of a white male with a poor credit history, then a court might find that the landlord purposefully denied the woman a lease based on her race or gender.

Here is another illustration involving landlords and tenants. In many states, if a tenant leaves rented premises before the lease runs out, the landlord must "mitigate" the landlord's damages, that is, must minimize the amount that the tenant owes by trying to re-let the premises. A court may look at certain types of facts that are relevant to whether the landlord is using reasonable efforts to mitigate. What types of factors are relevant? They will include whether the landlord advertised the availability of the premises, or used a realtor, or rejected suitable tenants, or asked new prospective tenants for a much higher rent.

You can now see that individual cases do not exist in an historical vacuum. It follows that sometimes there are ways that you can put together lines of cases to derive a new principle. Of course, the job of the lawyer who opposes the new principle is to show that the cases can be distinguished—that they are not as much alike (or similar, or analogous) as the proponent of the synthesis claims that they are. In fact, the opponent of the synthesis will try to synthesize the precedents in a way that forms a different rule or to create an exception to the rule.

Exceptions to Rules (or New Rules)

As the common law grows by induction and synthesis—the development of rules from a series of cases—it begins to develop exceptions to rules to meet new situations. Assume that over a period of time, a court develops the rule that killing another human being is murder. Soon, however, the court becomes troubled by the injustice of applying that rule to a case in which someone kills another in order to protect her own life. The court thus develops an exception to the rule that killing another human being is murder. The exception is, "unless the killing is done in self-defense."

As more cases come along, and the law expands, an exception may become so complex that it becomes a rule—or a set of rules—in itself. Thus, we may speak of "the self-defense rules"— a group of rules that evolve in response to a series of cases that present variations on the general situation of killing for self-protection. One of those rules, which may vary among jurisdictions, requires a person to retreat before using deadly force in self-defense, at least if she may retreat safely. Still another rule gives a person the privilege to use deadly force in self-defense, without the need to retreat, if the person is in her own home.

The main point to remember is that many rules have exceptions, and that exceptions sometimes become significant enough that they become new sets of rules in themselves.

Applying General Rules: Deduction

By contrast with the inductive method that formulates general rules from concrete cases, the technique of deductive reasoning applies general rules to particular facts, or, as lawyers say, applies the law to the facts. Courts and lawyers use this type of reasoning when general rules already have been fashioned, by statute or by previous judicial decision (that is, by induction).

A common law illustration begins with the procedural requirement that a court must grant a judgment as a matter of law when the evidence is such that reasonable persons could not differ on the outcome. Let us say that there is a substantive rule of state tort law, fashioned from precedents, that says that a plaintiff cannot establish a medical malpractice case without offering expert testimony (testimony from other doctors) that the defendant doctor was negligent. The plaintiff presents facts from which many lay persons would conclude that a doctor behaved negligently, but does not offer expert testimony. Thus, the plaintiff has not met the requirements of the substantive rule. The defendant moves for judgment as a matter of law, and the court will grant that motion. Given a substantive rule that requires expert testimony to support a malpractice case, jurors could not reasonably find for a plaintiff who did not present expert testimony.

Deductive reasoning is syllogistic in its pattern. In legal applications, it starts from a general rule (a major premise—that the plaintiff must present expert testimony to prove medical malpractice). It focuses on a particular set of facts (the minor premise—the plaintiff failed to present expert testimony). Then it moves to a conclusion, that the plaintiff did not prove medical malpractice because there was no expert testimony, which requires a judgment for the defendant. In formal logic, the conclusion is compelled by the premises. Lawyers who argue for a particular result try to fit the governing rule and its application to the facts of a case into this syllogistic pattern to compel a judgment for their clients. You usually will use this pattern for your writing assignments. That is, you will analyze an issue by starting with the general rule, explaining that rule, and analyzing the facts of your case in light of that rule.

Issues based on the language of statutes usually require deductive analysis. For example, a state statute requires a will to be signed by two witnesses in order to be valid. This statutory language requiring two witnesses is the major premise. In a particular case, a minor premise would be the fact, offered by a litigant to validate the will, that a will was signed by two witnesses. Applying the statutory requirement, we must conclude that the will is valid, at least as to the requirement of the number of signatures.

However, few issues will be that simple. You should understand that deduction as we illustrate it here supplies only a pattern for legal analysis. The simplicity of that pattern may hide the difficult analytical work that precedes the spelling out of the pattern. Sometimes the difficulty lies in supplying the major premise, that is, the accepted rule, because the issue has not yet been decided in that jurisdiction. In that case, the lawyer or the court must first determine the rule in that jurisdiction. (Remember the battery issue and the tray in Chapter Two). Sometimes the rule is not clear, for example, when statutory language can be interpreted in more than one way. Then the lawyer or the court must first analyze the statute and interpret its language to derive the major premise.

Often the difficulty lies in formulating the minor premise by characterizing the facts to fit the rule or to show that they do not fit. Consider, for example, a statute that requires a person who sells real property to sign the deed, saying that "a valid deed must include the seller's signature." The statute supplies the major premise. Suppose John K. Smith writes only his initials, JKS, on the deed for the sale of his home. Ask yourself whether under those facts, the deed is valid. Are Smith's initials his signature? If not, the deed is not valid. There may not be a precedent with the exact facts of this hypothetical, and it is likely that the legislature did not provide a definition of "signature." In order to analyze this issue, and to determine whether Smith's initials were a signature, you will have to reason by analogy to similar cases involving the statutory term "the seller's signature" (the next section provides a brief introduction to reasoning by analogy). You then have to create other syllogisms—or reasoning—in order to form the premises to your conclusion. The conclusion of one syllogism will be the major premise of the next one.

For the deed signature example, you would analyze the precedents to determine whether signed initials are valid as a signature. If you decide that signed initials are valid if the person wrote them intending to confirm the terms of the deed, you may construct the major premise of the next syllogism, "A person's signed initials on a deed is a valid signature if the person wrote intending to confirm the terms of the deed." The minor premise would be "Smith wrote his initials intending to confirm the terms of the deed." The conclusion is that the deed signature is valid. How do you know that Smith intended to confirm the terms of the deed? You need the facts of what happened at the deed signing to construct your story about Smith's intent.

Sometimes an argument is not completely written as a syllogism; one step is omitted. This is called an enthymeme. A court may just say that Smith wrote his initials to confirm the deed and the signature on the deed is valid.

Reasoning By Analogy

A powerful tool for law work, one almost instinctively used by people with legal training, is reasoning by analogy. We have been using examples of reasoning by analogy throughout this book because it is the essence of a lawyer's work. A simplified introduction to this form of reasoning in the legal context lies in the phrase, "this case is like that case," a statement that implies that the two cases should be treated the same. In a prior case—the "that" case—facts 1, 2, and 3 were present, the court applied a particular rule, and the plaintiff won. In the case that's being argued—the "this" case—facts 1, 2, and 3 are also present, so the plaintiff's lawyer would contend that the same rule should apply and the plaintiff should win. People use this form of reasoning for many purposes, not just legal ones, especially when they analyze a new problem. To analyze a new problem, you look for existing solutions to problems of the same kind to see how those who solved the prior problems examined them. If the two problems are enough alike, then the solution should be the same in the new case as in the prior cases.

Besides helping you to identify similarities in cases, reasoning by analogy also will aid you to analyze differences between and among cases. We discuss that skill in the section below on "Distinguishing Cases." As you go through law school, it will become second nature to you to find such distinctions. That is a developed ability that is important to lawyers. Yet, you should not neglect the skill of being able to find similarities between cases. Sometimes we call that harmonizing cases.

The ability to find common ground in situations of potential conflict has uses in the law that go beyond case analysis. We have observed that lawyers are argumentative and that much of the argument in which lawyers engage concerns the comparison of similarities and differences between cases or problems. Yet, one of the most useful attributes of many talented lawyers lies in their knack of helping adversaries to narrow and reconcile their differences and to achieve agreement.

Here is an example involving two torts cases that shows how the ability to analogize cases may be helpful on the intellectual side of law. Assume, first, that a court has decided that it is a battery if a twelve-year-old boy playfully kicks a classmate during school hours, seriously aggravating a previous wound to the classmate's knee that is concealed by his trousers. The court reasons that the kicker's intent to make a contact was sufficient to constitute a battery, even if the young defendant did not intend harm to his classmate. In the model of case analysis we are developing, that decision provides the rule, which for these purposes we might state as being that an intended contact in violation of social norms is a battery.

Now consider a later case, in which a male employee "affectionately" hugs a female co-worker, who has made plain that she dislikes on-the-job hugs. The female employee suffers an immediate and unexpected facial paralysis, which medical testimony indicates was a fortuitous result of the hug.

On the surface, these two cases might sound like they do not have a lot in common—horseplay by kick in an elementary school classroom and hugging by a co-worker in the workplace. When we analyze the cases together, however, we can begin to see that they share a common legal thread. Both cases involve a deliberate contact, by someone who subjectively may have thought he was just "fooling around," which causes an objectively unforeseeable but serious physical injury. Thus, you might contend that the cases are analogous, and that the hug, as well as the kick, was a battery. To be sure, there may be room for argument about whether the cases are enough alike that they should come out the same way. Reasoning by analogy, like induction, is a matter of probabilities, not certainty. Our basic point is that lawyers use reasoning by analogy to see potentially crucial similarities between cases, as well as to synthesize a generally applicable rule.

Distinguishing Cases

Many times attorneys and judges find it necessary to identify controlling distinctions between cases. A time-honored way for a lawyer to argue that an earlier decision does not bind the present litigation, and for a court to decide that way, is to *distinguish* the precedent.

The technique of distinguishing cases presents a kind of reverse image to reasoning by analogy. Instead of using analogy to show how a case at issue is like a previous case, the attorney or judge will stress what he regards as relevant differences between the cases.

One example involves the gift case in earlier chapters, in which we established the principle that a person who gives access to personal property delivers that property. If a person who is hospitalized with a serious illness gives her daughter the key to her desk drawer and tells the daughter that the stock certificates in the drawer are for her, a court may decide that the mother "delivered" the certificates to her daughter when she gave her the key by giving her the only means of access to the certificates. But if a healthy woman gives the key to her daughter and says that the certificates are for her, and then changes her mind and decides to keep the certificates, the woman's attorney may say, "my client never delivered the certificates and so never completed the gift because a gift requires delivery. In the earlier case, the mother was very ill and couldn't go to her desk herself. That is a very different situation from this case. They are not analogous. My client could have handed over the certificates herself if she really meant to complete a gift. But she didn't. The decision in the earlier case is distinguishable—it doesn't control here, and my client still owns the certificates."

Another example is the rule we created inductively on pages 63–64, of a person who performed a task without knowing that another person had offered payment for the task. We earlier hypothesized three cases with respect to that rule. Now consider a fourth case that comes along. In this case, the third person knew before he performed a task—let us say washing the defendant's windows—about the defendant's statement to another person that he would pay someone to wash his house windows. This plaintiff should win his suit for payment, because he knew about the offer before he performed the requested task even though the offer was not made to him. In the other three cases, the plaintiffs did not know of the offer when it was made. The court would know about the rule not to require payment, but would understand that the rule was confined to the particular facts of the earlier three cases. The court would distinguish the case before it from the three precedents.

Alternative Arguments

A form of reasoning that lawyers use that often perplexes first-year law students is that of an alternative argument. An example of an alternative argument is one in which a lawyer, defending a client in a contract case, first tells the court, "This contract is invalid because it is unconscionable,"[3] giving reasons why the contract is unconscionable. Then, however, the lawyer continues, "Even if the contract is not unconscionable and is valid,[4] my client did not breach it," and gives reasons why the client did not breach. In alternative argument, the lawyer sets up a logical chain of claims or defenses and then analyzes and argues each in turn. The lawyer concedes the first point (the contract is valid and not unconscionable) for the purposes of argument in order to reach the next issue (my client did not breach the contract), but uses the concession only for that purpose.

Another example of an alternative argument, with a constitutional basis, is this: A person charged with violating a disturb-

---

3. Meaning, essentially, that the contract is so unfair it should not be enforced.

4. Legal jargon for this is the term "assuming arguendo," which means "as-sume for the sake of argument." A lawyer might say, "assuming arguendo that the contract is not unconscionable ..."

ing the peace ordinance argues first that she did not violate the ordinance, that is, she did not disturb the peace. She then argues as an alternative that even if she did disturb the peace, she still cannot be convicted because the ordinance infringes her right to free speech and thus violates the First Amendment. When lawyers argue in the alternative, they don't admit that either argument they proffer is not valid. Instead, they provide two different bases upon which the court could decide for their clients.

Being Relevant

One of the most crucial skills for any lawyer to develop— really, for anyone in ordinary life to develop—is the art of being relevant. Especially for those law students whose prior education has consisted largely of giving back memorized facts to the teacher, this will take some learning. Relevance, for these purposes, consists in saying things that properly apply to a particular situation, for example, identifying the particular statutory language that applies to the facts of a problem, or emphasizing facts that are crucial to proving or disproving a particular contention.

The law of evidence provides a gatekeeping function for trials that is based on relevance. Consider a trial of a man for murdering his wife. The prosecutor seeks to introduce evidence that the defendant once was engaged to eight women at the same time. This evidence is irrelevant and no court will admit it. Although these facts might put the defendant in a bad light with some jurors, there is no logical linkage between evidence of multiple engagements and a tendency to murder a spouse.

An evidentiary question arose in the much publicized trial of O.J. Simpson for murdering his ex-wife and another victim. The issue was whether the prosecution could introduce evidence that Simpson abused his wife in the years before the murder. The court admitted some of the evidence on the basis that it was relevant to whether the defendant had a tendency to commit violent acts against his wife. Whether you agree or not, you probably will conclude that this evidence presents a much stronger case for the prosecution than the hypothetical evidence of prior engagements.

The Use of Hypotheticals

Many law teachers use hypothetical cases to develop a topic in class. These "hypos" make you analyze the case under discussion from a variety of perspectives. A primary purpose of hypos is to help define the scope of the rules that emerge from a case.

Hypos also introduce you to the world of law practice. Practicing lawyers really do operate, almost as a reflex, by asking questions of themselves and of others, about hypothetical cases— the cases just across the line from the one they are dealing with. A principal reason they do that is because they may be called to account by adversaries and judges. Opponents will try to embarrass you with hypotheticals to show up the flaws in your logic: "If the court holds for you in this case, it will have to hold for Party X in this hypothetical case, and wouldn't that be stupid?" Judges themselves may put hypos to you to help sharpen their own thinking about the limits of your claim or defense. You will see this when you participate in moot court. Your moot court partners or your law partners—if they are good partners—will put hypos to you to prepare you for what judges or opponents may ask. If you are on your own, you would do well to create your own hypotheticals. Ultimately, someone else will.

There are two particular values in hypotheticals that relate to earlier points in this chapter. First, they help you to reason by analogy. Is this case or this hypothetical enough like a precedent case to make them legally comparable, so that the rule of the prior case should apply, and the party whose position is analogous to that of the victor in the first case should win? Incidentally, one way to deal with a professor's Socratic questioning is to answer her hypotheticals by using analogies and distinctions. A second benefit of hypotheticals is that they force you to a test of relevance: Does the precedent I want to invoke apply persuasively to the case before me now, and in which specific ways?

*

8
Interpreting Language

Law school, and law generally, provide both challenges and opportunities in the use of language. In law school, the difficulty of the challenge will depend in part on your prior experience with the plastic possibilities of words. In practice, your ability to use language perceptively and creatively will create unlimited opportunities.

An article in a scientific publication, although written about the evolution of humans from prehistoric beings, captures how lawyers put concepts into words, and how they use words to create arguments. The writer says,

> Language is not simply the medium by which we express our ideas and experiences to each other. Rather it is fundamental to the thought process itself. It involves categorizing and naming objects and sensations in the outer and inner worlds and making associations between resulting mental symbols.

The writer then declares that "[i]t is, in effect, impossible for us to conceive of thought (as we are familiar with it) in the absence of language, and it is the ability to form mental symbols that is the fount of our creativity."[1]

___

1. Ian Tattersall, 282 Sci. Am. No. 1, at 56, 62 (Jan. 2000).

The Same Word May Mean Different Things

Words that you have grown up believing have particular, rather fixed meanings—"ordinary" meanings—may turn out in legal contexts to stand for things that are different from what they signified to you before. We will give just a couple of examples that will take on more significance when your teachers put flesh on them in concrete legal contexts.

Consider the word "intent." Most non-lawyer readers probably think they have a well-defined idea of what "intent" means—something like a fixed purpose to accomplish a goal. As you plow into legal terminology, however, you will learn that intent does not simply mean purpose, or desire. It may also mean something a little less purposeful—for example, in the law of torts, it may mean acting with substantial certainty that a particular result will occur.

A "substantial certainty" definition of intent will control the outcome in particular cases. An example is a case in which a child pulled a chair out from under an elderly woman, who suffered serious injuries in the resulting fall. A jury might decide that the child did not have a specific purpose to cause the plaintiff to fall, but that on the basis of his life experience, he would have been substantially certain that she would fall as a result of his pulling out the chair. Thus, if a court defined "intent" to include "substantial certainty" rather than only "desire" or "purpose," it would open the gate a little wider to claims for personal injury based on "intent."

Another illustration concerns the word "malice." Most people probably have a pretty fixed idea that "malice" means something like "spite," implying a sense of vindictiveness. As you get into the language of the law, however, it will become clear that courts give several meanings to this one word. For example, in the area of defamation law, the Supreme Court has endowed the term with a very specific meaning. Instead of necessarily signifying spite or vicious intentions, the word "malice" may mean "reckless disregard of the truth or falsity" of a remark that injures reputation. The harm caused by a reckless publication of defamatory remarks is not pleasant to contemplate, but it may not necessarily involve the kind of malice that most people associate with that word. Thus, the definition of "malice" to include "reckless disregard" may permit more suits than a definition that requires spite.[2]

The law can complicate one word even more; a court might use the term malice in two different ways in the same defamation case. For one purpose—determining whether an action can be brought for defaming someone who is well-known to the public—the word may mean "reckless disregard." For another purpose—the decision of whether to award punitive damages[3]—it might mean something more like "spite." Thus, a defendant could have published a defamatory statement with "malice" in the sense of "reckless disregard" of whether the statement was true, justifying an award of compensatory damages[4] in favor of a public official, but not with the kind of vindictive "malice" that a state might require to justify punitive damages. Interestingly enough—really, confusingly—the Supreme Court has defined "reckless disregard" in defamation cases by the term "actual malice," a usage that you might ordinarily think would accentuate the requirement that a claimant must show spite or vindictiveness. This simply underlines the point that words often have meanings in the law that are not their ordinary meanings.

Pouring Meaning into Phrases

A good part of the job of courts and of lawyers is to interpret words and phrases. Rather vague phrases like "equal protection of the laws," or "due process of law," or "cruel and unusual punishment" do not come to us defined for all time and all situations. Is it "cruel and unusual punishment" to impose the death penalty on a murderer? There is a difference of opinion on that question. Is it a deprivation of employees' "due process of law" to limit the hours that they may work because it deprives them of their property? Early in the 20th century, there were serious differences of opinion on that issue. Courts often resolve

2. As a matter of constitutional law, the Supreme Court's use of the "malice" standard in this context actually limited the opportunities that previously existed for certain people to sue for defamation. Our point, however, is that the Court's use of the term "malice" is different from the ordinary connotations of the word.

3. Punitive damages are additional damages awarded to punish a defendant's especially culpable conduct. State rules vary on how egregious the conduct must be, but one test requires that it must be reprehensible. Punitive damages are awarded in only a small percentage of cases.

4. Successful plaintiffs in injury cases usually recover compensatory damages, which are designed to compensate someone—a term often used is "to make whole"—for the consequences of a wrong by the defendant.

disputes over the meaning of words by interpreting this kind of vague language.

In addition to their role in deciphering such vague phrases, courts also must determine the meaning of words that superficially seem less vague, but still require interpretation. Consider, for example, a statute of limitations[5] that applies to "improvements to real property." If a factory is real property, and a crane by itself is a very large piece of personal property, is a crane that has been installed in a factory an "improvement to real property"? There has been some disagreement on this issue, with the courts focusing on such questions as the permanence with which the crane is attached to the factory premises, how crucial the machine is to the operation of the plant, and whether it was custom-designed for incorporation into that particular plant. Thus, even a fairly straightforward statutory term like "improvement to real property" requires interpretation. In litigation, courts must supply its meaning, and lawyers try to persuade the court to adopt one meaning rather than another.

Stretching Words

Although lawyers always have to interpret words and give them content, you may come to think that they sometimes try to stretch words, and that sometimes courts do stretch them. For example, the Constitution grants to Congress the power to regulate commerce "among the several States," a phrase usually known as the interstate commerce clause. Until the nineteen thirties, most people would have given that phrase a relatively literal meaning, calling up images of vehicles or people actually moving across state lines.

Imagine, then, the surprise of an Ohio farmer who challenged a penalty imposed on him under a federal statute for exceeding the statute's marketing quota for wheat grown on his farm for his own use. To what must have been the farmer's dismay, the Supreme Court said that his production beyond his quota had a potential impact on prices of wheat that moved in interstate commerce that was significant enough that Congress' power to regulate that commerce extended to his individual farm. In fact, the Court said that the marketing quota constitutionally

---

5. A statute of limitations bars a person from initiating a lawsuit beyond the time period permitted by the statute.

could cover even wheat "consumed on the premises," as food for livestock and flour for home baking. The Court reasoned that wheat that the farmer consumed himself "supplies a need ... which would otherwise be reflected by purchases in the open market."[6] This famous decision illustrates that one of the reasons that lawyers are wonderful folks—or people who twist the truth, depending on your point of view in a particular case—is that they can give this kind of content to words.

There are limits. Courts would not interpret a statute that specifically allows an administrative agency to regulate the labeling of refrigerators to empower it to regulate the labeling of automobiles. Would a statute that permits an agency to regulate safety in the "workplace" permit it to promulgate regulations for the safety of domestic workers in homes? That might not be out of the question, because a home may be a workplace, although it is not a likely result. But one does not have to answer that question to appreciate the plasticity of language in the law.

Another example appears in a much-discussed decision in which the Supreme Court said that a statute exceeded the power of Congress to regulate interstate commerce. At issue in this case was the Gun-Free School Zones Act, which made it a federal crime knowingly to possess a firearm in a place that the defendant knew or reasonably believed was a school zone. The defendant in this case was convicted under that statute because he brought a handgun to his San Antonio high school. A majority of the Court decided that the legislation was unconstitutional, so the defendant could not be convicted under it. The Court said the "the possession of a gun in a local school zone is in no sense an economic activity" that through repetition of that behavior in other places "might ... substantially affect any sort of interstate commerce."[7] The Court took into account its decision in the case of the wheat farmer, which it said was "perhaps the most far reaching example of Commerce Clause authority over intrastate activity"—that is, activity within a single state. However, it distinguished that case because it "involved economic activity in a way that the possession of a gun in a school zone does not."[8]

---

6. Wickard v. Filburn, 317 U.S. 111 (1942).

7. United States v. Lopez, 514 U.S. 549, 567 (1995).

8. *Id.* at 560.

[*Id.* means that this footnote cites to the same case as the one in the preceding footnote.]

Using Policies to Define Words and Phrases

When courts confront a dispute about the meaning of legal terms, for example if a term is ambiguous—that is, capable of more than one meaning—they often will interpret the words to harmonize with the policies in which these terms are rooted. Suppose a statute revokes a person's will made prior to the person's marriage unless "provision was made for the surviving spouse by settlement before or during marriage, or the survivor is provided for in the will." (The effect of the statute's revocation of a will protects a surviving spouse because the surviving spouse will inherit a share of the estate that is defined by another statute.) Mr. and Ms. Green signed an agreement before their marriage that provided that neither spouse would claim any rights to the other's property when the other died. Mr. Green had a premarital will that did not include Ms. Green. He did not change that will after they were married, and thus died with that document being his will.

When Mr. Green died, Ms. Green was destitute, having forfeited her seniority and pension when she left her job at her husband's insistence. Because of the premarital agreement, she would receive nothing from Mr. Green. She claimed that his premarital will was revoked by the statute because he had made no provision for her, arguing that to make "provision" meant to give property, which he had not done. Thus, she contended, he died without a will and she was entitled to a statutory inheritance share as his surviving spouse.

Mr. Green's administrator, acting on behalf of the estate, claimed that Mr. Green's will was not revoked because Mr. Green had made "provision" for his spouse by their prior agreement. The administrator argued that "provision" meant only that the decedent made prior preparations concerning the spouse. The dictionary defines "provision" as having both meanings: "the state of being prepared" (supporting the estate's position that the premarital agreement was the couple's "preparations"), and also "a gift" (supporting Ms. Green's argument that her deceased husband had not given her any property).

The court presented with this problem agreed with the estate's argument that the statutory term "provision" meant only "make preparations." It decided on this meaning of the term because it determined that the policy behind the statutory language "provision was made" was one of guarding against unintentional disinheritance, and that the premarital agreement showed that Ms. Green's disinheritance was planned and not unintentional. Had the court decided that the purpose of the statute was a different one, for example, to ensure support for a surviving spouse, it would, no doubt, have interpreted the statute as Ms. Green had argued, requiring a financial provision of property. In interpreting the particular term "provision" in this case, the court used the policy behind the law to interpret the statutory words. The next chapters will elaborate more on judicial use of policy.

Interpreting Statutes

A lot of the work that first-year law students do involves common law, but that should not obscure the fact that a substantial amount of practicing lawyers' work consists of reading and interpreting statutes. Many students are apprehensive about analyzing statutory topics. Although some of the preceding material in this chapter deals with statutes, this Part specifically introduces some basic steps of statutory analysis and by doing so, seeks to relieve some of that anxiety.

1. Read the Statute

Point one would also be point 100, if we had space to make 100 points. It is obvious as it can be. It is also very difficult for law students to believe its literal truth. *Read the statute.* Say it again with emphasis, and add a rule: *READ THE STATUTE AND NOTE ITS EXACT LANGUAGE.*

It may be useful to introduce a contrasting point. When you are briefing an appellate case, it sometimes may be a good idea to paraphrase what the court said. That way you force yourself to put the court's conclusion into your own words. By contrast, that is not a good idea when you are reading a statute. There may eventually be room for interpretation, but you start with the exact words of the legislature. Never try to paraphrase a statute.

Failure to read a statute, and to take seriously its exact language, is an error that students often make. The point may not come across until you make a few mistakes of that kind. There will come a time, however, when the idea that you must read statutory language exactly will have worn a groove in your brain.

After you have familiarized yourself with a statute, look for the particular statutory language that your assignment involves and focus on that part of the statute. If you are briefing a case involving a statute, include that language in your case brief. The case that you read for class or the problem you have for a writing assignment will require you to analyze how that specific language applies to particular facts.

2. Plain Meaning

Lawyers use some fairly standard techniques to interpret statutes. Although the actual interpretation can be difficult, the basic techniques are not.

First, not surprisingly, the most obvious step is to look for the plain meaning of statutory language. The crux of the "plain meaning rule" is that, if the language has a plain meaning, then the court will not consider any other evidence of what the statute means. It must interpret the language using only the statute itself. The plain meaning rule is really what is called a "no extrinsic evidence" rule: the court will not consider evidence extrinsic to— that is, outside of—the statute. For example, if a statute permits a seller of goods to disclaim all responsibility for injury caused by its goods only if the disclaimer is written in red ink in one-inch type, the seller cannot introduce evidence that the legislature really meant only that the disclaimer must be conspicuous.

Another example of plain meaning would treat the Constitution of the United States as a statute. Consider Article II, section 1 of the Constitution, which says, speaking of the President, "neither shall any Person be eligible to that office who shall not have attained to the Age of thirty five Years."

Suppose that an exceptionally serious and able young politician who is 33 years old comes to you and says he wants to run for President. He argues that the phrase "thirty five Years" was just a way in which the makers of the Constitution expressed their opinion that the President should be a mature person with ripe experience in public life. He asks why he can't argue that the "thirty five" requirement is a guideline and not a hard and fast rule. Your answer would have to be that he must wait one more election to try for the Oval Office. "Thirty five" has a plain meaning: thirty five.

Although the plain meaning rule is the first step in interpreting a statute, unfortunately, words rarely have just one meaning, and some words that are "plain" to people in one area of life may not be plain to people in another. As is apparent from our example on pages 82–83 about the wills statute, even the seemingly simple phrase "provision was made" has two recognized meanings—to prepare for or to make a gift. Many words take their meanings from context. The word "estate" in a deed or contract might refer to a particular piece of property. The same word in a will might mean all that a person owned at death.

3. Legislative History

If statutory language does not have one plain meaning, and it often does not, then the court will determine what the legislature intended by the statutory language. To do so, it will examine other evidence, that is, evidence of the legislative intent extrinsic to the statutory words. Indeed, recent interpretations permit courts to consider such extrinsic evidence even if the statute may have a plain meaning, in order to determine if the legislature simply could not have intended the plain meaning. The type of evidence most often used to determine legislative intent is the legislative history, that is, the documented trail of information created as a statute makes its way through the legislative process. This trail includes the introduction of the statute as a bill, its consideration by a committee, the committee vote, the vote on the floor of the legislature, and then signature by the executive.

Each of these stages of the process produces some documentation, for example, legislative committee reports. Congressional committees often publish extensive reports concerning bills that become federal legislation. All of this material may yield some clues to the intended meaning of the statute's language. Sometimes the clues are explicit explanations; often, however, they are not, and the lawyer must create a story, based on a view of the purpose of the statute that is favorable to her client, about how the language should be interpreted.

Other types of evidence about the meaning of legislation may come from other parts of the same statute. If the legislature used the exact language at issue in other sections of the disputed statute, then a lawyer would interpret that language to be consistent in its meaning throughout the statute. If, however, the legislature used similar, but different, language elsewhere in the statute, then perhaps it intended to impart different meanings to those terms. For example, if the legislature used "domicile" in one part of a statute, but "residence" in another, then it probably intended different meanings to those words. Another indirect kind of evidence would be amendments offered to a bill that failed to pass. These may give an idea of language the legislature did not intend to adopt.

Many lawyers who represent clients interested in proposed legislation will spend part of their time creating legislative histories. They will, for example, formulate questions for one senator to ask another senator during debate on the Senate floor about the meaning of a particular phrase in a bill, and will also fashion appropriate responses. These statements are published in the Congressional Record and become part of the legislative history. Questions of interpretation arise when there are conflicting statements of that sort in the legislative history of a bill. Legislative history is a tool that courts use for interpretive help when the meaning of statutes becomes the subject of litigation and the meaning is not "plain." Proponents of legislation have that in mind when they draft the question-and-answer dramas by which members of Congress "explain" the "meaning" of a bill.

4. Ambiguous or Vague Language

As is evident throughout this chapter, the language of legislation may be ambiguous or it may be vague. Ambiguity—a word has more than one meaning—is sometimes a result of careless or hurried drafting. By comparison, vague language— language where the boundaries of meaning are not fixed—may reflect the fact that legislation, by its nature, represents a compromise between warring forces. Statutory language may be vague because it was necessary for proponents of legislation to make some ideas—like "reasonable amount of time" or "reasonable protection"—fuzzy in order to entice enough supporters to pass a bill.

5. Canons of Statutory Construction

You would use the analysis we have outlined above to interpret the purpose of a legislature as it bears specifically on the meaning of the words in a particular statute. Another type of analysis is that of statutory construction. The goal of this approach is to determine what is usually meant by a particular kind of language, or by a particular type of statute, when the person doing the interpretation does not know what was actually intended. This process uses what are known as canons of construction. In this context, canons are like maxims—fundamental principles.

Below we give four examples of these canons, presented in rough pairings of ideas. The first canon, expressio unius, says that the expression of one thing excludes other things not mentioned. The second, ejusdem generis, says that when a general word follows a list of specific things, persons interpreting the language may look to the specific list to give meaning to the general word. The third and fourth canons are, respectively, that courts should narrowly construe statutes "in derogation of the common law," and that courts should broadly construe "remedial statutes." We have added another canon about interpreting criminal statutes. In a way similar to the third and fourth canons, this canon also concerns the question of whether to interpret a statute broadly or narrowly.

Expressio Unius

This canon is in legal Latin and its full description is "Expressio unius est exclusio alterius." That means, roughly, that to express one thing in a document is to exclude other things that have not been mentioned.

Assume that a statute makes it a misdemeanor to let "swine, cattle, or sheep run at large." The sheriff arrests Mr. X because he finds Mr. X's goat on the highway, but the prosecutor tells the sheriff to let Mr. X go because the law does not support the arrest. The sheriff might argue, "I know the law says swine, cattle, or sheep, but goats are close enough." The prosecutor will emphasize to the sheriff that this statute makes it a crime—even though a minor crime—to let certain livestock run loose. The prosecutor will probably explain that one must assume that in making a very specific list of offenses, the legislature meant only to punish the exact behaviors on that list, and to exclude all others.[9] The prosecutor might also explain her decision not to prosecute by referring to another canon, one that says that criminal statutes should be strictly construed. The reason supporting this canon is that a person should not be punished for a crime unless he has clear warning in the statute that the conduct is criminal.

9. It is possible, however, that the legislature in fact may not have intended its list to be exclusive.

Ejusdem Generis

Another commonly used canon of construction—also in Latin—might have applied if the statute had made it a crime to allow "swine, cattle, sheep, or other such animals to run at large." In that case, a court could apply the statute to goats by using the canon known as *ejusdem generis*, which means of the same genus or class, and applies to catch-all words after an enumerated list. Animals could be of the same kind as the three listed creatures if they are four-legged and are common farm animals, such as a goat.

However, given that the three listed animals are also commonly used for human consumption, and if goat meat is not usually eaten by people in that jurisdiction, then a court might conclude that the statute does not include goats. That would be because under an interpretation that focused on the common characteristic of the listed animals as livestock used for food, goats would not be of the same class as the other three animals. The statute also might not apply to a dog or cat because they are animals typically used as household pets. If you want to consider a more difficult question, ask how a court should respond to the case of a pig that a farm family has adopted as a house pet. To answer that kind of question, you often need to know the purpose of the statute in order to identify the common characteristic the catch-all phrase is meant to capture.

Narrow Construction of Statutes in Derogation of the Common Law

Another principle of statutory construction fits rather closely here. This is the maxim that when a statute changes the common law, courts should interpret it narrowly.

An example from civil litigation concerns tort damages. Let us say that the common law in a particular state allows theoretically unlimited damages for intangible harms connected with physical injury. The legislature, seeking to decrease recoveries for personal injuries, enacts a statute that limits injury victims to $500,000 for "pain and suffering." A jury makes an award to an injured plaintiff that includes an item of one million dollars, labeled as representing "loss of capacity to enjoy life." The defendant seeks to reduce this award by $500,000, invoking the statutory limit on "pain and suffering" damages.

The defendant would argue that when the legislature used the phrase "pain and suffering," it had in mind a broad cluster of intangible harms that cannot easily be quantified in dollars. A court, however, might refuse to apply the "pain and suffering" cap to "loss of capacity to enjoy life." Since the statute cuts back on common law remedies—it is "in derogation of the common law"—the court may well (although not undoubtedly) construe the legislation narrowly against the party who is relying on it, in this case, the defendant. The court might explain that if the legislature had intended to limit "loss of capacity" damages, it knew how to say so, but didn't.

Incidentally, the great maxims of statutory construction often tend to spill over into one another. For a court to construe this statute narrowly could be said, in effect, to apply the canon "expressio unius": to express "pain and suffering" is to exclude all other forms of injury. Some might even argue that this interpretation applies the "plain meaning" rule.

Broad Construction of Remedial Statutes

A somewhat contrasting idea is that courts should broadly construe "remedial" statutes. Assume that in a particular jurisdiction, the courts have never allowed damage claims for water pollution, effectively recognizing the dependence of the state's economy on its chemical industry. They also have never allowed nuisance claims for offensive animal odors, indirectly recognizing that the second most important industry in the state is livestock farming.

With the passage of time, however, the state becomes progressively urban and suburban, and homeowners whose houses sit near rivers begin complaining to their legislators about chemicals in the streams. After hearings that amass information on the public perils and inconveniences of toxic and ill-smelling chemicals dumped into streams, the legislature passes a statute that permits individuals to bring damage actions for "air and water pollution."

Along comes a suburban homeowner who complains that the odors of a nearby pig sty make life very unpleasant for his family. He sues the owner of the sty for violating the pollution statute. The sty owner will argue that when the legislature passed the statute, the primary evil mentioned in the legislative hearings was that of chemical pollution. Thus, he will contend, "air . . .

pollution" means pollution by environmental chemicals, not the smell of pigs. Yet, though residents of the state previously could not have brought claims for animal odors, the court might well (although not necessarily) construe the words "air ... pollution" to include the aroma from the pig sty. If it does, it probably will rely on the idea that a statute that is avowedly remedial—that is, expands legal remedies or creates new ones—should be construed broadly.

If it has occurred to you at this point that sometimes maxims of statutory construction clash with one another, congratulate yourself. Naturally, the sty owner would argue that because the state's courts did not allow suits on animal odors before the passage of the statute, the court should construe the statute narrowly. Thus, arguably we now have two maxims in conflict—a narrow construction rule for statutes that change the common law and a maxim of broad construction for remedial statutes.[10]

You should get used to this kind of conflict and uncertainty. Moreover, you should view it as good news. It is exactly this sort of ambiguity—and the room for creative argument that it offers—that provides employment for lawyers.

*   *   *

Illustrations of use of legal reasoning and the interpretation of language to decide cases

Below are three illustrations of modes of reasoning and interpretation that are discussed in Chapter 7 and in this chapter as they are employed by courts.

Case 1: A constitutional provision: Analogies to precedent

In a constitutional law case, *Gonzales v. Raich*,[11] the Supreme Court determined that Congress had the authority to prohibit California from allowing its residents to grow their own

---

10. If you are interested in this subject, when you're ready to read law review articles you may want to read an article by Karl Llwellyn in The Vanderbilt Law Review, Remarks on the Theory of Appellate Decisions and the Rules or Canons About How Statutes Are to be Construed, 3 Vand. L. Rev. 395 (1950).

11. 545 U.S. 1 (2005).

marijuana for medicinal purposes. The decision turned upon the Court's interpretation of the U.S. Constitution and the power it grants Congress to regulate interstate commerce. The precise issue was whether Congress's banning of medicinal marijuana in California fell within the meaning of the constitutional phrase "interstate commerce."

To determine whether regulation of home-grown marijuana fell within interstate commerce, the Court relied on an analogy to a precedent Supreme Court case involving Congress's regulation of home-grown wheat.[12] In that case, the Court had determined that Congress had the power to regulate the amount of wheat that farmers could grow on their own land, even when the wheat was intended only for the farmers' own personal consumption and not intended to be sold. The Court concluded that farmers could not grow a surplus of wheat over the allotted amount, even if only for their own consumption, since doing so would inevitably have an impact on the national wheat market—especially if many other farmers followed suit. Inevitably, those farmers who grew and consumed their own supply of wheat would no longer need to rely on the national wheat market to feed themselves and their families. Home-grown wheat for personal use would thus decrease the amount of wheat being bought and sold among states on the open market. The Court thus decided that Congress could regulate home-grown wheat under its power to regulate interstate commerce.

The Supreme Court found the similarities between the medicinal marijuana case and the precedent of home-grown wheat to be "striking." Like the home-grown wheat, home-grown marijuana would inevitably have an impact on the national marijuana market, although it is an illegal market. The Court reasoned that the production "of the commodity meant for home consumption, be it wheat or marijuana, has a substantial effect on supply and demand in the national market for that commodity." The Court held that, under its constitutional power to regulate interstate commerce, Congress could prevent California from allowing its residents to home-grow medicinal marijuana. Do you agree?

12. See pages 80–81.

Case 2: An advertising offer: Distinguishing precedent

Another illustration of the use of precedent is a colorful 1999 contracts case in which a Pepsi consumer sought to enforce what he believed was a Pepsi television advertisement's firm offer of a Harrier Jet, a 14–ton, $23 million military aircraft, to any consumer producing 7,000,000 promotional points from Pepsi cans.[13] In a Pepsi commercial, a voiceover said, "Introducing the new Pepsi stuff catalog." The catalog contained an order form that included 53 items that could be ordered for "Pepsi Points," but that list did not include any "entry or description" of a Harrier Jet. In the commercial, a student arrived at school in the Harrier Jet, creating a violent storm of wind. The following words appeared at the bottom of the television screen: "HARRIER FIGHTER 7,000,000 PEPSI POINTS." The Plaintiff and his associates pooled the 7,000,000 points for the Harrier Jet and brought suit after Pepsi denied that its commercial constituted an enforceable offer of the jet.

In deciding whether the television commercial constituted a firm offer or simply a "tongue in cheek" "jest," the court turned to well-established contract law. Quoting the Restatement of Contracts, the court noted that advertisements and order forms are "mere notices and solicitations for offers which create no power of acceptance in the recipient." The exception to this rule is when an advertisement is "clear, definite, and explicit, and leaves nothing open for negotiation." To determine whether this exception applied to the Pepsi case, the court distinguished an old precedent involving a published newspaper advertisement announcing "Saturday 9 AM Sharp, 3 Brand New Fur Coats, Worth up to $100.00, First Come First Served $1 each."[14] A male plaintiff who showed up at the store but was denied the coat on the basis of his sex challenged the store as having made a firm offer through the advertisement. The plaintiff won his suit on the basis that he had "fulfilled all of the terms of the advertisement and [since] the advertisement was specific and left nothing open for negotiation, a contract had been formed."

The court in the Pepsi case distinguished the Harrier Jet commercial from the fur coats precedent since the Pepsi commercial "[could] not be regarded in itself as sufficiently definite, because it specifically reserved the details of the offer to a separate writing, the Catalogue." The commercial did not discuss

---

13. Leonard v. Pepsico, 88 F.Supp.2d 116 (S.D.N.Y. 1999).

14. Lefkowitz v. Great Minneapolis Surplus Store, Inc., 86 N.W.2d 689 (Minn. 1957).

the specific detailed steps that the plaintiffs had to take in order to receive the Harrier Jet. Moreover, the Pepsi ad never identified the person who could accept the offer, whereas in the fur coat case the ad sufficiently specified "first come first served." Perhaps more obviously, the prospect of an individual purchasing an expensive Harrier Jet at an exceptionally reduced price from a soft drink manufacturer was simply much less realistic than being able to purchase fur coats for $1, provided that the merchandise was still in supply. Having distinguished the Pepsi commercial from the fur coat ad, the court decided that "no objective person could reasonably have concluded that the commercial actually offered consumers a Harrier Jet," and entered judgment in favor of PepsiCo.

Case 3: An international agreement: Using an administrative agency's definition of terms

Here is an example from a case in a federal appellate court[15] that involved interpretation of the Warsaw Convention, an international agreement regarding airline accidents on international flights. The case involved the court's interpretation of the treaty's relevant language, which it did by examining precedents, and ultimately by following guidelines of a federal agency. The plaintiff was a passenger on an international flight on which the plane ran into turbulence and the captain announced that all passengers should take their seats. The plaintiff was injured when he hit his head on the cabin ceiling as he was coming down the aisle to get to his seat. He based his claim on Article 17 of the Warsaw Convention,[16] which imposes liability on a carrier for a passenger's damages "if the accident which caused the damage so sustained took place on board the aircraft." The plaintiff's injury took place "on board the aircraft," but is turbulence an accident?

The Warsaw Convention does not define "accident." The federal appellate court that had to decide the turbulence case first looked to precedent, but it had no applicable mandatory precedents. Other federal circuit courts discussed the question only in dicta. The language most apt to the case appeared in a

15. Magan v. Lufthansa German Airlines, 339 F.3d 158 (2d Cir. 2003).

16. For these purposes, the Court uses the same techniques to interpret the Convention's language as it uses for statutory language.

Supreme Court case that was not about turbulence in which the Court said that "When the injury indisputably results from the passenger's own internal reaction to the usual, normal, and expected operation of the aircraft, it has not been caused by an accident and Article 17 of the Warsaw Convention cannot apply."

Using the Supreme Court's statement as a platform, the trial court had reasoned that turbulence can commonly occur on a flight and can be a "usual, normal, and expected operation of the aircraft," and thus would not qualify as an accident under Article 17. However, turbulence can also be severe, unusual, and dangerous, and qualify as an accident. What was available to the court to decide what kind of turbulence this case involved? The trial court looked to the administrative agency with expertise in air travel, the Federal Aviation Administration, specifically to how the agency had classified types of turbulence using detailed descriptions including "light," "moderate," and "severe." Although the plaintiff had said that "he found walking almost impossible," the district court decided that the turbulence was "light" or "moderate" and that "light" or "moderate" turbulence could not be an "accident" under the Warsaw Convention, and granted the defendant's motion for summary judgment. The appellate court held, however, that this decision was erroneous as a matter of legal interpretation. And, specifically referring to the testimony of the plaintiff and other passengers about the severity of the turbulence, it said it was wrong for the trial court to decide that there was no "genuine issue of fact regarding the degree of turbulence experienced" on the plaintiff's flight, and that the case should go to trial.

9

Balancing Competing Interests and Factors

A great deal of law—and specifically for our present purposes, of the work of courts—consists of weighing and balancing, that is, to "weigh" the importance of various policy factors pertinent to a decision and to "balance" their importance against other factors. Courts also weigh the parties' competing legal arguments, and relevant facts in particular situations, to determine which party has proved his case.

Law as Influencing Behavior

Many decisions that the law makes to resolve disputes, and to deal with the underlying conflicts of social and economic policy, proceed on the assumption that law influences behavior. This premise underlies many rules of law, contained both in statutes and judge-made rules. Ordinarily, we hardly think about many of the ways that law affects behavior, so much are they a part of our lives.

Consider a few obvious examples:

- Many rules of contract law force us into formalities that we might not otherwise observe: Put it in writing. Sign both copies. Don't bury important ideas in the fine print.

- Tort rules guide conduct by informing us what level of risk is socially unacceptable: Do not drive over the speed limit, for if your speeding hurts someone, you will have to pay for their injuries. Do not let produce accumulate on your supermarket floor, or you may have to compensate those who slip and get hurt. Those two examples, directly embodying disincentives for undesired conduct, illustrate negative advice aimed at "deterrence." Tort law also effectively communicates advice about desirable conduct like, "Doctor, listen to your patients." Ordinarily, we might not think of that as a deterrence-oriented suggestion, since it tells someone what to do, rather than what not to do. However, as is the case with classic negative deterrence, the key is behavior control, since the clear implication is that a doctor ignores the advice at the risk of malpractice suits.

- The criminal law goes beyond the law of torts: Don't drive over the speed limit, or you may go to jail. Absolutely, don't drive while drunk, or you may go to jail for a long time. Thou shalt not kill, and if you do, you may be executed. Even, thou shalt not cheat. These illustrations represent, once more, negatively framed deterrence. Again, too, the law in effect offers some positive advice, for example, keep good records of your company's sales. Here an implied threat for noncompliance is the risk of a prosecution for tax fraud. Framed in terms of what to do, rather than what not to do, such counsel embodies an incentive to avoid unpleasant treatment by officials.

- The rules of property law advise us about all manner of behavior: Have your land surveyed so there are no disagreements about where the fence belongs. If you own a parcel of land but do not actively use it, visit it now and then to signal your ownership. If you make a mortgage loan, be sure to record it. Do not keep pigs in suburbia.

- The rules of procedure also influence conduct: Do not file a claim unless you have found some law to support your case, or the court may impose sanctions on you. File your motions on time. Do not continue a litigation if you come up short on evidence. Even, think about settling this case.

Balancing of Interests

If we view law as a set of rules and standards for governing human behavior, we need not reach beyond everyday experience to understand that a principal reason we need those rules is to minimize conflict. Even casual observation of daily life reveals frequent interactions between and among people that will cause disputes or exhibit potential for interpersonal controversy. The seller of corporate stock that neglects to tell a buyer that the corporation is being sued for everything it owns; the motorist whose fast driving causes a fatal injury; the "night-person" homeowner in a community of small lots who blasts his sound equipment at 3 a.m.—all these situations present cases likely to require dispute resolution.

In resolving disputes and fashioning rules, American courts more or less consciously attempt to balance competing social interests as well as the individual interests of the parties. Some of the cases we just mentioned illustrate this process of weighing and balancing. For example,

- The problem of whether a seller of stock must tell a purchaser about events that create significant risks to the corporate treasury underlines the difficulty that the law often faces in deciding how much information a seller must give to a prospective buyer. A strong element of our moral traditions condemns cheating and sharp practice. But another, somewhat competing element, urges that buyers must be self-reliant. An economic perspective suggests that the answer to the question of how much information one party to a sales transaction must give to another depends on how much it would cost each to obtain the information.

- The law must weigh facts and policies when dealing with conduct that physically injures a person. Consider, for example, the case of a speeding motorist who runs into a pedestrian and kills her. Since the driver was speeding, the criminal law may punish him in some way, and the pedestrian's family may sue the motorist for the financial consequences of her death. But should the criminal pun-

ishment be a fine? If so, how much? Should it also involve
jail time? If so, for how long? Should the money that the
motorist must pay the victim's family be measured only to
compensate the victim's family for losing her, or should it
include "punitive" damages, which themselves serve a
kind of punishment purpose? What precisely were the
facts? Just how fast was the motorist driving? In how
densely populated an area? Was he drunk or under the
influence of a controlled substance? Was he driving in a
way that distinguished his behavior from a manner in
which almost every motorist drives at some time in any
given month? Was he driving at the speed at which most
motorists drive on that stretch of highway most of the
time, which happens to exceed the posted speed limit by
ten miles per hour? Was he driving someone to the
hospital? What will be the likely effect on that particular
driver's future conduct of a specific form of criminal
punishment or a particular amount of civil damages?
What will be its effect on drivers in general?

In cases of this sort, courts must weigh assumptions about
the behavioral effects of different kinds of remedies, the social
consensus (if one is discernible) about the level of culpability of
particular types of conduct, and an intuitive sense of how people
in society would react to a particular type of penalty or award.
When a trial judge says, "five years in jail," or an appellate court
affirms a judgment for $150,000 compensatory damages and
$500,000 punitive damages, they are balancing all these consider-
ations.

- The need to balance competing property interests is evident in the case of the homeowner who uses a very loud
  stereo well into the wee hours of the morning. If you are
  his neighbor, you would see only one right. That is, a right
  rooted in your interest in peace and quiet after a reasonable hour—what *you* think of as a reasonable hour. If you
  are the stereo owner, you would see yourself as exercising
  an important right—the right to use your property as you
  wish. Maybe you would even believe, and certainly your
  lawyer would argue, that you are somehow exercising your
  right to free expression. When courts decide nuisance
  cases, or when city councils write noise regulation ordinances, they balance these rights. A city council probably

will set rough guidelines about when someone can generate loud noises. It may impose outright prohibitions on some forms of noise. For other kinds of noise, it may announce quantitative standards, for example, rules expressed in terms of decibel levels, perhaps also referring to specified hours of the day or night. Each of these decisions represents a social weighing of interests in conflict.

- A further example, from the area of constitutional law, concerns the law of defamation and its relation to the First Amendment's prohibition of restrictions on speech. A few analysts of free speech issues argue for an "absolutist" position, saying essentially that there is never a persuasive reason for government to regulate speech, even defamatory speech. Others insist, by contrast, that in this area of human controversy as in others it is exactly the role of courts to weigh competing interests and the policies that support them. These commentators would say, for example, that despite the attraction of the idea that the cure for vicious speech is always more speech, sometimes speech becomes so offensive or harmful that its destructive effects outweigh the social interest served by freedom of communication.

- Some very personal interests that are litigated present questions that are especially difficult because of their high emotional content. For example, suppose that a husband and wife use in vitro fertilization to conceive embryos, and they have the embryos frozen in order to start a pregnancy later on. The couple later divorces while the embryos are still frozen. The ex-wife wants to have possession of the embryos so that in the future she can implant them and give birth to children. She claims that she has a "right" to be a parent. The husband wants the embryos destroyed. He claims that he has a "right" not to be a parent. How should the court weight these two proposed rights?

The Concept of Factor Analysis

An approach that parallels the balancing of interests in the setting of legal standards is the technique of factor analysis.

Where the balancing of interests may evoke the metaphor of a scale and two sets of weights, the technique of factor analysis might trigger the image of a smorgasbord menu. It enables the court to draw upon a catalog of several factors, sometimes presented as a list, from which it selects what it considers the most relevant factor or factors as the basis for its decision. The sources of this catalog may be prior judicial decisions or statutes.

It is useful to have in mind the way in which a cause of action that involves factor analysis differs from one defined by elements. An elements claim, such as a cause of action for an intentional tort like battery, requires the plaintiff to prove each element of the definition of that tort—for example, the defendant's intent, contact with the body, and the plaintiff's lack of consent. By contrast, in the case of a cause of action that involves factors, the plaintiff will offer facts that relate to those factors, but her success will not necessarily depend on offers of proof under each factor. Rather, the successful plaintiff will convince the court that the circumstances of the case are favorable to her with respect to the most important factor or factors in the list, or that, on balance, her proof satisfies enough factors to outweigh the opposing claim.

Legislatures sometimes write statutes that contain lists of factors for courts to consider. One typical example is a statute directing courts to divide a couple's marital property between them at divorce, taking into account several relevant factors, including

(1) the contribution of each spouse to the acquisition of the property

(2) the value of other individual property set apart for each spouse

(3) the duration of the marriage

(4) the economic circumstances of each spouse

(5) the age of each spouse

(6) if there are children of the marriage, the custodial spouse's need for the family home.[1]

A court deciding how to apportion the property of a divorcing couple with children, possessing modest means, might decide that a spouse with a job outside the home had the stronger case

---

1. Taken from the original Uniform Marriage and Divorce Act § 307.

on factor (1), despite the other spouse's contributions in home-making. It might decide that factor (2) counted for nothing because neither spouse had individual property set aside. However, the court might conclude that there was a significant disadvantage to the spouse who had not pursued a career during a long marriage, and who thus argued that it would be difficult to find work. This would cut in favor of that spouse on factors (3), (4) and (5). Moreover, if there are minor children, the court might conclude that the spouse who does not have outside employment should have custody of the children and that that spouse should get a bigger split of the property to account for the expense of raising the children while they are young—an application of factors 3 through 6 in favor of that spouse.

Some people think that lists of factors are cop-outs—that they provide judges an excuse to do almost anything they please. Or, in more legal terms, they give the judge too much discretion. For example, some people might be apprehensive that a family court judge dealing with a division of marital property would think that the economic circumstances of each spouse should dominate all other factors. Moreover, a major concern of critics is that to allow judges that much discretion leads to a high risk of unpredictable decisions. A more mechanical rule—for example, requiring that each spouse gets 50 percent of a couple's combined assets—provides a more predictable outcome and more efficient decision-making.

Factor analysis does present the risk of unpredictability, and also increases the possibility that judges will impose their personal biases. However, defenders of factor analysis think its discretionary aspect—the way it permits judges to determine the weight of each factor or to choose the most relevant factor from a list— also presents advantages. Indeed, a primary justification for the use of factor analysis is that it forces conscientious judges to focus on the most relevant facts, often including the individual circumstances of the parties, as well as policies and precedents, to determine which factors are most important for the decision. The flexibility provided by these standards may lead to an outcome that is more fair in the circumstances than the results produced by a rigid rule.

When courts weigh the individual interests of parties or set priorities among several factors, they fulfill an important role of judges, that is, to exercise *judgment.* The law often does not emerge as a neat grid of mechanical rules. The very idea of law, as we have emphasized, arises from dispute and controversy in individual cases. Of course, the law tries to impose order on messes, and appellate review provides some of that order when appellate courts impose guidelines on lower courts' exercise of discretion. But often the result is not an entirely tidy package. Factor analysis can provide a flexible means of sorting out several elements of an intellectually complex situation. The judge who seriously reviews a catalog of decisional factors will be the more honest, and the more persuasive, the more she reveals how she sorted out and ranked those factors.

It is fair to ask how factor analysis relates to the process of judicial weighing and balancing. Properly done, factor analysis results in a form of balancing. Candidly done, it can help judges who write opinions to persuade their readers that they have done justice.

10

Policy Foundations

Non-lawyers probably tend to think of law as a technical set of rules. They are not wrong, up to a point. There is a side to law that is relatively mechanical. Here is a mechanical rule: it is an offense to drive more than 40 miles per hour. Mr. D drives 55. He has broken the rule and committed an offense.

But in more cases than most people might ordinarily think, the law is anything but mechanical. There are exceptions even to the apparently ironclad rule mentioned above. One may drive above the posted speed when operating an emergency vehicle or taking a woman in labor to the hospital. More importantly, one cannot begin to understand or interpret a rule unless one understands the policy basis for the rule. The question is not so much "what?" as "why?"

There are many policies that underlie various rules of law. This chapter does not attempt to present an exhaustive catalog. We do try to identify some of the most important policies, or rationales, for decisionmaking. Although we may not have presented the very one that your professor in torts or contracts or civil procedure will invoke in tomorrow's class, we have put together a number of often mentioned ideas. We suspect that for most students, these concepts will inform, or even dominate, discussion in many of your classes.

Some Basic Jurisprudential Concepts

This section summarizes some basic ideas in the philosophy of law that courts apply to a wide range of specific legal topics.

1. The Descriptive and the Normative

An introductory point concerns the distinction between "descriptive" or "positive" analysis and "normative" concerns. Many analysts of law concern themselves principally with describing things the way they are. In theory, this is a "scientific" enterprise. In some academic contexts, scholars will refer to this endeavor as descriptive or positive analysis.[1] For the purposes of this summary, the relevant point is that description should not have ideological overtones.

The normative, by contrast, deals with the "ought." Those who examine the law normatively will make a bow to the facts that descriptive analysis turns up (although, of course, on important questions there is likely to be disagreement about what the facts are). However, the normative question is, how *should* one decide a particular controversy? Assume, for example, that an analysis of factory work indicates that production is more efficient in states where employers do not have to pay compensation to workers for industrial injuries than in states that require employers to pay for such injuries. If you accepted the definition of efficiency that was offered in that analysis, that might be a fact. But that positive analysis would not necessarily settle the question of whether factory owners *ought* to pay compensation to their injured workers. Such issues present normative questions, and ought issues often are difficult ones.

Those opposing compensation may say that employees should take their chances with risks that they freely choose to confront. Those who support compensation might say that compassion for injured workers should outweigh, in this case, a philosophical commitment to freedom of choice. They might argue that from an ethical point of view, the burden of such

---

1. The term "positive" has several refinements of meaning. A related meaning that you may encounter is one that emphasizes the development of models of reality that produce accurate predictions of real world behavior.

injuries should be assessed to the enterprise as a cost of doing business. Moreover—just to bring positive analysis back into the discussion—advocates of compensation might confront a descriptive facet of the anti-compensation argument directly and say that it is not a fact that workplace risks are freely chosen. They might use statistical surveys based on worker interviews to show that duress compels employees to accept certain risks that they are not free to choose.

2.   Is the Law Neutral?

An important and continuing argument about the system of justice concerns the question of neutrality of decisionmaking. There is a strong tradition of belief that this should be a principal goal of judges. In the purest version of this view, judges should— and can—put aside their personal biases and make decisions that are free of their own political and ideological conceptions. That is an ideal, and many believe that to strive for it will promote respect for courts and for the law generally.

Counterposed against this view is one that urges frank recognition that judges carry around a lot of baggage of personal experience and philosophy and inevitably will apply their preconceived premises to their decisions. Some people will go further and suggest that judges *ought* to apply their biases, perhaps even arguing that it is quite appropriate for interest groups to lobby for the appointment of judges that represent their political points of view.

Law students should be apprised of an important feature of present academic life that reflects ideological struggles in the world generally, and that relates to the issue of neutrality of decisionmaking. This is the rise of schools of thought about the law that feature avowedly ideological approaches, sometimes focusing on the impact of the law on particular groups. We will briefly discuss some of these approaches, including such schools of thought as feminism, critical legal studies, and critical race theory, in the next chapter.

Many who take these positions will stress that law and decision-makers are not, and cannot be, neutral. Indeed, with reference to the criticism that their own positions are ideological, they will respond that the traditional ways of analyzing the law are themselves ideological. They will argue that an especially pernicious quality of traditionalist approaches lies in the way they mesh their ideological content with professions of neutrality.

3. Reason and Arbitrariness

One idea that recurs throughout the law is that rules require reasons. When we demand the "rationale" for a rule, we are basically asking its proponents to give us reasons for it. Those reasons may be dry and abstract, or they may be full of juice and richly related to life. In either event, when we ask for reasons, we are saying: Persuade us. Convince us. Tell us why we should have this rule.

If you reflect on this idea, you will come to see that it is central to our legal system. To take an exaggerated example, let us say that a police officer discovers Mr. A dead on the sidewalk, and finds Mr. B casually leaning against a utility pole in the next block. Without any other facts, the officer arrests Mr. B for the murder of Mr. A. Could a court allow a conviction of Mr. B for the murder? Why not? Because it would be arbitrary—the very opposite of a reasoned decision. This fits into the law as the law actually is applied because such a conviction would violate due process. One of the most fundamental meanings of due process is that the decisionmaker must have a reason for her decision.

4. Clarity and Notice

Another important jurisprudential principle is that the law should be clear. This idea links up with the strong opposition the law manifests to arbitrariness. If the rules are muddled, or too vague, they do not give a signal to people about how they should behave. Particularly in the case of rules that impose sanctions for their violation, this is unjust. It is especially important that the criminal law be clear because people should have notice of the kind of behavior that will brand them as criminals.

The requirement that people should have notice of the law is an independent principle that applies not only to the criminal law but to law generally. An often used example of lack of notice is that of the Roman emperor who inscribed the laws so high up on a column that no one could read them. If rules are hidden away, or if they are not clear, then people cannot know them, conform their behavior to them, or even challenge them. This is unfair, in addition to often being inefficient. How can you obey a rule when you do not know it exists? Although various levels of governmental units do not have to give direct actual notice of each law to all members of the community, they must publish their laws at all levels: constitutions, statutes, ordinances, and administrative regulations. For example, the federal government publishes the *Federal Register*, a daily collection of proposed and newly adopted administrative rules and regulations. Among other things, the *Federal Register* also publishes presidential documents and notices of public meetings.

5. Predictability and Stability

Another goal of the law is that of predictability, a goal that fits in especially well with the requirements of a business-oriented society. Business persons have to know what the rules are so that they can order their productive lives. Much of the law of contracts revolves around this idea. A lot of current controversy about the effects of tort law turns on assertions that expanded liabilities for personal injury leave businesses uncertain about when they will have to pay compensation for injury and how much they will have to pay.

Yet it is not just business persons who desire predictability in the law. People generally have a stake in rules that are relatively stable and that will be enforced in much the same way from day to day. For example, they count on property rules to uniformly assure them clear title to the homes they purchase and for reliable guidelines about how to make an effective gift. We all make plans—short-range and long-range—based on the ideas that we can know today what the law will be tomorrow and that those who resolve our disputes will behave consistently.

6. Treating Like Cases Alike

In our discussions of stare decisis in Chapter Four and analogies in Chapter Seven we introduced the idea that like cases should be treated alike. This principle has an obvious linkage to the desire for predictability as well as to respect for precedent. People would like to think that if they behave in a particular way that has been approved or allowed by a prior rule, they can count on having that conduct judged in the way it has previously been judged. One reason for this way of thinking is quite practical. The knowledge that your conduct will be treated as similar conduct has previously been treated helps you to plan your life.

Beyond that, there is a philosophical basis for the principle. It lies in a sense that inconsistency of results on similar facts is simply unjust. You have only to consult your intuition to validate this belief. Ask yourself how you would react to the application of opposing rules to identical events that occurred one month apart. It is a safe bet that you would say, "That is unfair." The principle therefore has an ethical foundation as well as roots in pragmatic needs to develop strategies for business and personal life.

7. Flexibility in the Law

An important counterweight to such goals as clarity and predictability is that the law should be flexible. Haven't you thought, on occasion, that someone in a position of authority was rigid or unbending? Sometimes following a rule out to its logical conclusion does not yield what people would call justice. It is for that reason that practically everyone values flexibility in decision-makers, at least some of the time, and that the law creates exceptions to rules. It is also for that reason that some legislation requires that courts exercise discretion rather than apply a mechanical rule, even though discretionary lawmaking is less predictable than the application of fixed rules. We want the law to be able to bend enough to take particular circumstances into account.

8. Responsiveness to Social Change

A particular challenge to the effort to keep the law stable and predictable arises from the need to make law responsive to changing social conditions. Rules conceived for simple social and economic situations may require changes to respond to more complex environments, both with respect to the solution of disputes and the effort to prescribe standards for conduct. Here are a few examples.

- Rules of contract governing acceptance of an offer, designed for an age when the fastest transmission of written information was by the mail, should be re-evaluated at a time of fax machines, e-mail, and agreements made on the Internet.

- Rules concerning personal injuries caused by products that served a time when most goods were sold face to face must change when confronted with systems of mass production and sales that extend over long chains of distribution.
- Rules of procedure that responded to an era when it was considered part of the game to spring surprise evidence on opponents have given way to elaborate systems of pretrial discovery of evidence in the possession of the other party.
- Rules of property designed for a society that thought it proper that the eldest son of a family should inherit all its land have been replaced by inheritance rules that distribute property equally among children of both sexes, regardless of age.

These are only illustrations of situations in which courts and legislatures have found that the need to respond to changes in society outweighs the need for predictability and certainty.

9. Policies and Balancing

As we suggested in Chapter 9, policies may conflict. For example, suppose a person is driving while intoxicated. He crashes, suffering injuries that he alleges were especially serious because the car he was driving was not adequately designed to withstand foreseeable collision impacts. Should he recover damages for his enhanced injuries from the car manufacturer? On one hand, the state has a strong interest in deterring drunk driving. On the other hand, the state has a strong policy of imposing a duty on manufacturers to produce safe products. Which policy outweighs the other?

10. The General vs. the Specific

An age-old question that runs through the law is whether rules should be general or specific. We will begin with a general answer—some of both.

How much care should a supermarket owner take against the risk that a customer will slip on something in the store aisles—a spilled beverage or a stray grape? The answer that the law usually gives is a general one, which some people may say is vague: the standard of conduct for supermarket owners is that of "reasonable care."

We could have a much more specific rule that says that a market is liable if, at least every twelve and one half minutes, it did not have someone clean each aisle where things might spill.

Which rule do you like better? We will guess it is the more general one, because there are so many things one would want to take into account in deciding whether it is appropriate to make a market pay for a slip-and-fall injury: the number of spills, the number of injuries believed to be caused by spills, the average age of the shoppers, the policies followed by other markets, the size of the market, the number of employees.

There will, however, be some circumstances in which we would prefer a more precise, even quantitative rule. Perhaps, in certain workplace settings, we would want to say that a barrier that guards against the risk of falls must be 54 inches high. That is not because 54 inches is a magic number. It is because that height represents an estimate about the probability of falls by employees over any lower barrier, perhaps allowing some margin for error, and a practical judgment that that probability would be unacceptable. An important justification for such a rule is that it tells the factory owner just what she has to do. The owner may not much care whether the number is 54, or 50, or 58. She principally wants to be given a specific standard.

Or maybe she does care, because each extra inch of height on the barrier is costly. But it may be worth it to her to have a specific rule rather than one that just says, "use reasonable care," because that vague language may effectively force her to set up a barrier that is 60 or even 62 inches high, just to be safe.

Another consideration, which may cut in the other direction, is efficiency in the lawmaking process itself. It may be costly to go out and do surveys about how the average height of workers and the height of barriers relate to accident rates. We might conclude that a standard like "barriers of reasonable height" would be much cheaper to devise, and not much more costly to enforce, than a rule that specifies barrier heights in inches.

There is no easy rule that tells you when to be relatively specific and when to be relatively general or vague. Just be aware that your professors will tease you from time to time with this problem. Understand, moreover, that this is serious teasing, because it reflects the exact kinds of choices that courts, legislatures, and administrative agencies must make in the everyday world of judging and lawmaking.

The contrasts evident above between the values of predictability and of flexibility, and the tension between the general and the specific, will teach a lesson that is difficult for many law students, but familiar to all lawyers. This is that one must be able to analyze problems through a variety of lenses and be prepared to bring to bear a variety of rationales in the effort to solve problems. The ability to do that is a distinguishing feature of the well-trained law student and the creative lawyer.

11. Different Kinds of Rationality

Lawyers are fond of demanding rationality in rules. But the content of rationality may vary depending on the legal context, for example, as between trial and appellate courts and between courts and legislatures. Judges—in particular, appellate judges—are likely to hold other judges—in particular, trial judges—to rather high standards of rationality. They will insist that trial judges adhere to a relatively well-defined legal logic, for example, in ruling on motions and in fashioning jury instructions.

Appellate courts will be somewhat more lenient in setting rationality tests for juries. For example, in affirming some large damages awards for intangible elements of injury like pain and suffering, they may say something like this: "We would not have awarded as much money as this jury did, but we cannot say that the size of the award is 'shocking to the conscience' "—that is, that it is irrational.

Courts also will be relatively lenient when they review certain types of legislation to decide whether it is constitutional, for example, legislation regulating economic behavior. Litigants often call on courts to do that, claiming that a statute violates a constitutional provision such as the due process clause or the equal protection clause. In that type of situation, a judge who reviews legislation challenged on equal protection grounds may conclude that the statute is personally distasteful to her. However, courts often will say something like this in refusing to hold unconstitutional statutes dealing with such matters as economic regulation: "We refuse to sit as a superlegislature to weigh the wisdom of legislation."[2] Exercising even more self-restraint, the Supreme Court has declared, "We cannot say that the regulation has no rational relation to that objective and therefore is beyond constitutional bounds."[3]

Our general point is that rationality has many faces, depending on the subject matter of disputes and whether courts are reviewing the product of other judges, of juries, or of legislatures.

Approaches to Justice: Different Lenses

The next three sections briefly summarize three principal approaches to justice. You might liken them to different lenses on a camera. Each emphasizes certain features of the subject, while tending to exclude others or put them in the background. (1) "Corrective justice," at least in its pure form, centers on achieving the just result between the litigants in a dispute. (2) "Instrumentalism" emphasizes the need for courts to go beyond the individual merits of litigants' claims to consider the policy consequences of decisions in particular cases, and thus contrasts with the pure concept of corrective justice. (3) "Distributive justice" involves the idea of redistributing wealth and represents a much broader idea of entitlement than does corrective justice, one that applies not only between individuals, but among classes of persons.

1. Corrective Justice

The concept of corrective justice enters many discussions of the law. In fact, volumes have been written on this idea. First articulated by Aristotle in Book V of his *Nicomachean Ethics*, corrective justice requires an injurer to compensate the loss incurred by his victim to the extent of the gain the injurer has received through his wrongful conduct. Corrective justice fixes on the relationship between particular parties and the actual harm caused. One way to phrase the basic idea of corrective justice is

2. Ferguson v. Skrupa, 372 U.S. 726 (1963) (upholding a statute that regulated "the business of debt adjusting").

3. Williamson v. Lee Optical Co., 348 U.S. 483 (1955) (upholding a state statute that made it unlawful for persons who were not licensed optometrists or ophthalmologists to fit lenses to a face).

to say that it centers on redress for wrongs; corrective justice seeks to make things right between the parties. A central feature of the concept is its focused response to individual controversies. Corrective justice provides a way to sort out rights and wrongs in particular disputes. In its most rigorous form, corrective justice excludes considerations of policy that go beyond the individual dispute between the litigants.

Often, the "gain" acquired by the injurer under the framework of corrective justice is not as self-evident as in the case of a thief who steals goods from another. For example, take the case of a motorist who injures another driver while driving well above the speed limit. Here, the injurer arguably benefitted from his violation of state-regulated speed limits that are imposed on all drivers. Similarly, an automobile manufacturer who produces shoddy products that result in an injury to a consumer has received an advantage through the use of substandard materials, securing a monetary profit in the form of lower manufacturing costs. In both cases, the driver and the manufacturer must recompense their victims' loss with money representing the advantage each has received through his injurious conduct.

2. Instrumentalism

A contrast to the party-centered method of rationalizing legal judgments that characterizes the purest form of corrective justice is an approach that is widespread in the American way of looking at the law. It often goes under the name of "instrumentalism." Many of your teachers will emphasize—or assume—an instrumentalist approach to the law. That is, they will assume that when one analyzes a legal dispute between particular individuals, one must consciously take into account the effects that a decision one way or another will have on society more generally.

Consider, for example, the question of whether a low-income purchaser who buys a consumer product—say, a television set—at a very high interest rate should be able to get out of the sales contract on the theory that the contract is unconscionable. Perhaps some courts would conclude that it would be fair to let the consumer get out of the contract—"fair" as between the parties. But under one instrumentalist approach to the problem, a court might reason that to free buyers from their contracts on a fairness basis would destabilize consumer markets for home electronics by increasing sellers' expenses. The result, in fact, might be to raise the overall price for television sets, with particular harm to the poor consumers that the court presumably would be trying to protect by voiding the contract. The instrumentalist approach employed by a court that refused to hold the contract unconscionable, which would take into account the larger policy implications of the case, would therefore yield a different result than at least a highly individualized form of corrective justice. This is not to say that the results produced by corrective justice and instrumentalism cannot coincide, but sometimes the approaches will produce different outcomes.

Instrumentalism has its place in public law controversies as well as disputes between private parties, like contract cases. One Supreme Court justice has said that in interpreting constitutional provisions, judges should consider the consequences of their decisions. Carefully pointing out that judges who "emphasize[] consequences" are "aware of the legal precedents, rules, standards, practices and institutional understanding that a decision will affect," he says that "to consider consequences is not to consider simply whether the consequences of a proposed decision are good or bad," but rather "to emphasize consequences related to the particular" provision of the Constitution at issue.[4]

3. Distributive Justice

Rather distinct from the concept of corrective justice is the idea of "distributive justice," which for present purposes we may define as a normative concept—an "ought" idea—of how economic goods *should* be distributed, according to moral criteria such as the principle of equity. Again, we do not suggest these are airtight categories. However, American lawyers generally think of distributive justice as a job for a legislature. We sometimes allow Congress and state legislatures to take from the rich and give to the poor—notably, through the tax system. A legislature literally redistributes wealth. If you think about it, you will recognize that frequently half the headlines on the front page of any newspaper deal with this issue in some form, especially when Congress or a state legislature is in session.

4. See "Breyer rebuts 'originalists' in Tanner Lecture," Harvard Law Bulletin, Jan. 2005, at 8.

Of course, some judicial decisions may have redistributive effects. A decision that changes a general rule in pollution cases might have substantial redistributive effects between industries and homeowners when it favors a group of homeowners harmed by a factory's discharge of toxic materials into air or water. Sometimes we allow judges to do this kind of distributive justice, but our system tends to be wary of allowing courts to serve as redistributive agencies. One way to express the general reason is that we think of income distribution as a "political" rather than a "legal" matter. Given a belief that courts should be as neutral as possible, we try to steer judges away from making political, redistributive decisions—as much as possible. By contrast, we are much more prone to accept the idea that legislatures can transfer money from one class of people to another in the name of community ideas of fairness, although under constitutional limits, such as the prohibition in federal and state constitutions against taking property without due process of law.

Courts and Legislatures Compared

A view widely shared by American lawyers and judges is that courts exist primarily to resolve disputes, employing relatively specific rules, while the main function of legislatures is to make relatively general rules for society, often arbitrating among the claims of competing interest groups.

Most students of the American legal system would agree, at some level of generality, that it is best for legislatures to resolve issues concerning moral choices that society must make, as well as questions about large-scale distribution of wealth. The argument is that elected representatives, representing the political will of the people, are best qualified to fight out big social questions. Legislatures also have a greater fact-finding capacity than do judges, a capability that is also necessary for decisions on large social issues.

By contrast, courts generally are deemed best able to deal with interstitial questions—issues that lie in the cracks within large questions of morality and within controversies about the distribution of resources between and among groups. Thus, generally speaking, no legislature has improved on the judicial administration of a standard of negligence that defines it as conduct that falls below a "reasonable standard of care." Part of the reason for this is that the concept of negligence must be applied to thousands of different situations, making it impossible for a legislature to fashion a code so precise that it would cover all those occurrences.

There are, however, areas of overlap between judicial and legislative roles as analysts traditionally distinguish them. Thus, a legislature might decide that a pattern of issues has arisen so often in litigation that it should adopt a specific rule to resolve those issues. Consider, for example, a personal injury case in which a firm had complied with a governmental safety regulation but someone was hurt. Should the fact of the firm's compliance conclusively establish that it was not negligent with respect to injuries that the regulation was designed to prevent? Although sometimes a corporation might "really" be negligent even though it fulfilled the letter of a safety regulation, a legislature might decide that to save arguments about such questions that would otherwise arise in scores of cases, it should make a flat rule: one who obeys a safety regulation issued by an administrative agency may not be held negligent. A court could also announce such a rule on its own. By contrast, courts might hold that compliance with regulations can be used as evidence that a defendant was not negligent, but is not a hard and fast defense.

More dramatic examples of tensions in this zone of over-lap—tensions less easily resolvable—appear in certain aspects of judicial review of legislation to determine whether it is constitutional. Some of the most publicized modern illustrations are the decisions of the Supreme Court on segregation of public schools and on abortion. In holding that it was a denial of equal protection to segregate school children by race, the Supreme Court effectively took over the resolution of a large social issue on which several state legislatures—presumably representing the majority will of their constituents—had made decisions that the Court considered unconstitutional. The Court's activity in this area has represented, at least in part, a moral choice.

The Supreme Court's current jurisprudence on abortion also embodies its determination that some anti-abortion laws made by state legislatures, reflecting strongly held moral premises, violate deeply rooted principles of constitutional policy. The continuing political argument on this issue is another powerful example of the tension over the question of whether the legislature or the court is "supreme" in an area of disputed moral principles. One law professor wryly summarized the way people play word games on this subject when she said, "Judicial legislating is an allegation people make when they disagree with the outcome."[5]

Concepts of Judicial Administration

This Part presents policy considerations that focus on judicial administration—in simple terms, how courts run their own business. It is not immediately evident to many beginning law students that an important factor in judicial decisionmaking is the impact of decisions on the court system itself. If one thinks about the point, however, it appears logical. Courts cost money. Courts are a last resort for dispute resolution, at least in our society. We want people to try to work out grievances among themselves, and we wish to use social resources to resolve disputes only if there is no other (peaceful) way to do that.

1. Requirement That There Be a Dispute

One device that courts use to control their workload is to require that there really is a dispute—you may hear of this idea in your civil procedure or constitutional law courses in connection with the requirement that there be a "case or controversy" before the court. Courts use this concept to insist that the parties present a focused, present-time argument about a concrete issue. Judges say, in effect: Don't come to us because you think you are going to have an argument in the future. Don't ask us for "advisory opinions." We are not consultants; for that task, use a member of the clergy, or your friends and neighbors, or your psychotherapist, or even your lawyer. The courts exist only to resolve actual disputes.

2. Discouraging Frivolous and Fraudulent Litigation

Judges try to insure that courts use their resources only for serious matters; they will not allow "frivolous litigation" and they are hostile to fraudulent claims.

---

5. Heather Gerkin, quoted in "Did Florida Court Interpret the Law or Write It?," N.Y. Times, Nov. 30, 2000, at A22 (speaking of the controversy over the presidential election of 2000).

When courts condemn "frivolous" lawsuits, they sometimes are announcing their belief that there is no ground in law for a claim and that the claimant's attorney should have known that. They are saying that an attorney is trying to build a legal structure where there is no foundation—either no legal rule that supports that claim, or no facts to which to apply a valid legal rule, or no reason to argue that the court should adopt a new rule that would validate the claim. Sometimes they are saying that the plaintiff's allegations are too trivial for a court to take notice. For example, in rejecting a plaintiff's suit for mental suffering alleged to be caused by a bill collector's tactics, one court referred to "the 'wide door' which might be opened" if it allowed the claim, a door open "not only to fictitious claims, but to trivialities and mere bad manners."[6]

To be sure, there is a fine line between a frivolous claim and an argument that the court should extend an established rule or create a new one. Because under the rules of professional ethics, an attorney must represent her client zealously, courts that draw the line too restrictively against novel legal arguments may be accused of stifling that representation.

A different concern is outright fraud by litigants, for example, a litigant who fabricates facts in order to present a complaint that cannot be dismissed. Besides being morally wrong, and a breach of professional ethics for the attorney, this kind of conduct can have destructive effects on people's perceptions of justice. A fraudulent claimant may, in effect, extort money from a defendant who settles because he would rather pay the nuisance value of a fraudulent suit than fight it.

3. Administrative Efficiency

Beyond wielding their axes against transparently frivolous or fraudulent litigation, courts invoke other concerns of administrative efficiency to turn away disputes. They may tell a litigant that his or her grievance inspires their sympathy but that it just would be too costly, or otherwise too impractical, to do the judicial work necessary to resolve that claim.

One example is cases involving the shock felt by so-called "bystander witnesses"—people who are in the vicinity when

6. Medlin v. Allied Inv. Co., 398 S.W.2d 270, 274 (Tenn. 1966).

someone else suffers physical injury in an accident. These "by-standers" do not sustain a physical contact themselves but they sue for mental suffering—or perhaps even physical consequences, such as a heart attack—because of the fright of seeing a terrible event.

Fifty people might observe an accident, and ten of them might suffer consequences from seeing the event that legitimately sends them to the doctor. But courts try to minimize the chance that parades of claimants will come before them, especially when the alleged injuries are somewhat harder to pin down than the injuries typically caused by direct physical contact. In order to sort out these cases, courts have created relatively limited categories of people who can recover for injuries suffered as bystander witnesses. Principally, these will be relatives of the person who suffered a direct physical injury. In fact, in order to prevent the indefinite extension of liability, courts probably will limit the persons who can recover to very near relatives—members of immediate families, or perhaps only spouses, or only parents if the victim of the physical injury is a minor.

4. Promoting Settlement

In their effort to achieve administrative efficiency, courts often focus on promoting settlement. Indeed, most federal courts assign a set percentage of cases to mandatory settlement conferences. The kinds of substantive legal rules that courts choose will frequently affect the inclination of parties to settle cases, although sometimes that effect occurs in different ways. On some occasions, a relatively vague rule will promote settlement; because of the parties' uncertainty about the law, they will decide that it is better not to take a chance on the outcome of a trial. At other times, a rather precise rule will make clear the negotiating territory for settlement. Assume, for example, a negligence suit for loss of an arm. Assume further that a pattern of case law indicates that the state's appellate courts, in reviewing jury verdicts in personal injury cases, view the worth of an arm as $150,000. That will give both the plaintiff and defendant a basis for a settlement figure (which will be some amount less than $150,000) that will save both sides the expense of a trial.

Obviously, a principal element of the judicial desire to have parties settle their cases rather than litigate them is that courts want to keep their own workload manageable. But settlement does more than conserve judicial resources. It saves time, money, and often grief for litigants. Moreover, many people would invoke a philosophical reason for favoring settlement: it enhances community values to encourage disputants to work out their disagreements with each other.

5. Open Courts

Since you already have learned that lawyers have a comeback to almost any argument, you should not be surprised to find that there is a basic idea that competes with administrative efficiency. We can sum this up as the "open courts" idea. In fact, many state constitutions include what are sometimes labeled as "open courts" provisions, which seek to assure that the courts will be hospitable to citizen grievances.

Many judges are inclined to be relatively liberal about the kinds of complaints they will entertain. Of course, judges are sensitive to the pressure to control their caseloads—who wants to make more work for herself than she needs to? But American flags wave in the background when attorneys argue that courts should be more, rather than less, open to complaints. One might even say that open courts are an important distinguishing feature between democracies and totalitarian governments. The point does not appear that boldly in the decisions, but the idea is there, in the judicial subconscious, when there is a close question about whether to let a case in the courthouse door. Indeed, a relatively full judicial workload arguably is a good rather than a bad thing, because questions of law often include issues that deserve airing in a public forum.

Limiting the Judge's Role: Self-Restraint and Activism

As just one institution in the governance of human affairs, courts have a limited function in the overall scheme of law. Many law school courses, especially first-year courses, tend to focus on judicial cases. However, that focus may implicitly convey the idea that judges can, or should, play more of a role than they do.

In fact, the ethic of judicial self-restraint is deeply embedded in the system. Most lawyers, whatever their political views, do not ordinarily view the role of judges as one of dispensing compassion, for example. At the least, judges who respond to humanitarian concerns tend to dress them up in the garb of relatively neutral sounding reasons.

Part of this attitude arises from the idea, mentioned above, that the purposeful redistribution of wealth is generally a function for the legislature. Another set of concerns underlies the traditional, restrictive view of the judicial role. We fear judges injecting their personal moralities into individual disputes. Some observers may stress that judges cannot avoid doing that. Most people, however, probably would agree at some level that our sense of fairness in decisionmaking significantly depends on our belief in the decision maker's neutrality, or at least impartiality. This view exerts a powerful drag against judges overtly making choices between or among competing moral ideas.

To be sure, the very idea of the common law, as well as our tradition of constitutional law, provides some room for judicial activism. In the constitutional area, courts from time to time invalidate legislation—that is, they hold that statutes are unconstitutional. This is a form of activism, because it consists of the court—often a non-elected court—telling the legislature, which by definition represents the political will of the people, that it cannot have its way.

Courts dealing with common law cases also take activist roles on occasion, often without even thinking of themselves as being "activist." Notably, courts may formulate new theories of liability or expand existing grounds for lawsuits. One illustration comes from property law, where courts now imply a covenant (a promise) in residential leases, known as a warranty of habitability. Under that theory, the landlord covenants to the tenant that the premises are fit for residential use. Prior to these decisions, landlords did not owe a duty to keep rented premises habitable.

Sometimes courts go beyond simply creating new categories of actions. In their bolder acts, courts occasionally will provide remedies that unavoidably redistribute resources between or among relatively broad classes of people. For example, some federal trial courts have virtually taken over the management of certain state prisons, at least for a time, where prisoners significantly lacked basic protection and care. When courts do that, they effectively compel state governments—and thus taxpayers—to deliver more money for the benefit of prisoners.

It is beyond the scope of this book to give a full description of the principles governing the scope and limits of judicial activity. It is enough to stress here that, under the traditions of the common law, judges may adopt new liability doctrines, but also that most American judges have it bred in their bones that they should be very careful and selective about when they take steps that can be described as legislating. A good part of the reason lies in our sense that judges should not make broad social choices, nor should they impose their own moralities on litigants or society more generally. Deep roots of that thinking lie in our fear of tyranny, and in the idea that the legislature, composed entirely of elected representatives, is the principal foundation of our democracy. Less dramatic, but still fundamental foundations for the constraints we place on judges lie in the doctrine of stare decisis, and in the idea that the law should be stable and certain so that ordinary people know what the law is and can rely on it.

11

Choices Among Policies

The competition among interests we have described in Chapter 9 gives rise to the need for decisionmakers to reconcile, or sometimes to choose among, the social policies described in Chapter 10 that underlie those interests. Those policies frequently clash with one another.

The Struggle Over the Goals of the Law

Judges always will be influenced by the pull of individual claims of justice in particular cases. It is useful to reiterate, however, that American courts, especially appellate courts, tend to be "instrumentalist"—that is, they look beyond the claims of the parties for individualized justice to the social implications of their decisions.

The law schools have provided important stimuli to the policy analysis of law in which courts now engage. In some law schools, students will find that there is quiet—sometimes not so quiet—warfare among their teachers about the primary goals of law and policy. Some teachers who have a law and economics slant, for example, will focus exclusively, or in very large part, on using the law to achieve efficiency. Others will suggest that the law should focus primarily on equity, or will emphasize redress of historic injustices. Some will say, or assume, that the power of the law lies in its ability to choose among different goals, and to accommodate several different sets of rationales and aspirations.

You ought to be aware that your teachers come to the law with intellectual baggage. Be prepared, as a pragmatic matter, to adapt to the particular prisms through which individual teachers view the law. This does not mean that you have to bow down to ideas that seem screwy to you. It does mean that sometimes you have to be alert to where a teacher is "coming from." Moreover, even if you violently disagree with a professor's views, you might learn something. At worst, you will learn that there is another side to issues on which you hold strong views. That realization, in itself, is part of a lawyer's equipment.

Justice–Oriented Concepts

There is a wide spectrum of ideas in the law that employ the terminology of "justice." Many people probably think of the problem of justice as basically involving issues concerning the distribution of wealth. That is certainly one version of justice, but its applications do not have to be as simple as the redistributive exploits of Robin Hood. A sophisticated set of ideas about justice in recent philosophical literature derives from the work of John Rawls. In very simplified form, the Rawls approach asks the decisionmaker to consider the distribution of goods that she would choose if she did not know, in advance, the place in life she would occupy at the time of the relevant litigation or legislative enactment. How would you like wealth to be distributed if you did not know beforehand whether you would find yourself in the top third, the middle third, or the bottom third of the economic ladder?

Notions of ethics and morality tie in with the idea of justice. The justice orientation of some people, including some law professors, inclines towards equity; among other things, these people believe in relatively equal distributions of goods among the population. Others see that as a basically unethical position, because it fails to reward effort and the virtue that effort represents. Particularly if your past education has not focused on these questions, you may find that teachers who challenge you with them force you to do some of the hardest thinking you must do in law school.

Here are capsules of just a few of the positions that various teachers may advocate, sometimes out of conviction and sometimes to make you think.

The wealth maximizer will contend that the principal goal of law is to increase the total store of goods in society. One ethical justification draws on the practical assumption that the more goods are produced, the more they will be spread around, thus benefitting the poorer as well as the richer segments of the population.

The libertarian will argue that the law should resist intruding in people's affairs—it should "stay off their backs"—letting people live their own lives and work out their own bargains among themselves so far as social peace allows. Libertarians frown on labor unions and civil rights laws. They will argue that union wages command more than an efficient share of the income of companies and that civil right laws, on balance, produce more discrimination than would exist without them. People who take the libertarian position also tend to oppose various kinds of regulatory regimes, such as the regulation of safety in the workplace. They would suggest that, in that environment, people should be able to decide whether they want to face a particular risk at a given wage without the interference of a paternalistic government.

Critical legal studies (CLS) scholars occupy a spectrum of positions about law, all of them critical of law as a tool of oppression. CLS scholars question the underlying principles of the law. One thing that the so-called "crits" emphasize is that law is not neutral, but dominated by power. Questioning the validity of the underlying principles of judge-made law, they assert that all law is political. They strongly oppose the notion that decision-makers can be dispassionate and can put aside their experiences, perhaps even their emotions, when they decide disputes. Why does a particular judge construe labor legislation in favor of management, time after time? The roots of this judicial behavior, a crit might explain, lie partly in the fact that the judge was the child of a corporate manager, grew up with people in that stratum of society, and imbibed assumptions of conservative, moneyed people about justice. Beyond that, many crits would insist that the judge is, at one level of consciousness or another, a tool of the managerial class.

The CLS movement has broken into several other groups, for example, Lat Crits, queer crits, and race crits.

Some practitioners of *critical race theory* carry this style of argument into legal controversies involving race, while sometimes criticizing CLS advocates for ignoring issues of race. Critical race theorists believe that race affects everyone's perceptions and understanding of the world. They assert that the racial distinctiveness and cultural experiences of racial minorities have been ignored and marginalized by majority white society. Indeed, some contend that most civic institutions are pervasively racially biased and oppress minorities. Like many CLS commentators, critical race theorists also reject formal legal analysis and the idea that law can be neutral. They reject the idea that formal law, such as the decision in *Brown v. Board of Education*, can bring about meaningful equality in our society.

An important technique of critical race theorists is to use narratives to tell stories that reveal the experiences of minorities and underline the deficiencies of the law in not taking account of those experiences. Critical race theorists may insist, for example, that legislators and judges who are not African–American cannot understand the African–American experience and are thus unqualified to make laws dealing with racially sensitive subject matter or to preside over litigation in which that experience was a crucial factor. They especially criticize the criminal justice system in this country for discriminating against African–American defendants. An example in the civil litigation area, illustrating how critical race theorists might question the use of whites on juries as well as white judges, would be a civil suit by an African–American plaintiff alleging maltreatment by white arresting officers.

We should note that critical race theorists themselves do not all agree on all issues. For example, some question whether, on balance, integration and affirmative action benefit African–Americans.

One brief summary of *"LatCrit"* philosophy refers to "this group's commitment to antisubordination and inclusive critical engagement of oppression within the Latina/o community."[1] A summary of " *'Queer' legal theory*" describes "a critical investigation of the ways in which white and straight supremacy interlock to create social and legal conditions that permit or encourage the

---

1. Robert Westley, Introduction Lat Crit Theory and the Problematics of Internal/External Oppression: A Comparison of Forms of Oppression and Intergroup/Intragroup Solidarity, 53 U. Miami L. Rev. 761, 761 (1999).

practice of permutated bigotries against the multiple diverse sexual minorities of the United States."[2]

As is so with critical race theorists, *feminists* are not a monolithic category. Their common enterprise, to be sure, involves the analysis of law through the prism of being female and often focuses on improving the status of women. Generally, feminists view society as inherently patriarchal. Early modern-day feminists—of the 1960s and 1970s—advocated equal opportunity in all areas to which the law applies, including employment, education, and family law. Some later feminists—the "difference feminists"—have instead advocated that women should be treated differently from men, in order to compensate for past disadvantages and to obtain meaningful equality. Like critical race theorists, they say that formal equality under the law does not bring actual equality. An even later strand of feminist thinking has come to emphasize women's individually different experiences. Like critical race theorists, feminists in this tradition use narratives and storytelling to manifest their diverse experiences and to demonstrate the patriarchal nature of the law and its unresponsiveness to women's concerns.

Many current issues divide those who call themselves feminists. The issue of surrogate motherhood[3] provides an example of their diverse points of view. Some feminists oppose surrogacy but others applaud it as an exercise of reproductive choice. Those who argue against the practice see it as a way of enslaving women, a patriarchal and medical conspiracy to control women's bodies. They criticize surrogacy as harmful to society, both as promoting baby selling and as degrading to the individual surrogate, whom they label "a rented womb." By sharp contrast, feminists who favor surrogacy argue that to prevent women from entering into voluntary contracts is itself degrading and paternalistic.

Feminists, however, will generally come together on certain ideas. You will not find any feminists laughing about the idea that negligence law has "never spoken of the reasonable woman." In fact, you probably will find few torts teachers—feminists

---

2. Francisco Valdes, Queer Margins, Queer Ethics: A Call to Account for Race and Ethnicity in the Law, Theory, and Politics of "Sexual Orientation," 48 Hastings L.J. 1293, 1296 (1997).

3. The term surrogate mother refers to a woman who contracts, usually with a childless married couple, to carry a baby and then give the baby to the couple for adoption. The baby is either conceived by artificial insemination of the surrogate with the sperm of the contracting male, or by in vitro fertilization of the contracting couple's sperm and eggs.

or not—who invoke that idea, which used to be considered good humor, even a staple of some teachers' classroom instruction. To take an even clearer example, the impact of feminism has made it clear that rape is not amusing. It may surprise you to learn that this was not necessarily the case in criminal law classes less than a generation ago.

Some Basic Economic Ideas

Many law professors introduce principles of microeconomics into their classes in order to help to explain the law, or in some cases to challenge it. Many casebooks also include notes and questions involving economic theory. Those teachers and books that employ economic theory will go much deeper than we do here. We aim to present, for reference, a convenient set of capsulized ideas that recur in the application of economic ideas to law. If you become weary of the details of economic analysis— the leaves on individual trees in the economic forest, so to speak—you may want to refer to this summary as a way of viewing the whole forest. By the way, some advocates of the use of narratives use their story-telling techniques as a challenge to the emphasis on economic analysis of law; for example, they use narratives to add concrete human experiences to economic abstractions.

1. Scarcity, Prices and Demand; The "Free Lunch"

Economic analysis generally proceeds on the premise that goods and services are scarce. This principle covers automobiles, stereo equipment, law school coursebooks, certificates of deposit, and visits to the dentist. Because the supply of these things—and people's resources—are limited, people often face choices about what to buy. Acquiring one of these items sometimes means forgoing another, so people concentrate their spending on purchasing the things they want the most. Generally, they indicate the strength of their desire to possess a good by how much they are willing to pay for it.

A related concept is that there is a close relationship between the price of a good and the amount of the good that people demand. Generally, as the price of a good increases, there will be a decrease in the number of units of that good that people will purchase. Conversely, when a producer lowers the price of a good, people will buy more of it. The conventional economic chart of this phenomenon, which will generally match up with your intuition, is called the "negatively sloped demand curve."

You have probably heard the phrase that "There is no such thing as a free lunch." Sometimes there may well be, but economic theory teaches us that, one way or another, we usually wind up paying for a good. Your college alumni office may invite you to a buffet supper party at which you do not have to pay for food or drink. If you value your minutes and hours, however, you may realize that your own expenditure of time creates a cost— the lost opportunity of doing something else you might otherwise have done. This "opportunity cost" will come home to you when you have to listen to the inevitable fund-raising appeal. Thus, you have "paid" for supper.

A topical example is the use by law students of electronic research services—Westlaw and Lexis. To superficial appearances, these come free to you. But the cost of the library's contract with the providers of these data bases inevitably will find its way into the price of your tuition.

Undoubtedly, this kind of analysis can get rather tortured. It will lead you into thinking that if a good friend buys you lunch, it is not out of the goodness of his or her heart, or simple friendship, but because he or she wants something. However far you want to take this approach, there is often something to the idea that free lunches are not truly free.

2. Free Markets

The economic theory presented in law school classes generally assumes free markets, or at least begins with a model of unregulated markets in which people are free to sell and buy goods and services at mutually agreed prices. Freedom of choice is a philosophical underpinning of economic analysis, paralleling the premise that there is competition in the marketplace. Two basic ideas tied in with markets are those of shopping ("searching") and bargaining. It is assumed that, within the limits of their resources, and given competing demands on those resources, consumers will shop for the goods that best fulfill their needs and, where it is possible to make deals with sellers, will bargain over price and other features of goods and services. A lack of competition inhibits a consumer's ability to bargain, however, and in the case of monopolies may make it well-nigh impossible.

The idea of shopping, or searching, shows the importance of information in markets, and it is useful to focus on the fact that information is not costless. You might buy a CD player for $150 at store X, not knowing that store Y, in easy walking distance, sells the same device for $117.50. Had you only known, you might say. But it would take some searching to acquire the information. Information, then, like the CD player itself, is a costly economic good.

If you have not had training in economic theory, you may get frustrated, from time to time, with certain assumptions that economics-oriented professors make about the nature of markets. You may think it is somewhat silly to talk about bargaining for price on a can of supermarket tomatoes, for example. However, the fact is that because you—and other consumers—are free to shop, all of you together engage in a masked form of bargaining about price with all sellers of canned tomatoes. Those sellers, because of competition, are always pricing their goods with an eye to what consumers are willing to pay, and to the level at which they think their competitors will set prices.

An important premise to keep in mind about free markets is that people should be able to make their own choices—about what consumer goods to buy, what kind of recreation to engage in, who to marry or live with. The devil, from this point of view, is paternalism. In law, it is government intervention that prevents or constrains free choice. Perhaps the most famous anti-paternalism declaration is John Stuart Mill's declaration in his essay On Liberty that "the only purpose for which power can rightfully be exercised over any member of a civilized community, against his will, is to prevent harm to others." Mill insisted that, with respect to conduct "which merely concerns himself," a person's "independence is, of right, absolute." In practice, there are many kinds of laws that restrict personal autonomy, for example laws that require motorists to wear seat belts or motorcyclists to wear helmets. But anyone who takes the "free" part of free markets seriously will tend to oppose paternalistic restrictions on personal choices.

Learn to treat the theoretical assumptions you encounter about markets in the same way you should treat the conventional use of legal hypotheticals. Do not be unduly quarrelsome, get used to economic theory, and make it your servant.

3. Efficiency

There are several basic definitions of efficiency, and volumes of variations. We begin by propounding one simple idea: The quest for economic efficiency involves, among other things, the effort to put resources to their most socially valued use. That is a neutral (some might think cold-blooded) concept. It does not have to do with fairness,[4] or ethics, or morality. The question is only what the people in a given economy, taken together, declare with their dollars (or pounds or yen) is most valuable to them.

This definition of efficiency implies that the efficient solution may not necessarily be the fair solution. A newly built factory that pollutes the air over several homeowners' dwellings may violate some people's sense of fairness. Efficiency-oriented economists will suggest, however, that if we are to take seriously the idea of putting resources to their best use, a flourishing factory that in effect uses a few homes as a sink for its pollution may be the most efficient use of the air over those homes. Moreover, if one thinks in terms of comparing benefits and costs, one may decide that consumers of the factory's products will value those products highly enough that the economic contribution of the factory to society, including the jobs that it provides, will far outweigh the annoyance, and perhaps even the ill health, that the pollution causes to a few homeowners.

Well and good, you may say, but those homeowners were there first. Some of their properties have been in their families for generations. The efficiency-oriented economist might respond, "I understand your concern, but you are talking about fairness and even sentimentality, not efficiency." Efficiency, on the one hand, and fairness in wealth distribution or in the allocation of resources, on the other hand, are distinct concepts. You may resist this idea. However, you should understand that efficiency-oriented economists do not necessarily contend that one should not be concerned about fairness. They simply observe that if what one wants is efficiency—and, perhaps the greatest good for the greatest number—the efficient solution may be unfair for some people. They also point out that when disputing parties offer contradictory versions of fairness, efficiency analysis will help us to see how much it will cost to achieve one brand of fairness or another.

---

4. We discuss the concept of fairness below, at pages 139–141.

Note, at the same time, some wrinkles in this form of analysis. Some of these variations have to do with the question of how one values both resources and costs. For example, one might put a value on the good health of the homeowners that outweighs the value of the pollution-causing factory. Alternatively, the homeowners might contend that a court should recognize a theory of social value beyond that represented by market prices. They might argue, for example, that the value of having stable communities is worth as much in an intangible sense as the factory's production is worth at market prices. Or, they might secure some experts in historic preservation to testify about the benefits society would realize from preserving their homes as historic places.

The homeowners might also refer to such intangible costs as the increased tension that the pollution inflicts on their everyday lives and their relationships, the fact that their children cannot play outside after school, and the general destruction of community values. Some people might value those costs at more than the production of the factory, which would suggest that the factory should be liable even if the sole standard for liability is inefficient conduct. These might be hard arguments to sell to many economists, but we are just trying to point out that there is some flexibility in definitions of value and cost. The practical effect of valuing intangibles at significant levels might be to raise the cost of pollution to a level where the imposition of liability on the polluter would be judged efficient, as well as fair.

4. Property Rights

Linked to economic analysis of law, and particularly to questions of efficient resource allocation, is the concept of property rights. How do we define what a property right is, and how do we determine when someone has one, to whom the right should be assigned, and what the consequences are of having such a right? Consider the different sorts of legal problems where these issues may prove fundamental.

- Mr. A begins openly occupying a piece of land to which Ms. B had title, and stays there for 15 years, during which Ms. B never shows up or demonstrates any attachment to the land. The doctrine of "adverse possession" may transfer the property right to Mr. A.

- A coal-fired railroad engine gives off sparks that cause fires on farmland that borders the tracks. Should the farmers be able to recover damages from the railroad company? Is there only one relevant "property right"— that of the farmers to the undisturbed agricultural use of their land? Or is there a countervailing "property right"— that of the railroad to pursue its lawful business of carrying passengers and freight?

- The X Company drills for petroleum in coastal waters, causing an oil spill that kills a large number of fish in fishing grounds that have consistently yielded profits to Y, a fisherman. Does Y have a sufficient "property right" in fish that swim in the open sea to sue X Company for the loss of his profits?

- A county extends the runways of an airport it owns to accommodate bigger jets, which cause much more noise over a larger area than previously was bothered by jet noise. If it does not compensate the homeowners whose property is newly affected by the noise, will the county be "taking" private property without just compensation, which is prohibited by the Fifth Amendment to the Constitution?

- The owner of a shopping mall wishes to keep political groups from handing out leaflets to customers on the premises. Can the owner enforce an action for trespass to stop the handouts without violating the group's First Amendment right of free speech?

- A state government wants to force owners of oceanfront property to give up strips of land so that members of the public can reach the beach. If it did so without paying for the strips of land, would it be unconstitutionally "taking" private property?

These few examples will give you a flavor of the ways in which the definition—and assignment—of property rights may affect the results in cases in diverse areas of the law. Among other things, they introduce the fact that the assignment of property rights often will be critical to the determination of whether an application of a legal rule is efficient or not. They also underline the importance of the distinction between private property and public property, and the need for law to play a role in resolving disputes about the limits of both.

5. Incentives and Disincentives

Economists put special stock in incentive effects for their own professional purposes, and sometimes devise rather technical measures for them. You, however, can go a long way in *legal* analysis by using your common sense about the tendency of particular legal rules to influence behavior.

One fundamental point is that incentives can be either positive or negative. Some rules will inspire people to more intense levels of certain kinds of activity. Other rules will provide disincentives—they will discourage particular types of behavior.

Consider, for example, the rule of contract law that presumes that one who signs a contract has read the document. The tendency of this rule is clear: it creates an incentive to read contracts, because it tells people who are preparing to make an agreement that there will be no profit in later claiming that they did not read what they signed. Almost every rule of law, from the simplest to the most complicated, may be argued to have incentive effects.

An illustration of a rule that creates disincentives is a rule that permits a court to award punitive damages for fraud. Such an award would be added to damages that give the plaintiff the difference between what he has received in a transaction and what he would have received if the bargain had been as the defendant represented. The so-called "benefit of the bargain" rule is a traditional measure of contract damages. The threat of having to pay an award that not only reflects the economic loss caused by a fraud (the lost benefit of the bargain), but adds a sum for the defendant's ethical transgression (the punitive damages), is likely to make people think more than twice about telling lies concerning the value of their goods.

Lawyers will often argue about the factual basis for assumptions concerning the incentive effects of rules. For example, an empirical disagreement may arise about whether one party to a fight to which both parties assented should be able to recover damages from the other for injuries that the other inflicted. Those who argue that there should be liability declare that such a rule will discourage fighting, since the prospect of having to pay damages to an opponent will make people much more cautious about engaging in brawls. The people who argue there should be no liability, however, contend that if one knows that he will not be able to recover for injuries that he himself suffers in a fight, he will be discouraged from slugging it out. Thus, both sides say that the rule that favors them will deter fighting.

This problem, featuring diametrically opposed assertions about the effects of yes-and-no rules on behavior, presents a good example of the sort of issue concerning incentive effects on which there is not likely to be solid social science research. For practicing lawyers, such an issue would leave a lot of room for effective advocacy that appeals to the experience and intuition of the judge or jury. The illustration also demonstrates to the law student that often there is plenty of room for plausible-sounding arguments on both sides about the incentive effects of particular rules.

6. Externalities

The idea of an "externality" is another concept that both lawyers and economists can use as a tool of argument.

We mostly tend to think of externalities as being negative effects from the conduct of others. An obvious example is smokestack pollution from a factory that causes illness in persons who live nearby. Another pretty clear example is A's loud stereo noise that keeps B from reading this book. A somewhat subtler illustration appears in the argument that a particular kind of gas tank design on a car is associated with an unacceptably high degree of injury to passengers when rear-end collisions smash the gas tank. In suing on the basis that the design is "defective," a person burned in a collision-triggered explosion would in effect claim that his injuries were "externalities" of the design.

An argument that goes along with the concept of externalities is that those who cause them should have to "internalize the externalities." In plain English this means that the polluter should have to pay for illnesses caused by his pollution, or that the car maker should have to compensate those injured by the gas tank design. The damages award will force the firm to absorb—internalize—the costs rather than to impose them on others.

When lawyers and economists play games with the externalities idea, it will make a lot of difference how one describes whose ox is being gored. For example, in the stereo case above, A might claim that it is B's hypersensitivity to sound, rather than A's playing of her music, that is the cause of B's complaint. Therefore, A would argue that there is no externality attributable to her. Perhaps even the smokestack owner would claim that whatever externality there is arises from the very presence of the nearby residents, whose sensitivity to smoke impinges on his ability to produce useful goods in his factory. That argument would have particular force if the residents built their houses after the factory had started production.

A further twist is the concept of the "positive externality." If I have excellent flower beds in my garden, that confers an esthetic benefit on my neighbor. Indeed, since my neighbor provides neither fertilizer, seed, nor labor to my garden, she may be said to be a "free rider" on the positive externality of my flowers. She benefits from the flower beds without contributing to them.[5]

Of course, a firm or person might generate negative and positive externalities at the same time. If a hamburger stand starts up business next door to my house, its negative externalities include loud crowds and people dropping wrappers on my lawn. Its positive externalities for me, if I like hamburgers, would include an increased ability to secure a quick and tasty dinner. How would you describe the cooking odors? For strict vegetarians who could not stand anything connected with the cooking of meat, the odors always would be negative externalities. For those who like the smell of frying burgers, they would be positive. In fact, the same hamburger lover might consider cooking odors to be positive externalities at dinner time and negative externalities when they waft through his window late at night.

7. The Moral Hazard

Economists describe a moral hazard as a state of affairs that creates incentives for people to behave in inefficient, or even criminal, ways that will throw the losses associated with that conduct onto others. The law frowns on moral hazards. Consider these examples.

- A federal insurance program permits people to get insurance for homes that they build in areas with high risks of flooding. When this program draws people to build in flood plains, the moral hazard is that the taxpayer will have to pay for the improvidence of the insured homeowners.

---

5. See pages 141–142 below for a discussion of "free riders."

- An insurance company issues a life insurance policy on the life of A to B, a person with no family or business relation to A and no financial dependence on A's life continuing. B murders A for the insurance money. The issuance of the policy created the moral hazard of the murder, because B had no stake in A continuing to live and a positive incentive to end A's life.

8. The Coase Theorem

In the course of their studies, many law students will encounter an idea called "the Coase theorem." This idea, much used by professors who like to do economic analysis of law, takes its name from a Nobel Prize-winning economist, Ronald Coase. For those who have not studied economics, it may seem opposed to intuition. We suggest, however, that you consider it for its potential power to shed light on legal problems.

Coase argued that when two parties interact with a result that ordinary people would characterize as one party causing injury to the other, it will make no difference to "resource allocation"—essentially to efficiency—who will have to bear the cost. At least, this will be so if there are no "transaction costs"— if the parties could work out deals and bargains concerning the behavior at issue without expense. In dealing with this form of analysis, you must keep in mind the assumption that in the absence of transaction costs, parties in a free market will bargain to efficient results. It is also important to understand that Coase himself understood very well that transaction costs permeate most of life. In fact, he spent a significant part of the article in which he invented his "theorem" explaining the potential implications of transaction costs for legal rules.[6]

Coase's principal example[7] concerned a rancher's cattle trespassing on the crops of his farmer neighbor. Coase premised that in a purely marketplace setting the farmer and the rancher would bargain out the issues that would inevitably arise. If, for example, the law refused to impose liability for crop damage on the rancher, the farmer would pay a "bribe" to the rancher to get him to decrease the size of his herd, which would effectively reduce the loss to the farmer's crops. Coase concluded that whether the law imposed liability on the rancher or let the loss

---

6. We will focus on transaction costs at pages 138–139 below.

7. Ronald Coase, The Problem of Social Cost, 3 J.L. & Econ. 1 (1960).

remain on the farmer, the *economic* outcome would be the same. Here is the reasoning that applies to this admittedly pristine example: If the law would let the loss stay with the farmer, he would bribe the rancher to reduce his herd. If the law would impose liability on the rancher, he would reduce his herd to avoid paying damages. Either way, the herd would be reduced, and the result would be efficient, given the amounts that consumers in the broader world are prepared to pay for beef and corn.

You may respond that if the court lets the loss stay with the farmer, this seems a miserably unfair result, whether it is efficient or not. The farmer will be out of pocket because of the rancher's trespassing cattle. You might say, indeed, that this sounds like a classic example of an "externality." The answer of efficiency analysis to this criticism is one that we provided in an earlier section: Efficiency and fair wealth distribution are quite separate things, even though on some happy occasions they may coincide. Your own instinct may favor achieving a "fair" result by imposing liability on the rancher. However, you should understand that, under the Coase theorem, if there are no transaction costs, it would make no difference to resource allocation—i.e., an "efficient" result will be achieved—whichever way courts decide the liability issue. Let us be clear, to the point of repetition. Efficiency-oriented economists do not necessarily say you should not adopt fairness as your principal goal. Their invocation of the Coase theorem simply emphasizes that if what you really desire is efficiency, you should not allow fairness-oriented sentiments to obscure what may be efficient rules.

9. Transaction Costs

Volumes have been written about the Coase theorem, and we have given you just a primer. But even this primer would be incomplete if we did not introduce the major qualification of the theorem—the assumption that there are no "transaction costs." The reason that Coase could assume that there were no transaction costs in his hypothetical of the cattle and the crops is that the rancher and the farmer didn't need lawyers or even e-mail or fax machines to discuss their dispute. All they had to do was bargain face to face amidst the marauding livestock and the corn. But once one plugs in items like the cost of getting information and the cost of negotiation, a new set of questions arises.

One useful way to describe this set of issues—and indeed a lot of law and economics problems—is to say that an important task of decision makers is to search for the party who is in the best position to minimize relevant costs—the "least cost avoider." Consider, for example, a case involving a factory that pollutes water in a stream that serves ten thousand homeowners. Courts may reason in such a case that it is more efficient to have a rule that requires the factory to use pollution control devices than one that effectively forces the homeowners to band together to bribe the factory owner. The theory is that it would be prohibitively expensive for the homeowners to organize themselves to put together a pot of bribe money; this is a transaction cost that is inefficiently high. In addition, many homeowners might try to ride the coattails of those who are doing the work on the issue. They would free ride—take advantage, without bearing any of the negotiating cost themselves—on the efforts of the more energetic homeowners to stop the pollution.[8]

You could turn the argument around, of course. You could focus on the expense to which the factory owner would be put to locate and bribe several thousand homeowners to let him keep polluting. And you could spin out the argument, contending that it would be cheaper for the homeowners to acquire filtration devices to combat the pollution, or perhaps even to move, than to make the factory owner locate them and bribe them or to force him to install pollution control devices. Acquiring information and engaging in the transactions that are necessary to complex agreements are often costly. That is why transaction costs, and more generally the search for the lowest cost avoider, represent an important part of economic analysis of law.

The concept of the least cost avoider sheds light on a recurrent problem, which concerns information about the characteristics of the goods and services about which people make contracts. The question of how much information one person is obligated to give another about the goods or services at issue may be addressed in neutral economic terms by asking how much it would cost (or has cost) each party to acquire, or to divulge, the information.

10. Fairness, Overreaching, and Coercion

Even a highly professional analysis of the efficiency of legal rules will not solve every case—perhaps not most cases. Ideas of

---

8. See pages 141–142 on "free riders."

fairness continually influence the judicial mind, sometimes at a subconscious level, and persuade courts to reach what they consider fair outcomes. Of course, the concept of fairness may mean very different things to different people, and competing concepts of fairness will often lead the people who hold them to arrive at opposite results in concrete cases. This section deals with a few of the meanings that people give most frequently to the term. As a general matter, it is a word that should put your mind on critical alert. When someone says she wants only to be fair, you automatically should ask, "What do you mean, 'fair'?"

One important meaning of fairness relates to the way that resources are spread among individuals. As we suggested above, judges have been inculcated with the idea that the equitable distribution of wealth, or even of risky circumstances of life, is pretty much a subject for the legislature, for example, through rates of taxation or occupational safety and health legislation. Even so, judicial decisions often reflect concerns with achieving fairness between litigants.

Another meaning of fairness has to do with perceived inequities in power relationships. Some cases that especially appeal to courts on fairness grounds involve plaintiffs who appear very vulnerable in the particular circumstances, and perhaps defendants who seem to be overreaching.

There is controversy about how far courts should go to redress perceived imbalances in bargaining power. In the area of contracts for the sale of consumer goods, for example, some controversy exists about whether courts should declare certain contractual terms to be "unconscionable"—in effect, so unfair that they should not be enforced. The Uniform Commercial Code permits courts to refuse enforcement to contracts that they find to be unconscionable. However, the reason that some people react uncomfortably to the unconscionability doctrine is that they think it is hard to find a principled stopping place for it. If I say that Company A is unfairly "taking advantage of" Consumer B because Company A is a wealthy business and Consumer B is poor and uneducated, then does it present a philosophical problem to allow that consumer to make contracts at all? Moreover, would placing such a limit on the ability to contract make society a lot less free than it is? Could it have overall effects that harm more people than the unconscionability doctrine aids? For example, might it discourage merchants from opening stores in economically depressed neighborhoods, because merchants fear that courts will find their sales practices to be unconscionable in those settings? This is how the arguments run.

There are, to be sure, some situations in which even the most efficiency-focused economists will say that they will not tolerate the use of economic power. For these situations, we employ concepts like coercion and extortion. A classic analogy for coercion—which goes well beyond the use of economic power—is the robber putting his gun to the citizen's head: "Your money or your life."

There is no freedom in that "transaction"—a lot less freedom, even, than the case in which someone with a sixth grade education buys a television set from Company A for twice the price charged by Company X, just a few blocks away. We make the armed robber's conduct a crime, but we are a lot less sure about calling it illegal to charge prices that are "too high." We are hesitant to have the law condemn that conduct even though most people would be willing to concede that there is not much freedom for buyers when there is no Company X nearby and the buyer lacks transportation to take her to a place where price competition exists.

Now suppose that someone says that he will provide you "protection" against your tires being slashed by vandals, when you both know perfectly well that if you do not pay up, it is he who will do the slashing. Is that extortion?

Or suppose someone builds a factory that does not make automobiles, or air-conditioners, or cardboard boxes. The factory makes only smoke, and it does so only in order to force surrounding landowners to pay the factory owner not to make smoke. Is that extortion? After all, the factory owner is producing something—smoke!

Among other things, these examples highlight the fact that at some point, overreaching—and "unfair" conduct generally—may also become inefficient. One way to define that point is to say that it occurs where the market is no longer free. Armed robbery, at least, is an unambiguous example of an unfree exchange.

11. Free Riders

A favorite target of economic criticism related to legal policy is the "free rider" problem. Often, when a group of people desire a particular outcome, a small number of them will work creatively to achieve that goal. Their work will produce benefits that all the others in the group will enjoy without contributing to the effort of the activists. Let us say that it would be a great advantage to a village, in which 100 people live, to build a road to the next village. Working in their spare time, 50 village members do the plowing, scraping and surfacing to build the road. All 100 villagers, however, will use the road to their benefit, both through commerce and visits with relatives and friends. The 50 who did not help are free riders.

Of course, this type of situation creates incentives to be a free rider. Everyone who lives in the village knows that the road will benefit them, regardless of whether they help build it. Thus, they have an incentive not to help build the road because they can do something else with their time and they will benefit anyway. One way to deal with this problem would be to charge for use of the road, perhaps giving the volunteers a discount or a free pass. An analogous situation—and a more difficult problem to solve—occurs in another setting when associations for the preservation of wilderness areas succeed with lobbying campaigns that benefit many non-members. The non-members are free riders, but it may not be so easy to charge them their fair, or efficient, share of the benefits produced by the association.

12. The Tragedy of the Commons

The "tragedy of the commons" is another idea that draws on the potential tension between individual self-interest and cooperation. This concept has been used to support the case for assigning property rights to private owners rather than to the public. A simple form of the argument may appeal to your intuition. I have a stake in a tidy lawn, and I will keep it clipped. I have a property right in "my" lawn. But if I share a big backyard with three other people, and none of us individually owns it, it is rather likely that that parcel of land—a "commons" that belongs to everyone in general but no one in particular—will get weedy. None of us has sufficient incentive to keep it up. And if one of us does, the others will be free riders. This arguably is unfair, as well as inefficient.

If you would like to tease yourself, though, assume that the real estate involved is not a patch of land that lies among four homes, but the Grand Canyon. Would you think that turning that piece of real estate over to a private corporation would keep it

free of candy wrappers and optimally pristine? Or would government better serve the common enterprise? Can people cooperate
best in preserving natural wonders through the medium of private marketeers? Or would it be less of a "tragedy" for the
Government to operate that particularly grand "commons"?

13. The Prisoner's Dilemma

"The prisoner's dilemma" also speaks to the problem of
reconciling isolated individual incentives. The basic idea is familiar to anyone who has seen a cop show on television where two
people, suspected of participation in a serious crime, face grill-
ings in separate interrogation rooms. The prisoner's dilemma
arises from the fact that one suspect does not know what the
other suspect is saying to the police.

Academic treatments of the prisoner's dilemma vary somewhat in their presentation and how they articulate their assumptions. However, here is a synthesis of several of these treatments:
The prosecutor wants to convict both prisoners at the maximum
sentence for the serious crime—say ten years—but has evidence
to convict each only of a lesser crime that carries a one-year
sentence. The only way that the prosecutor can convict at least
one prisoner at the ten-year maximum is to extract a confession
to the serious crime from one prisoner and to strike a deal in
which that prisoner will testify against the other. So the interro-
gators of each prisoner offer each a deal for a one-year sentence
if he confesses first, with this testimony setting up the other
prisoner for conviction of the more serious crime and a ten-year
sentence. However, as the hypothetical is typically presented, if
both confess to the serious crime at the same time during
separate investigations, they each get a five-year sentence. The
prosecutor's nightmare is that if both prisoners stay silent, the
worst that can happen to them is that each will receive the one-
year sentence on the lesser charge.

In this situation, where neither prisoner knows about the
thinness of the evidence the prosecutor has, silence would be the
strategy that would yield the best payoff to both prisoners, since
the worst it would bring them is a sentence of one year apiece.
But the prisoner's dilemma is this: the prisoners cannot communicate and each lacks information about what the other will do.
Because each must choose his own strategy, the incentive for
each is to confess and testify against the other. If one confesses
before the other, it will result in a one-year sentence for him, and

ten years for the other. If they both confess, each will get five years. In this situation in which neither knows what the other will do, the best strategy that each is capable of perceiving for avoiding a ten-year sentence is to confess. Their motivation to take that step, which will be more costly to the two combined than silence, is that each fears that the other will confess more than each believes that the other will join in stonewalling.

Some aspects of the prisoner's dilemma metaphor present useful analogies to problems often faced by free people and businesses as well. A problem is that people in the pursuit of their narrowly defined self interest may wind up making deals that are actually inferior to those that could be made if they got together with others in roughly the same position and worked out arrangements advantageous to each. If people had full information about the situation confronting them and could communicate with one another so that each understood the benefits of cooperation—advantages that the prisoners do not have—they would choose the cooperative strategy that provides benefits to all, rather than going it alone in pursuit of a misperceived advantage to each alone.

Under the roof of economic theory, there is plenty of room for people to blunt their inclination to press for a solution they perceive to benefit only them, and to work for a goal that includes the welfare of others. However, just because lawyers are always complicating things, we have to add that if business competitors go too far in cooperating between or among themselves, they may be guilty of an antitrust violation. That would be the case, for example, when companies selling competing products agree to keep their prices at the same high level, with the result that consumers pay more than the price that would exist if the cooperating "competitors" were really competing. In any event, part of your law study will involve the question of how to balance competition and cooperation.

14. Public Choice Theory

In some courses, teachers will refer to a concept known as "public choice theory." That has been defined by legal scholars as "a set of premises and hypotheses having, as its core, the conviction that well-organized groups, seeking to advance their members' self-interest at someone else's cost, tend to win out in the public policy market."[9] The term chosen to capture this idea may not ring true with you, but the insight is a common sense one. It visualizes some parts of life as being part of a game in which some win and others lose. In that environment, lobbying and political pressure by groups can gain a bigger share of the economic pie. One question the theory will raise for you is whether that view of the world appeals to your sense of what justice is all about. You may want to consider a strong critique by a law professor. He says that when people talk about "the lure of 'it's all politics' or 'common law judges basically do what they want'" when they confront cases of "agonizing complexity," he finds it "extraordinarily challenging" to convince students that law is more "than just another expression of self-interest and will."[10]

15. A Note on Selfishness

An issue that underlies many of the policy clashes that you will confront in law classes concerns the assumptions we make about self-interest. One strong position is that, describing the world as it is, the rewards of life go to the self-interested. Those who endorse this view—for example, sociobiologists—argue that our genes seek to maximize their own survival and, by extension, so do we. As a principal promoter of the idea of "the selfish gene" put it, "[t]he universe that we observe has precisely the properties we should expect if there is, at bottom, no design, no purpose, no evil and no good, nothing but pitiless indifference."[11]

A contrasting position stresses the competing idea of altruism. Altruism involves conduct that most people would consider unselfish, for example, the behavior of people who risk their lives to save others neither "expect[ing] nor consider[ing] possible rewards for their acts."[12] You can imagine the sorts of arguments that would occur between defenders of an unvarnished selfishness model and advocates of altruism.

Why do soldiers brave death to rescue a stranded comrade? Some might contend that the rescuers think that the chances of

9. Cynthia R. Farina & Jeffrey J. Rachlinski, Foreword: Post–Public Choice?, 87 Cornell L. Rev. 267, 268 (2002).

10. Peter Strauss, Getting Beyond Cynicism: New Theories of the Regulatory State, 87 Cornell L. Rev. 690, 695 (2002).

11. Richard Dawkins, God's Utility Function, 273 Sci. Am. No. 5, 80 at 85 (November 1995).

12. Kristen Monroe, Michael Barton and Ute Klingemann, Altruism and the Theory of Rational Choice: Rescuers of Jews in Nazi Europe, 101 Ethics 103, 120 (1990).

their own survival will be heightened because of the skills that even a wounded soldier would contribute to the group. Somewhere in the subconscious of the rescuing soldiers, these commentators would insist, is a selfish motive.

There are intermediate positions. Each soldier might reason that if he did not participate in a rescue, the other members of the squad would not be likely to rescue him if he got into a similar spot. We could certainly discern selfishness in that motivation. Or perhaps the members of the squad would decide that if they do not rescue the wounded soldier, morale will drop and their general chances of survival would be diminished.[13]

Sociobiologists would themselves suggest that a soldier would aid in the rescue, perhaps without thinking through costs and benefits in a refined way, because impulses of that sort are embedded in the genes through generations of living in social environments. This response, labeled "reciprocal altruism," is behavior by one person that benefits another on the assumption that someone will provide a benefit in the future to the "altruist" or someone who is genetically related to him. Yet we would not want to ignore the quite different argument that the real reason that people rescue others is because of a learned, ingrained moral sense that it is right to do so and perhaps even that it would be wrong not to do so.

* * *

Which views will your professors hold on efficiency, justice, morality, and ethics? We are inclined to say that you will be lucky if your little platoon of teachers each year presents different points of view on the law. That would broaden your education.

We think you will be luckier still if those teachers who hold strong points of view are open to competing arguments. You will have to get a feel for this in particular classes. Frankly, you will have to estimate how open individual teachers will be to your presentation of ideas that oppose their own, in class or on examinations. We hope they would be disposed to consider opposing ideas, but you will have to play the game according to your sense of your teacher's hospitality to arguments against his or her own position.

---

13. Some people would say that this is simply an attempt to maximize the number of lives saved within the squad. Here, we will not go more deeply into the disagreements that occur between advocates of the selfish gene hypothesis and efficiency maximizers.

Empirical Questions

Judicial decisions and preambles to legislation often state premises based on assumptions about the world, including assumptions about how people actually behave, which may be heavily disputed. For example, in one case Minnesota Supreme Court justices disagreed on the question of whether to allow a tort action against a non-custodial parent who kidnaps a child from the custodial parent. The majority, refusing to allow such an action, said that "[t]his tort will not deter parental abduction."[14] But a dissenter asserted that to allow tort actions would "serve the best interests of the child by encouraging the return of absent children by imposing a civil damages remedy."[15]

Sometimes questions about how people actually respond to legal rules can be answered by social science research. Often, however, judicial "empiricism" relies on guesswork and intuition. For judges, and even more for legislators, sometimes the answers to questions about influences on behavior can be both multi-faceted and intuitive.

A Concluding Word on the Value of Argument

Our discussion in this chapter of goals and rationales of the law should bring home to you the fact that many of us carry around several different, and sometimes competing, views in our minds about proper policy in particular situations. Consider one simple example, a case in which a buyer claims that a seller did not disclose some crucial information that she had about the product or service she was selling. In a case like that, you might have several reactions, almost all at once: that encouraging buyers to search for more information makes markets more competitive; that it is immoral for sellers to withhold such information; that ethically we should reward buyers who discover qualities of products that do not appear on the surface; that sellers possess crucial information mostly because of luck; that people who have acquired such information did so because they were industrious rather than lucky; and the egalitarian view that people are entitled to equal access to the good things in life, including information.

---

14. Larson v. Dunn, 460 N.W.2d 39, 46 (Minn. 1990).

15. Id. at 52 (Popovich, C.J., dissenting).

If you are willing to play this type of ping-pong game of arguments, it will sharpen your mind. And you will become more sensitive to the fact that courts always must choose among competing rationales when they decide difficult cases. Among other things, they must consider the claim that there is only one rationale that governs a particular branch of the law as against the argument that an important task of courts is to decide which of several rationales is best applied in a particular case.

12

Remedies

The business end of the law lies in the remedies it offers. A court could tell a defendant in a tort suit that she was negligent and simply admonish her for her carelessness, or could scold a defendant in a contract action for breaking a promise. Usually, however, that will not satisfy a plaintiff who has suffered the consequences of the defendant's negligence or breach of contract and gone to the expense and anguish of a lawsuit. Except for the few plaintiffs who seek only vindication, those who are successful in litigation will always pose the practical question to the court, "What will you do about the defendant's behavior?" The remedy provides the answer.

Legal and Equitable Remedies

One way to divide the world of remedies is between legal remedies and equitable remedies. The principal legal remedy is damages—ordering one party to pay money to another, usually with the specific purpose of providing some sort of recompense to the claimant. A typical remedy in equity is to require the defendant to take some action or to prohibit the defendant from a course of conduct.

Damages

When a court orders a payment of money damages, the measure of damages becomes important. Some damage remedies seek to give back to the plaintiff what she has lost "out of pocket." Others aim to give the plaintiff the "benefit of her bargain"—for example, the value of what she was promised by a contract that the defendant breached. Certain damage remedies try to compensate for intangible losses, for example, by attempting to assign money values to harms like pain and suffering. Some such categories of intangibles, although they are difficult to quantify on a neatly principled basis, are nonetheless well-established.

Punitive damages are a separate, and presently controversial, type of remedy that plaintiffs may seek. Courts assign a cluster of rationales to support the award of punitive damages. Unlike the more usual damage awards in both tort and contract cases, punitive damages are designed not for the purpose of compensation, but rather, as the term suggests, to punish the defendant. Courts also rationalize punitive damages as a way to achieve an extra sting to deter people from very risky or highly culpable behavior in the future, and even as a device for effectively reimbursing the plaintiff for her attorney's fees.

Very high punitive damages awards have been the subject of litigation across the country. The champion of all punitive awards came in a verdict in a Florida products liability case brought by cigarette smokers. That jury fixed the punitive damages at $145 billion dollars, although the award was eventually overturned. The United States Supreme Court has rendered several decisions on the subject, of which the most famous case involved the oil spill that flowed out of the wreck of the tanker Exxon Valdez. In that case, in which the jury gave a punitive award of $5 billion, the Court ultimately reduced it to $507.5 million.[1]

Equitable Remedies and Related Categories

Equity began as a system of courts in England that dispensed justice when common law courts could not provide an adequate remedy. It has now become a system of remedies

1. Exxon Shipping Co. v. Baker, 128 S.Ct. 2605 (2008).

administered by trial courts generally. Wearing their equity hats, courts possess a flexible battery of these remedies. They recognize that sometimes money cannot redress a wrong effectively, let alone prevent an injury, and that the best remedy may be one that compels or prohibits some kind of action. This section summarizes a few of the most-used equitable remedies.

1. Injunctions

A classic equitable remedy is the injunction, of which the most well-known is the prohibitory injunction—an order by the court that the defendant must cease or refrain from doing something. Typical examples would be to stop the discharge of pollutants into the air or water and to stop trespassing on someone's land.

Sometimes courts will order individuals to do something rather than to stop doing it. These mandatory orders, which may be called injunctions or which may have different labels, might command a party to do something like install pollution control equipment. A court may condition a damages remedy on a mandatory injunction: if the defendant obeys the mandatory order, it will not have to pay damages.

There are several sub-classes in the injunction category for which the time element is crucial. Sometimes even without prior notice to the defendant, a court may issue a temporary restraining order (TRO), which immediately prohibits the defendant from conduct in which it has been engaging, for example, dumping chemicals in a waterway or abusing a spouse. The court may do this in situations in which it is not ready to make a definitive ruling about the legality of the defendant's conduct, but in which the plaintiff will suffer "irreparable injury" if the court does not act right away to stop the defendant.

After the court holds a hearing, it may elect to go to the next stage, the preliminary injunction, which orders the defendant to continue to refrain from the conduct at issue. If the parties cannot work out a satisfactory settlement, the litigation will then proceed to a trial. At that stage, the court must make an unequivocal judgment about whether the defendant should be permitted to engage in the behavior of which the plaintiff complains. If it concludes, on reflection, that the behavior is illegal or unreasonable, it will enter a permanent injunction.

2. Specific Performance

Specific performance is a very special kind of equitable remedy involving an order to do something. Occasionally awarded in contracts cases, this remedy seeks to achieve a result that, in some sense, money could not buy. Suppose that A contracts to sell B a mountainside house with a spectacular view of hills and valleys. Then A backs out of the deal, but offers to pay damages to B that represent B's expenses in getting ready to move. He even offers to compensate B for the recent increase in price of a nearby house, lower on the mountain than A's house, that B could have bought earlier at a lower price. B counters that there is no other house that has a view like A's house. The court might order A to convey his house to B because of the uniqueness of the harm—the loss of ownership of a house that arguably could not be compensated in money.

It may be difficult to persuade a court to compel specific performance, a drastic remedy. Often, important policies will weigh against requiring a promisor to do what he has promised. To take an exaggerated example, a court would be very reluctant to order someone to perform a surgical operation even though he or she was the best surgeon in the region for that type of procedure and had promised to do the operation. In support of a decision denying the specific performance remedy, the court might say that ordering people to perform personal services directly for others has an overtone of compelling slavery.

3. Constructive Trusts

One other example of an equitable remedy is the constructive trust. Suppose that C, the beneficiary of an insurance policy on D's life, murders D for the insurance money. E, who is D's only heir, brings an action against the insurance company for the proceeds on the policy, which otherwise would go to C under the policy terms. The court may impose a constructive trust on the proceeds in favor of E. That is not what we ordinarily think of as a trust—a fund voluntarily set up by a moneyed person for named beneficiaries. Rather, a constructive trust is a remedy by which a court orders someone who has legal title to money or other property, but whose title has been acquired wrongfully or in violation of some equitable principle, to convey that property to a person who has an equitable right to it. In creating a constructive trust, the court in effect stamps E's name on the insurance fund.

From a linguistic point of view, this is an example of something we mentioned above[2]: courts investing words that have well-accepted connotations with a meaning that rings rather oddly to ordinary persons. We can assure you, though, that after you come in contact with enough of these artificial usages, you will come to use them just like you employ ordinary language. We add one specific hint. When a court uses the word "constructive" to modify another word, it is likely that it is cloaking the other word with a special legal meaning.

Alternative Dispute Resolution

Other remedies come from what is labeled alternative dispute resolution (ADR), a group of procedures used to resolve disputes by means other than litigation. Usually ADR employs an agreed-upon third party to facilitate, or even to require, a solution. Many courts require that certain cases first go to ADR. One form of ADR, arbitration, is often used to resolve contract disputes; indeed, a contract term may require that the parties use arbitration instead of litigating. Arbitrators have the power to make orders that give or deny remedies, and often their decisions are not subject to judicial review. Another form of ADR is mediation, in which the third party tries to bring the parties together to reach a settlement acceptable to both.

2. See pages 78–79.

*

13
Legal Writing

Good legal writing ought to be like any good writing. When you read legal documents that contain jargon, that use language in a fuzzy way, or that are poorly organized, you are reading not just bad legal writing, but bad writing. Many lawyers write well, though, and everyone can improve his or her writing significantly.

The best writing habits grow over periods of years. If you have not been reading well-written prose for a long time, and you have not had teachers who forced you to rewrite and rewrite again, you start at a disadvantage. We do not kid ourselves, or you, that this little chapter will make you a good writer. Nor is it a comprehensive introduction to legal writing, which your separate course in that subject will provide. What we hope it will do is identify some of the most common problems that occur in the writing of law students, and to suggest ways to solve those problems. Because we begin by focusing on problems, a fair amount of the advice that follows is negatively phrased. When we can, however, we will try to say what to do rather than what not to do.

Should you have any doubt about how crucial writing is to attorneys, we suggest that you ask any lawyer you know whether writing is important to his or her work. We expect that the answer will line up with the result of a survey of young Chicago lawyers, who ranked oral and written communication as the "clear winners" among the important skills in legal practice.[1]

1. Bryant G. Garth and Joanne Martin, Law Schools and the Construction of Competence, 43 J. Leg. Ed. 469, 474 (1993).

The text of this chapter focuses on principal problems of structure and organization. An appendix gives advice on how to avoid a few specific recurrent problems. In general, we advise that you pay careful attention to your legal writing course. The skills you learn in that course will be important to your summer jobs, and vital to the rest of your professional work.

Having a Purpose and Audience In Mind

Before you begin to write anything, you must have an idea of what you want to accomplish. Do you want to tell someone you love him or her? Convince your credit card issuer that you did not incur a particular charge? Order a winter jacket from a catalog? If you are a lawyer, or are studying law, questions about your purpose are more likely to run in this vein: Do you want to convince a court that your client has a better case than does an opponent? Are you trying to explain to a client how to avoid litigation? Do you want to persuade a professor that you have analyzed a hypothetical problem intelligently? If you are a judge, are you attempting to explain why a sympathetic plaintiff must lose because the law is against her? Keep the purpose of your writing, the identity of your reader, and your reader's needs and expectations firmly in mind. Composition teachers and rhetoricians call this writing for your audience.

One characteristic common to both your professional and lay readers is that often they will be busy people. Thus, they will appreciate clarity and brevity in what they read. Indeed, not only will they appreciate those qualities, but your job may depend on them.

Organize Your Thoughts

Tied in closely with purpose is organization. A piece of paper before you is blank, neutral about your thoughts. You can put anything down on it you wish; the paper makes no judgments. It is you who must give content to the brief, or the memo, or the exam, and you who must organize the content to communicate effectively and to meet the expectations of your reader. A good writer organizes to provide information in the order in which her reader expects and needs that information.

Some people organize best by literally outlining their thoughts. When you outline your analysis of a legal issue, you break it down into its logical components. For example, when you analyze a claim that has a fixed definition, such as an intentional tort claim or a statutory issue, you organize the claim into its elements. Alternatively, if you analyze a claim for which the court must balance several factors, you might organize by discussing each of the factors and then comparing their importance.

If you analyze a battery claim—let us say for an exam or a memo about a problem like the case in Chapter 2 in which someone yanked away a tray held by another—you might start with this familiar form:

I. Battery tort

    A. Intent

    B. Contact

    C. Harmful or offensive

    D. Unprivileged

    E. Unconsented

For each element concerning which a legal issue exists, you would then proceed in this fashion: (1) Define the element (for example, what a contact requires in that jurisdiction). (2) Summarize the facts of precedents relevant to that element (kicking a dog on a leash is relevant to whether the defendant made contact with the person holding the leash). (3) Apply the law developed in the precedents to the facts of the case at issue (are the dog on the leash and the leash in the plaintiff's hand in the precedent analogous to the tray in the hand in the case you are analyzing?). (4) Draw a conclusion about whether the facts fulfill that element (yanking the tray fulfills the contact element of a battery).[2]

That is a time-tested way to organize and outline, using the elements of a claim, as well as a time-tested way to analyze each element. Many students, however, do not start with an easy flow of ideas. They may need to kick-start themselves. These students may best begin to get a feel for the problem when they start

---

2. For more persuasive documents, such as an appellate brief, you would start with conclusions about your case rather than neutral definitions.

writing prose sentences. The process of writing helps them to analyze and know what they want to say, even if this early writing is very rough. If your mind works that way, you will find that as you write, your mind will start to move logically from one idea to another. You may want to keep a list of ideas as they come to you. Often even people who take naturally to the traditional outline form will find that the process of writing helps them to see relationships among parts of the material that they did not discern at first.

Whether you outline first or start with a rough draft, an important thing to keep in mind is that you must revise your work, often several times. You should assume that your writing will change, for the better, as you get more of a grasp on the subject and as you rewrite your early drafts.

Logical Flow of Ideas; Transitions; The Problem of Jerky Sentences

An outline should make clear how the parts of your topic relate to each other. The best writing flows and carries the reader forward. If the information is not organized well, or a sentence is not clear, your reader has to go back and figure out what you mean. So, for example, when you re-read a paragraph you have written—it is a good test to read it aloud—you should ask yourself whether the paragraph is about only one topic, but also whether the ideas in the paragraph connect to one another—that is, whether the paragraph is coherent.

A recurrent weakness in student writing is the series of jerky, unconnected sentences that require the reader to go back and connect up the information herself in order to understand its content. To provide a bad example, let us suppose King Henry V had said, addressing his army before a great battle against the French at Agincourt:

"We're all English. We should fight together like brothers today. I'm a king. You're like a brother to me if you fight with me."

* * *

Now compare what Shakespeare had the king say:

"We few, we happy few, we band of brothers;
For he to-day that sheds his blood with me
Shall be my brother; be he ne'er so vile,
This day shall gentle his condition."

We are not suggesting that you should wax poetic in a legal memorandum or brief. Indeed, you will want to fashion complete sentences, so we would advise against a construction like "We few, we happy few, we band of brothers." However, consider what Shakespeare does that you *can* imitate: He employs the word "for" to effect a transition. Even the words beginning "be he ne'er so vile" carry the reader forward.

Now notice how much better your draft in modern English prose would be, as contrasted with our original jerky example, if you added just a couple of words at strategic places to tie your ideas together: "We are like brothers today; for if you fight with me, it is as if you were my brother. Although I am a king and you are a peasant, fighting alongside me here will make you noble."

In emphasizing the need to link up your ideas, we understand that the logical linkage between those ideas may seem absolutely clear to you when you construct jerky sentences. When you write, "I'm a king. You're like a brother to me if you fight with me," it may be apparent to you, in your own mind, that what you are saying is, "I am a king and you are a peasant, but if you fight with me today, you will be like my brother." But you are not saying that; you are leaving the reader to supply the linkage between your two sentences. Notice what even the little word "but" does in our later version; it provides a transition and a logical link. Since reading is hard work as it is, your aim should be to make the job as smooth for the reader as possible. It is the fulfillment of that task that makes good writing itself hard work.

Active Voice

It is usually desirable to use the active voice, in which the subject of the sentence performs an action, rather than the passive voice, in which the subject is the recipient of the action.

Consider the following sentence, which uses the passive voice:

"Sentences were written by Jim with subjects before verbs."

Now consider whether this version would make the point more sharply:

"Jim wrote his sentences using active voice."

Would you award the prize to the first sentence or the second one? It should be clear that "Jim wrote his sentences" is superior to "Sentences were written by Jim." In the active voice sentence, Jim is the "actor" who wrote the sentences. Active voice conveys a stronger message than does passive voice, and usually produces shorter sentences.

When you read these examples, you may think that the "sentences were written" sentence is a caricature, a joke. As teachers, however, we see hundreds of passive sentences like that every year. And you, like us, will also see excessive passive voice in many kinds of non-legal writing. Our aim is to give passive sentences power by making them active, or, in trendy lingo, to empower the subjects as well as the verbs.

Everyone yields to passive voice on occasion, often as a result of fatigue. Sometimes the problem is physical fatigue. Sometimes it is intellectual fatigue. In either case, fight through your tiredness against the passive voice. Until you develop the rhythm of positive expression, you might do well to do a separate passive-voice check on yourself every couple of pages that you write.

We do not say that passive voice may not be more appropriate than active voice on some occasions. For example, you may want to use passive voice when you do not know who did an action ("the package was wrapped in brown paper"). Or you may want to de-emphasize who did an action; for example, if you are defending a client charged with murder, you may want to say "the victim was killed." However, we assure you that most people do not have to worry about using the passive voice too seldom.

Besides checking your own drafts for passive voice, you may drill yourself on other people's writing—even other lawyers. To start close to home, you might scrutinize some pages at random in any of your casebooks, looking for passive voice in judicial opinions. Think of ways that you might change an offending passive sentence to give it more punch. Illustrative of how simple the exercise can be are some variations on a sentence from a state court decision:

1) [Passive-passive: The worst] "It was held by another court that when a landlord represented that a bed was safe, an express warranty action could be maintained."

2) [Passive-active: Surely better] "It was held by another court that when a landlord represented that a bed was safe, the plaintiff-tenant could maintain an action based on the express warranty."

3) [Active-active: Is this the best?] "Another court held that when a landlord represented that a bed was safe, the plaintiff-tenant could sue for breach of express warranty."

This exercise incorporates some lessons that go beyond our campaign for active voice. We did several things in the third version to give it more force than even the second version. We made the first verb ("held") active. Having made the last verb active in the second version ("maintain"), we changed that verb to the shorter and generally more powerful "sue." We got rid of the phrase "based on," which adds very little, if anything, to the message we are trying to communicate.

We might further have changed the end of the sentence to read, "could sue on express warranty." This is a judgment call. Although "could sue on express warranty" saves words, the word "breach" conveys some connotations of wrongdoing that might impart thrust to the sentence. Moreover, the phrase "breach of express warranty" is somewhat more exact, and rather more graceful, than the phrase "on express warranty."

However you resolve such matters of taste and judgment, it is important to understand not only that active voice writing is powerful but that a preference for it is often not just a matter of taste but of choosing the better technique.

Consider how our anonymous writer of bad sentences might have constructed a speech of Brutus, proposing the murder of Caesar:

"He should be carved by us as a dish fit for the gods, and not hacked up by us as a carcass fit for the hounds."

* * *

We hope you think Shakespeare did better:

"Let's carve him as a dish fit for the gods,
Not hew him as a carcass fit for hounds."

Nominalization: Natural Verbs as Weak Nouns

Besides using passive voice excessively, many writers use nominalizations excessively, and further weaken their sentences. Nominalizations are words that should be verbs, but instead are made into nouns. For example, if you say "John's decision was made too hastily," "decision" is a nominalized form of the verb decides. You can just say "John decided too hastily." Another example of a usage that recurs is "James had the intent ..." instead of "James intended."

Nominalizations weaken your sentences because as the subject of the sentence, they are abstract rather than concrete nouns. Because the word that should be the verb is now a noun, the verb that is used (was made) has no power. In the example above, the sentence's subject "decision" is an abstraction. A strong sentence uses a concrete noun as its subject and a verb that conveys the action of the sentence. We rewrote the sentence to use a concrete noun (John) as the subject and we used the verb (decided) to convey the action.

A recent unsuccessful nominee to the Supreme Court drew criticism for her poor writing style because it was abstract and depersonalized.[3] For example, she had published an article in a bar journal that included this sentence:

"When consensus of diverse leadership can be achieved on issues of importance, the greatest impact can be achieved."

How can we rewrite to get rid of the abstractions and put concrete words into the sentence? Try, "When our leaders agree on important issues, they will achieve the greatest impact." Other examples from that nominee's writing are:

- "Our organizing should result in implementation of programs fulfilling strategies and establishing goals." You could rewrite this sentence as: "We should organize to implement our strategies and goals."

- "More and more, the intractable problems in our society have one answer: broad-based intolerance of unacceptable conditions and a commitment by many to fix problems." A rewrite, after the colon, would be: "we must not tolerate

3. David Brooks, In Her Own Words,
N.Y. Times, Oct. 13, 2005, at A31.

> unacceptable conditions and we must commit ourselves to fixing society's problems."

Short Words, Short Sentences

The examples we gave above about passive voice show the value of simplicity and brevity. Notice that in Brutus's two lines of nineteen words (counting articles) on page 161, there is just one word that is more than one syllable. And that word, "carcass," carries particular force in a sentence that proposes the assassination of an emperor.

The law has a lot of long words. There is no way that one can jam "tortfeasor" or "mortgagee" into one syllable. That, however, makes it even more important to the power of your writing that you keep the other words short and simple. Thus, if your first thought is to write, "The social problem addressed by this legislation is considerable and complicated," you might consider, "This statute combats a great and complex evil in society." The latter sentence is active, and uses shorter and more emphatic nouns and verbs. This kind of rewriting requires that you look with a critical eye at your sentences, one by one.

Here is another illustration. If your first draft says, "The subject of this litigation, involving a philosophically challenging problem in personal injury jurisprudence, is whether...." we hope your next draft will start, "This case presents a difficult issue of tort law." You may think we exaggerate, but we see too many of the first type of sentences in these pairings and not enough of the second type. Judges would generally prefer to read the second type of sentence, which is lean and free of overblown language, in which an active verb immediately follows the subject, and in which the subject is a concrete rather than an abstract noun. The reason they would prefer it is the same reason you will prefer it, if you think about the matter; the second type communicates more effectively.

Another good general rule, like the suggestion that you use simple words and as few words as possible, is to keep your sentences short. We will give a bad example followed by a good example. For the bad example, consider the indented sentence just below, which tries to make the point we are now telling you about.

> The sentence you are reading at this moment presents an idea that makes the lesson of brevity evident in another way

that ties in with what we have said about simplicity of language and the use of relatively few words when you might be tempted to use a relatively great number of words, an idea that can be summarized by saying that you should attempt to write short sentences.

* * *

Now consider these two sentences:

The sentence you have just read gives an exaggerated example of our other major point about simplicity and brevity. That point is, keep your sentences short.

* * *

Notice that the two indented sentences just above present in 26 words, broken into two sentences, the same thought with which an eye-straining 67–word sentence consumed the first indented paragraph. Notice also, that when you break very long sentences into shorter ones, you can promote the flow between the sentences by carrying over an idea or word from the first sentence (in this case, the word "point"), to begin the second sentence.

We would suggest that practically all of the time, it will benefit you in your professional writing to work at achieving this style. Aim for shorter sentences, but mix your style so that your work does not read like, "Look, Jane, look. See Dick run."

We will close this Part with an example of writing by a lawyer in a legal context, from a master of the craft. It is the paragraph in which Judge Benjamin Cardozo presented his statement of the facts in *Palsgraf v. Long Island Railroad*, a case that appears in practically every Torts casebook:

Plaintiff was standing on a platform of defendant's railroad after buying a ticket to go to Rockaway Beach. A train stopped at the station, bound for another place. Two men ran forward to catch it. One of the men reached the platform of the car without mishap, though the train was already moving. The other man, carrying a package, jumped aboard the car, but seemed unsteady as if about to fall. A guard on the car, who had held the door open, reached forward to help him in, and another guard on the platform pushed him from behind. In this act, the package was dislodged, and fell upon the rails. It was a package of small size, about fifteen inches long, and was covered by a newspaper. In fact it contained fireworks, but there was nothing in its appearance to give notice of its contents. The fireworks when they fell exploded. The shock of the explosion threw down some scales at the other end of the platform many feet away. The scales struck the plaintiff, causing injuries for which she sues.[4]

Taken together, these sentences have something in common, something that you can emulate, even if you cannot capture Cardozo's special grace. The sentences are varied, but only two sentences are in the passive voice.[5] The subjects and the verbs come close together. The sentences move the reader forward from one event or thought to another. They are short: in a long paragraph, only one is more than 20 words, and that one only 27. These sentences march, and they are clear.

Practice, Practice, Practice

We have the pleasure every year of seeing some very good student writing. Yet however well students write, like anyone else they can always improve their writing. The key, for those who write well or less well, is to practice good writing. You will no more learn to write better without practice than you will improve at playing the piano or playing shortstop without practice. It is also crucial to start work on your written assignments very early. Your writing assignments will take longer than you think.

There is no royal road to writing well, but one quick fix is to spare a moment now and then to focus critically on a specific piece of writing. It may be useful to select a few passages in something you have to read for class, although any written material will do. Fix on a sentence, or a paragraph, that does not seem to communicate very well. Try analyzing it to see where it is weak. Rewrite it. Then rewrite your rewrite. This process will help to emphasize what a responsibility it is to write, but it also will underline the opportunity that writing presents for you.

Naturally, we advise the same fierce attention to rewriting of your own work. A principal reason to start your assignments early is that it will allow you time to rewrite. It is always possible, we concede, that you might have gotten something right on the first

---

4. Palsgraf v. Long Island R.R. Co., 248 N.Y. 339, 162 N.E. 99 (N.Y. 1928).

5. Perhaps Judge Cardozo wrote one of those sentences using the words, "the package was dislodged," in the passive in- stead of active voice because he did not want to focus on the guard's role. Judge Cardozo concluded that the railroad was not liable for Mrs. Palsgraf's injuries.

try. But almost always, you can improve a piece of writing by rewriting it. Hemingway rewrote the ending of *A Farewell to Arms* thirty-five times.

When you do rewrite, keep in mind some basic principles we presented above. Remember who your audience is and your purpose in writing. Write clearly, simply, and with active sentences and concrete nouns. Keep your sentences reasonably short, and tie them together logically.

We will add an important postscript: Make sure you spell correctly. You may have to deal with a judge, or a partner, or even a professor, who learned to spell before Spell–Check, which means that he or she *really* learned to spell, and may not indulge spelling mistakes that Spell–Check doesn't catch. That person will know the difference between "principal" and "principle," "statute" and "statue." Spell–Check does not.

Citation Form

Your course on legal research will introduce you to citation form, probably accompanying this training with either the volume popularly called the "Bluebook" or with the more recent ALWD Manual of Citation Form. Either reference will give you scores of rules about how to "cite" sources. "Citing" sources means giving your reader information about the source of the authority that you are writing about. Like the footnotes in academic papers or some non-fiction books, the citation tells your reader how to find the material you have used. In your first year of law school these sources typically are cases, statutes, books, and journal articles. Citation form for legal materials is very stylized, as it is for other disciplines. There is usually some logic to citation form, but whether you discern the logic or not, you must follow the rules, if for no other reason than the requirements of the discipline.

Think of all the ways that you might cite the great 1916 case of *MacPherson v. Buick Motor Company*, which appears at page 382 of volume 217 of the New York Reports, and also at page 1050 of Volume 111 of the Northeast Reporter. The pre–1991 Bluebook citation style for this case, requiring what are known as parallel citations (citations to more than one reporter in which a case is published), was *MacPherson v. Buick Motor Co.*, 217 N.Y. 382, 111 N.E. 1050 (1916). You will find that style in law reviews and many cases published before 1991 (not all cases, because many courts use their own citation forms.) The post–1991 Bluebook and the ALWD Manual require the following simpler citation, which omits the reference to the New York Reports and uses only the reference to the Northeast ("regional") Reporter: *MacPherson v. Buick Motor Co.*, 111 N.E. 1050 (N.Y. 1916). One could invent other citation rules. For example, one could require the use of MacPherson's first name, or the spelling out of "Company," or the spelling out of "New York" and "Northeast." However, unvarying rules relieve writers and editors of decisions that would otherwise be unnecessarily time-consuming, besides achieving the principal goal of allowing readers to find the source of the citation easily.

It is possible to engage in philosophical arguments about citation style, and sometimes you may disagree with a particular type of citation. However, no matter how frustrating the task, learn the style adopted at your school and slavishly follow it. As a practical matter, as a first-year student you will be using a few citation forms over and over again, and will have to look up others as they become relevant. The sooner you get into your head the most-used forms, the easier you will feel about not having to wrestle constantly with the mechanics of supporting your legal arguments. But, at the beginning, it will take you a long time to learn to cite cases and statutes in your written work. For your first assignments, you may spend several hours on citation form and you may hate every minute of it. As you practice more, you will be able to write the more common citations as a matter of course.

Just a Word on Research Techniques

Legal research is a complicated undertaking that you will begin to learn in your first year. Research now involves a combination of electronic sources and print media. Without even beginning to summarize the details of legal research, we offer a cautionary note about the use of electronic databases. Many of your professors grew up professionally with hard copy and not screen research. We know that most of our readers, not to mention our young grandchildren, are accustomed to using computers and often use them effectively. We ourselves find that they are valuable for many purposes. But a Dallas attorney sums up a world of warning in a complaint about "computer-educated law graduates" who "generally lack basic research skills" and do not know the "limitations of computerized legal research." He gives as an example a situation in which he needed a case in a hurry on a particular point of law and where a "computer-dependent associate reported that she could not find" such a case, although it "seemed obvious" to him that "some case would support" the argument he wanted to make. He continues, "So I went to the books, and found a suitable case in about 30 minutes." His associate, he says, "expressed shock: 'How did you find that? That's crazy—to find that one sentence in a sea of cases.' " He comments, "You would have thought I was a sorcerer."[6] Of course, he wasn't—he just was unwilling to rest on the idea that electronic databases were the entire known universe.

Appendix: Common Problems in Writing That Can Be Fixed

This Appendix presents solutions to a few problems that frequently afflict student writing—in fact, afflict all kinds of writing.

Subject–Verb Agreement

Plural subjects have plural verbs and singular subjects have singular verbs:

- "These statistics indicate," rather than "These statistics indicates."

- "This class of victims is not typical," rather than "This class of victims are not typical." Observe that the subject of the verb "is" is "class," not "victims."

Students often make errors in subject-verb agreement because they insert so many words and phrases between the subject and the verb that they lose track of which word is the subject. You can correct this problem, and write sentences that are easier to understand, by keeping the subject and verb as close together as possible.

Referents

Specify referents for words that are otherwise indefinite. Consider this passage:

6. Scott P. Stolley, The Corruption of Legal Research, For the Defense, April 2004, 39, at 40.

The court had established that a person's interest in emotional security deserves the same protection as her interest in physical integrity. In the *Smith* case, the court had hoped to take it one step further.

In this passage, the reference for "it" isn't clear. The writer would have made her meaning clearer by saying, in the second sentence, ". . . the court had hoped to take this principle one step further." Some people might argue that this is a judgment call, but we use this example to stress that when you are using a word for which you have not clearly established a referent, you should err on the side of clarity. The edited clause does this by substituting "this principle" for the indefinite word "it." Some writers might spell out the referent even more specifically: ". . . the court had hoped to take the principle of protection for emotional interests one step further." At some point, it is true, the addition of extra words will get verbose and awkward. The last example may be at that point. Always consider, however, how much more awkward it is when your meaning is not clear.

The Dangling Modifier

Most people probably do not consider dangling modifiers to be sinful, at least if sin is measured by what people write without thinking they have erred. However, the dangling modifier is still wrong. When you see the participle form in a word that ends in "ing" at the beginning of one of your sentences, be especially critical of yourself.

Let us say that you want to communicate that after a body of precedent had limited tort recovery to physical injury, a court allowed recovery for emotional harm. Now consider this description: "Flowing from the principle of protecting interests in bodily integrity, the court protected emotional interests." Given the meaning you wish to impart, what is wrong with this sentence is that it was not the court that "flowed"; it was the development of the law as it moved beyond the protection of one interest to protect another. It would be better to write, "Moving beyond the principle of protecting interests in bodily integrity, the court began to protect emotional interests." Here, it *is* the court that "moves," so your "moving" participle does not dangle, and the subject and the participle agree. Alternatively, if you insist on keeping the image of a "flow" in the sentence, you could write, "Flowing from the principle of protecting physical interests was

the idea that courts should also protect emotional interests."
Here, it *is* the "idea" that is "flowing."

If you believe we are being picky here, consider these
examples. The first is from a television news broadcast.

- "If found guilty, jurors will have to decide whether Kac-
  zynski gets the death penalty."

- "Having been dead for 24 hours, the searchers found the
  victim's body."

Consider also this sentence from a recent story about wind
turbines in China:

- "Blessed with vast, empty countryside and a seemingly
  permanent stiff breeze blowing across the steppes, the
  buzz of transformers is growing steadily louder in this far
  northern province . . ."[7]

Even if you think that dangling modifiers are not sins, you
can see that the jurors won't be found guilty, that it was not the
searchers who had been dead for 24 hours, and that the buzz of
the transformers was not blessed with "a vast, empty countryside."

Apostrophes

Apostrophes primarily serve two purposes: to form possessives and to form contractions. Many people use apostrophes
where they are not needed; it is hard for many people to avoid
wrong uses because we all see them used incorrectly so often.

   1. Possessives:

   a.   You make a noun possessive by adding 's. The apostrophe distinguishes a singular possessive noun from a plural
noun. To form the plural of most nouns, you add just an s, not an
apostrophe.

- Plural: The plaintiffs argue for a reversal. "Plaintiffs" is a
  plural noun. More than one plaintiff did the arguing.

- Possessive: The plaintiff's argument was brief. "Plaintiff's"
  is singular possessive. The argument involved is that of
  one plaintiff.

   7.   Howard W. French, In Search of a
New Energy Source, China, N.Y. Times,
July 26, 2005.

b. To form the possessive of a singular word that ends in s, you almost always add 's. There are a few exceptions, which you can find in a style or usage book.

- Jones's argument was long. "Jones's" is the possessive of one Ms. Jones.

c. However, you form the plural possessive by adding an apostrophe to a plural noun that already ends in s. To form the possessive of a plural noun that does not end in s, add 's.

- The plaintiffs' argument was long. "Plaintiffs' " is plural possessive. The argument involved is that of more than one plaintiff. You don't add an s after the s'.

- They painted the children's playroom. "Children's" is plural possessive. The playroom is for the use of more than one child. You do add an s after the apostrophe.

d. You use an apostrophe to show a plural in one situation: the plural of numbers and letters in order to avoid confusion.

- This word is spelled with three e's.

e. Do not use an apostrophe for possessive pronouns. The most confusing possessive pronoun for most people is "its." "Its" means that something belongs to it. There is no apostrophe.

- We must be careful about this computer virus because of its potential destructiveness. "Its" is the possessive form. If the writer had written "it's" he would have written the contraction for "it is," which would have appeared as "because of it is potential destructiveness," and would be incorrect.

- The court convened late because its time schedule was completely awry. Again, "Its" here is possessive, referring to the court's schedule, and is correctly written. If the writer had spelled the word as "it's," he would have written "it is time schedule," which would be wrong.

2. *Contractions:*

Use an apostrophe for a contraction where a letter is omitted.

- It's always wrong not to inform your client of progress in the case. This proper use of "it's" is a contraction of the words "it is." Unlike the possessive "its," the "it's" requires an apostrophe.

- There's nothing new to report. "There's," properly used here, is a contraction of the words "there is."

Contractions are a fairly informal way of speaking. You should not use them in memoranda and especially not in writing to a court.

14

Studying and Reviewing

Most law students find that law school, at least the first year, requires the hardest studying they have ever had to do. That is not surprising. Law school requires you, all at once, to absorb a different method of approaching problems, to learn a new language, to use new sources of information, and to employ a different technique of taking examinations.

This chapter offers a few basic suggestions about how to make your studying effective. As you seek to develop study habits that are productive for law school, you should take comfort in the fact that hundreds of thousands of people have done that with reasonable success.

How To Study, Generally

One of the most important requirements for effective law study, which is good preparation for law practice, is to manage your time. Especially during certain weeks of law school, you will feel that there simply is not enough time to do what needs to be done. And you will be right. As we have remarked before, you will find that everything takes longer than you think it will. That is because everything is new to you, and that is why it is crucial to organize and to set priorities.

A useful principle is to establish guidelines for how you use your time. Set target amounts of time to study, or to do the required research and writing, for each course. You needn't be rigid about this sort of planning. That is why we say "guidelines." It may turn out that contracts, which usually takes two and a half hours to prepare per class, will require three tonight, because the assignment is longer or more complex than usual. Or it may happen that because the assignment is benignly manageable, you will require only two hours.

The decision that recurs is where you should put that extra half hour. That is the priorities issue. It comes up in diverse ways, some of which involve choices that may total quite a number of hours to be allocated in one way or another over the course of a semester. Should you work harder on the course you think you understand best, hoping for an A or even an A plus rather than a B plus, and slack off on the course that you like least, assuming that in that course you can't do better than B but won't do worse than C plus? Should you reread your memorandum assignment one more time before it is due? We cannot answer questions like that for you. We do suggest you study subjects that seem hardest to you when you are freshest and least subject to frustration. Again, particular choices day by day are matters for your judgment. We also note the possibility that the course you like least may be the course in which you do best on the exam or the written assignment. Grades can be difficult to predict, and we recommend that you do not give up on any of your courses.

If you feel at sea the first few weeks of law school, struggling to manage your time, you should understand that everyone else is in the same boat. Moreover, you will be pleased to know that things will almost certainly get better. But not right away. You need experience to help you set priorities. We can also assure you that the experience of setting priorities in law school will prepare you for an even more difficult challenge—doing it in practice.

The Study Group Question

You will have to decide for yourself, perhaps after some experimentation, whether you want to join a study group, and how much you want to participate in jointly producing outlines. The way you study best—which may take some testing out as you confront this new discipline—will dictate this entirely personal choice.

A main consideration is time, and here you may wish to play economist. Does the benefit you get from the time spent in discussions with your group exceed the benefit you would receive from studying by yourself? Of course, you could crank into your equation the social features of the group. A study group, if the members are compatible, may provide a support group for you. If you do join a group, it will develop its own culture and its own rules about who contributes what—which may include congeniality, brownies, or a special feel for the Federal Rules of Civil Procedure. We do suggest that when you divide up work, you and your colleagues be sure to set clear responsibilities. You may have to figure in disadvantages as well as benefits. One member of your group may be personally obnoxious but may make brilliant contributions that offset his or her irritating ways. Whatever factors develop as the relevant ones, you must clarify your own priorities in making the basic decision about whether to join, or stay in, a study group.

When groups form, other people sometimes may feel they are being left out of cliques. Keeping that in mind, you should understand that either joining or not joining is an entirely normal choice. After surveying the scene, you should do what is best for you. In any event, remember that you can learn a lot from talking about your law school subjects. If you decide not to join a study group, then try to explain topics to someone else, or even talk the subject to yourself when you are taking a walk or a shower. Whether you join a study group or not, if you always have been fairly compulsive about studying, you may have to resist social pressures for you or your study group to study less.

Reviewing

At some point in each semester you should begin to review the material that is being covered in your courses. A lot of people do this by organizing course material into outline form; indeed, many students simply refer to reviewing as "outlining."

There is no mystery about why you do this, apart from the idealistic motive of learning the law for its own sake because it is intellectually challenging, stimulating and intuitively interesting. The pragmatic reason one puts together course reviews is to prepare for examinations.

Many law professors are now experimenting with ways, other than final exams, to assess students' abilities and their mastery of subject matter. This discussion, however, tends to focus on preparation for "traditional" law school examinations, the kind that most students will continue to face in many subjects. As you get a feel for the requirements of particular courses, in some cases you will want to modify the techniques that we suggest here.

Law school examinations typically feature hypothetical problems, often invented by the professor, that seek to test the student's developed ability to analyze the material presented in a particular course. Your task in reviewing is to prepare yourself to deal with those problems, or indeed any questions designed to test your command of the subject.

1. The Outline

The function of a review sheet, or outline, is to establish a framework of analysis for legal problems. You may find that you did not really understand the material in a course and the relationships among topics until you have worked on an outline. Your goal in making an outline is to deal with two interlinked bodies of knowledge and ability that professors will try to test: (1) Your knowledge of rules at a level from which you can apply those rules logically to particular problems (2) Your ability to apply the rules you have learned to problems involving new sets of facts, and to resolve the ambiguities and analyze the probable outcomes of such problems. As we will emphasize in the next chapter, competence in the second skill distinguishes a good exam.

You should organize your outline by topics, not by cases. One good way to choose your topic headings is to use the titles of the casebook chapters and their sections and subsections. The casebook author typically will have created a logical outline of the course in her organization of those sections. The information you include under each topic will come primarily from the cases and statutes in each section, but will also include material from the notes and comments in your casebook and from class discussions, as well as your own comments and questions. Other ways to organize your outline are by the topics in your professor's syllabus, or by the categories you personally develop after you review the material. The length of your outline depends on the course. Many outlines are as long as 30 or 40 pages. But as you get close to your exam, you may want to condense your outline to the main points that you can remember. By the time of the exam, you should further condense your outline to a checklist of topics, cases, and key words.

The course in civil procedure provides a good illustration of how to construct an outline. Almost certainly, a significant part of an examination in that course will test your understanding of the principal procedural checkpoints in litigation, which may be dealt with in separate chapters in your book. Thus, for example, your outline ought to include the highlights of what you have learned about the motion to dismiss. It should refer to the Federal Rule of Civil Procedure, Rule 12(b)(6), which provides for that motion. It should include short summaries (sometimes in just a few words, if you can boil them down that far) of cases that help to define the issues involved in the question of when a court should, and should not, grant a motion to dismiss.

Your professor or your coursebook may discuss competing interpretations of the law and the policy bases of specific legal rules; you will want to note such discussions in your outline. If there are cases in the coursebook that present differing points of view on the same question—that is, two opposed decisions, or majority and dissenting opinions in the same case, or two cases with different analyses of the issue—it would be useful to summarize the disagreement between opposing judges. A principal reason for this is that, often, controversial questions present an excellent opportunity for a professor to write an exam problem. Exactly because they are controversial, they help the professor to give you an opportunity to show your understanding of the difficulties of a problem, to weigh competing views, and to present a persuasive answer.

Besides summarizing cases, statutory provisions, and rules like the Rules of Civil Procedure, you should include in an outline anything that you think might be helpful in preparing you to show your relevant knowledge and your ability to resolve legal controversies. Perhaps the most obvious sources of outline material are questions that your professor asked in class and questions posed (or answers given) in the coursebook. It is only common sense that you should be careful to take notes on the professor's questions in class, since it is the professor who makes up and grades the exam. In fact, some of your most important notes may be those questions. They sometimes will reveal what the professor thinks are the most interesting issues in the course, which have a way of winding up on exams.

By the way, you shouldn't ignore the questions you have posed to yourself during class or in reviewing your class notes. The very fact that you have formulated those questions should carry you forward in your exam preparation. Often the first thing you have to do in solving a legal problem is to see what the problem is—to state the issue. Once you can do that, you can begin to apply the legal rules and principles you have gleaned from the course.

It also would be prudent to note in your outline particular ideas or phrases—for example, "buzz words"—that seem especially important or that appear to appeal to your professor. As one student said to one of us recently, "You have to walk the walk *and* talk the talk." That's your professor's walk and talk. He or she will grade your examination.

Your outline also might include ideas you have gleaned from treatises and hornbooks, as well as from law review articles that your coursebook cites, that your professor mentions, or that you have found yourself. As a practical matter, you may find it particularly helpful to read books or articles your professor has written. Many students find useful explanations in commercially published outlines. Some commercial outlines can be helpful, especially for topics you feel that you don't have a good grasp of. We recognize that some students rely solely on these outlines. However, we strongly caution against sole, or even principal, reliance on them. The reason, which we amplify below, is that the value of an outline comes from making it yourself.

At least the ideal of an outline is that it will be your own little treatise or hornbook on the subject of a course. The reason you fashion this little treatise is to prepare you, under the conditions of an examination, to analyze an unfamiliar problem case and discuss it in light of the principles and concepts that you have learned.

Many people do their reviewing literally in outline form because an outline enables them to place course material in an orderly framework and to see how different topics of the course relate to one another. The function of an outline is, after all, to help you to organize the material so that you will be able to see the issues in examination problems and discuss those issues with both knowledge and understanding. That is one reason why outlines that you write yourself are the most valuable. In fact, a few days before an examination, you can use your outline to take a dry-run exam based on one of your professor's prior exams or on a sample exam in a commercial prep guide. (Chapter 15 treats techniques for writing exams.)

2. Illustrations of Outlines

Here are two examples of outlines, offered purely for illustration of format. One uses material that is likely to be familiar in first-year curriculums, the subject of torts. The other example is from Estates and Trusts, a course that is typically an upper-year course. Both examples illustrate, in an abbreviated way, a form that identifies particular elements of the course, using specific applications and giving information about where the maker of the outline found the material.

a. Battery

Here is an example of an outline of the tort of battery. The material in parentheses provides examples of the source of the point discussed.

I. BATTERY: Definition—An intentional contact with the person of another that is harmful or offensive and is unconsented and unprivileged.

    A. Contact—An act that results in a physical touching of the person; can be indirect touching—it may be sufficient if the defendant touches an object closely connected to the plaintiff's body.

    1. Examples, including indirect contact

      —Plaintiff hits the ground after the defendant pulls a chair from under her (*Garratt v. Dailey*, casebook p. 33).

      —Defendant yanks a plate from the plaintiff's hand; this might be deemed a battery because the object is so closely connected with the plaintiff's body (class hypothetical).

    2. Rationale for allowing suit for an intentional, indirect touching: Battery emphasizes dignitary interest; in the plate case, yanking the plate violates that interest.

    B. Intent

    1. Meaning of intent

      A purpose to contact the plaintiff's body (ordinary meaning of intent for lawyers as well as non-lawyers); or

Knowledge with substantial certainty that there will be a harmful or offensive contact (*Garratt v. Dailey*, p. 33, five-year-old defendant).

2. Rationales for standard that requires at least knowledge with substantial certainty:

—Differentiates intentional torts from the negligence standard, which at a minimum requires that a defendant should have known of harmful consequences, whereas this standard requires knowledge with substantial certainty of at least offensive contact.

—Requires compensation from persons, even those who cannot foresee actual harm, "who violate social norms and injure innocent people."

—Standard even applies to children.

C. Intended contact must be harmful or offensive

1. Examples

Harmful—Actual physical injury (*Kelly v. Grimsky*, p. 42); or offensive—a breach of social norms concerning personal dignity; a less demanding test for the plaintiff than "harmful": It is a battery to kick a schoolmate in the shin, even without intending actual harm, when class has been called to order (*Vosburg v. Putney*, p. 27).

2. Explanation and rationale for lesser requirement of "offensive":

—Violation of a social norm—for example, the decorum of the classroom—justifies the imposition of tort damages even if the person who did the act did not intend actual physical injury;

—Discourages people from disobeying society's rules; moreover, as between a completely innocent person and someone who violated a rule even though he did not intend injury, it is fair that the rule violator should have to pay for the loss.

* * *

b. *Wills (an example of a shorter outline)*

Part of an outline for a wills course could be:

I. REQUIREMENTS FOR EXECUTING A WILL

A. Signature: every jurisdiction requires

1. Purposes of requirement: Gulliver article

   —Shows that testator adopted the writing as final; not a preliminary draft

   —Provides evidence of whose will

   —Prevents fraudulent wills

2. Jurisdictions that don't require signature at "foot or end":

   a. *Estate of Wineburg* (casebook p. 86): testator wrote her name only in the opening paragraph of the will: "This is Opal Wineburg's will." Intended only as an identification, not as signature adopting the will as hers.

   b. But, opening handwritten paragraph with the words, "This is my will, Joy Smith," shows signature intended to adopt the will. *Estate of Smith* (p. 97).

   c. Problem of how can "adopt" a document that not written yet.

3. Jurisdictions that require at foot or end:

   a. If there is writing below the testator's signature, the writing may invalidate the will if the writing was there when testator signed.

3. The Strategy of Reviewing

In an ideal world, you would start reviewing each course at about the sixth week of a semester, give or take a week, and you would squeeze out enough time to review each course each succeeding weekend. In the real world, most people will not do that. On a given Sunday afternoon when they "ought" to be reviewing, they may want to take a walk, or visit parents or friends, or watch television. And it's true that it's a good idea to take a break so that you don't burn out. But, you may have a legal memorandum due on Monday.

Having in mind that reality check, and the need to balance work and life (as well as to balance different kinds of work against one another) remember that the more you rework an outline, the more you will understand. This is because as you keep going over a body of material, you learn it more meaningfully. Your outline in the eleventh week of a semester will exhibit more understanding of material to which you originally were exposed in the fourth week than you derived when you initially reviewed that material in the seventh week, because the later review provides a broader framework. But the initial review in the seventh week will plant some seeds in your mind that will provide fertilizer for your review in the eleventh week.

The operational lesson is that reviewing a law course is a lot like piano practice, or studying calculus, or learning how to cook. The more you do, on average, the more you will get out of the enterprise. It is true that some students say that they have done better on certain exams for which they studied lightly than exams for which they prepared diligently. But averages are important, and in general, the keys are commitment and effort.

A serious strategic question eventually arises late in any semester: How much more new work should you do on your outline? We do not have a pat answer for that question. We can say only that at some point, you will decide that you have no more time to learn more details about the intricacies of motions for judgment as a matter of law, or what it takes to create an offer in contracts, or the elements of adverse possession in property.

It is at that point that your thirst for learning must turn pragmatically to a thirst for internalizing. Many students will tell you that in the real world, this means "memorizing." We use the seemingly more idealistic word "internalizing" because if you do enough reviewing of material that you have prepared, or played a meaningful part in preparing, then you will begin to absorb the material. It will become part of you in a way that just memorizing-to-disgorge does not achieve. To nail down the point, the fact that you prepared an outline (or review sheet) will make it more meaningful, and thus more instructive, than trying to memorize a commercial outline done by someone else who has not taken your particular class with your particular teacher. Memorizing-to-disgorge from a commercial outline is not good exam-taking preparation.

As it gets late in the semester and even during reading period, many students tend to spend all or most of their time reviewing for their first exam, and then spend only one or two days reviewing for each of the next exams. We suggest that you apportion your time more equally. Of course, you want to feel prepared going into your first exam, but it is a good idea to spend time during the study and preparation period reviewing for all the exams to come. It makes sense, of course, to spend most of the last study day on the course for the first exam.

We conclude on a note that may sound sermonizing, but we believe it describes how to get the most out of courses, usually in terms of your actual knowledge and frequently even on the grade sheet. Whether the issue is how much work you do in any one semester, or in any one course, or for any one class period, the crucial personal choice is how much you want to put into the enterprise.

*

15

Exams

Examinations are not particularly pleasant occasions for anyone, including professors. Remember, we have to grade them. The good news is that exams can be learning experiences, especially if one views the whole examination process broadly to include the activity of preparing for exams. Indeed, the principal part of your learning occurs in the process of reviewing, described in the last chapter. If you put some time into that task and if you review on a schedule throughout the semester, we guarantee that you will find a course more interesting than if you do not; you will see relationships in the materials that a more casual eye would not have discerned.

Solid preparation for an exam also increases the chance that the activity of writing the exam will itself be rewarding. After all, an examination should give you an opportunity to show what you know and, within certain limits, to be creative with that knowledge. Remember that solid preparation means that during reading period or whatever study time you have before exams begin, you spend some time on all your exams, not just the first one.

Law school examinations are usually essay exams rather than short answer or true and false tests, and they may differ from exams you are accustomed to taking. They will not ask you simply to regurgitate material you have memorized, but rather will ask for analysis of a problem. That requirement of analysis may take a variety of forms. For example, you may be assigned the role of an attorney representing a client. Another difference from your prior studies is that in most law schools, your semester grade in most courses other than legal writing will come from one exam at the end of the semester. So a lot rides on the one set of exams each semester. For example, membership on the law review or other student-run journals is determined in large part on your first-year grades, although many journals now allow students to try to "write on," that is, to write an article of acceptable quality during their second year of law school.

Nevertheless, we want to make an important point that gets lost in the anxiety surrounding exams. You should not think of your exam grades as a measure of your worth as a person. Remember that your exams try principally to measure your ability to analyze legal issues. Even in that regard, the questions may just be the wrong ones to test your skills, or you may be too tired to do well, or you may not have used your time well. Surely, law school exams do not measure many of the attributes that make good lawyers.

Two Introductory Tips and Some Preliminary Disclaimers

This chapter identifies what we perceive as major opportunities in exam-taking and problems that students can remedy, at least to some extent. We want to give two introductory pointers. The first is to check whether your professors make available their prior exams. If so, get copies so you can see what the exams look like and get an idea of what kinds of questions your professors ask. Our second pointer is to get enough sleep the night before your exam. Law school exams can be physically taxing and you don't want to be tired when you go in. In fact, you may want to bring some high-energy food to the exam.

We also want to limit our advice with a couple of observations. First, what we say here applies most focally to traditional law school essay examinations. We are talking most specifically about exams that consist principally of hypothetical problems fashioned to test your knowledge of a particular course and your ability to use that knowledge in an analytical fashion by applying the law you have studied to the hypothetical facts.

We will not specifically discuss the type of exam question that asks you to evaluate particular goals or policies of the law while not necessarily placing the question in a factual context. We believe that the advice in this chapter will be useful to those questions and to your other law school work as well, and indeed generally to your future work as a lawyer. However, our focus is on the traditional law exam format, which typically will require you to write an analysis of a few questions drawn from the topics covered during the semester.

Second, at some point talent will make a difference. When a runner wants to know how to improve his or her place in races, there are various tips that can help—about the start, the stride, and even how to lean into the tape. There comes a time, however, when the coach can say only, "Run faster." We cannot tell you how to attain the level of aptitude that the class genius possesses—how to "run faster." We do believe, however, that what we advise below will help you gain an extra stride here and there.

Key Word Outlines; Open Book Exams

Many students find it useful, just before taking an exam, to prepare from their larger outline an outline consisting of key words that capture what they perceive to be the most important subject headings or concepts in the course. If an exam is open book, students probably will carry in with them a sheet with this super-skeleton outline along with other materials. If the exam is closed book, they memorize the skeleton outline fully. They may remember it well enough during the exam without writing it down. If they do not, when it is announced that the examination has begun (but only then), they will scribble down the memorized list.

There is a difference of opinion about this kind of checklist. Some people think it helps you only marginally if at all. This is because whatever level of preparation you bring to the examination, the exam itself should inspire your recognition of each issue that a key word outline is designed to help you recognize. However, many students swear by such outlines, and in any event, preparing one provides a good last-minute review. Moreover, a key word outline may occasionally trigger a useful idea and help you remember some concepts that are relevant to exam problems. Our view is, any crutch in a storm, including psychological crutches.

We have to stress that if you are not ready when you walk into an exam, no open book or open outline is likely to help you very much. Some students think that if they are taking an open book exam they will be able after the exam starts to look through their casebook and their outlines to formulate good answers. We believe this is a mistake—you should go to every exam as if it were closed book. You will not have enough time to consult your materials except to refresh your memory about a few particular points.

Time Limits

Examinations have time limits. As one of our own teachers was fond of saying, the issue is not, "What are the best answers you can write on this exam?" Rather, it is, "What are the best answers you can write in three hours?" That probably is the average time for law school exams. Some teachers may give take-home exams that allow you 24 hours or more, but you may not regard that as a favor after you have endured one of those.

The main point is that you must gauge your time, whatever the limit is. Many professors will provide suggested time limits per question. Since they probably will roughly apportion their grading of different problems based on those suggestions, you would do well to follow them—not obsessively, but rather closely. If the question has sub-parts, allocate time for each part. Time limits, as we shall emphasize in a moment, make especially important for exams some advice we gave earlier about law school generally: organize and establish priorities.

Read The Question

It is vital that you read each question carefully. A serious misreading of a question is likely to produce proportionally adverse results. If you answer a question that a problem does not present, the professor has little to grade you on.

Many people read the whole exam first, or at least scan it, in order to familiarize themselves with it and get a sense of its overall scope. Even if you plunge right into writing the answer to the first question, quickly read the whole question first to get an idea of the issues. If what you thought might be an issue in Part A is certainly the issue in Part B, do some more thinking. Usually different parts of a problem will not focus on the same issue. You may have misread Part A but would not know it if you had not read the whole question first.

After a summary reading of each question, read the question again slowly with an eye to picking out the relevant details, that is, the details that are important to the issues you have identified. Zero in on the facts; they will be crucial to your answer. If your teacher has specified issues for you to discuss, stick to them. If she has not, then you must identify the issues.

Analysis and Application

Law school exams differ from certain kinds of undergraduate exams on which you may have received credit for disgorging memorized material, or material that you happened to know but that was not particularly relevant. Successful law examination answers, like any successful legal work, stick to what is relevant to the issues the question raises. They use the facts in the problem that are crucial to the answer and they *apply* knowledge to the problems presented, analyzing those problems rather than just identifying them.

In an open book exam, everyone can copy the rules from their outline or the casebook. But the professor is looking for an answer that goes beyond that and that explains how those rules will work, given those facts. In most questions, the answer is not a clear one; the interpretation of the rules may not be clear, or the facts raise uncertainties about the outcome. Analyze those uncertainties as fully as you can, rather than make snap judgments one way or the other. The professor wants to see how you identify and interpret the controlling language (for example, from a statute, common law, federal rules, or contract terms), and then how you think through the application of that language to the facts, showing the arguments and the counterarguments as you go.

Thus, for a typical essay exam question, your answer should identify the controlling legal rule, break down the rule to its elements and subparts, and identify and analyze any ambiguities and complexities in the rule. You should then apply the rule to the facts, using the cases you have covered in class, and the policies behind those interpretations, and explain the arguments for and against your conclusion.

A basic point here is that, for many issues, you will not want to stop with a syllogism. In addition, you will want to use analogies and policy arguments to develop your analysis (see Chapters 7, 10, 11), to demonstrate that you understand the difficulty of the problem, and to show that you can weigh conflicting interests and arrive at a conclusion.

Organize Your Answer

It is important to organize your answer. How should one begin organizing? People vary in what works for them concerning initial organization of their writing. Some like to prepare a little outline for an answer before they begin actually writing it, perhaps scribbling the outline right on the question sheet. Some prepare elaborate outlines, although we do not recommend this approach because it takes so much time. Others will write their way into the exam, pushing themselves to get some sentences on paper that respond to an issue. The process of writing itself helps them to organize as they proceed, especially as the adrenalin begins to flow. Then as they begin to think ahead, they may write a simple outline in the margin to help them remember what to include.

Do what works for you, but understand that the reader of an exam will appreciate it if she discerns a logical framework for your answer. That does not mean that the professor will not dig out the analysis if it is there. It does mean that between two answers that arrive at the same analytical conclusion, the one that shows its process of reasoning more clearly may receive the better grade.

But you do have to balance care in initial organization with the need to get started, for that may be more important than meticulous organization. Because exams have time limits, it is vital to get yourself moving. As we have noted, starting to write usually helps to get the adrenalin going. Occasionally, if the first question leaves you cold, you may want to start with another question. Or if Part A of a question is temporarily a mystery, and you understand the issue in Part B, start with Part B. If you do that, be sure to label carefully the question, or part, that you are answering so that the teacher will follow what you have done.

When you discuss specific causes of action, whether common law claims or statutory ones, remember to organize these claims by the elements or factors of their definitions, and by the types of facts that the courts use to analyze each element or factor. For example, if your problem involves an intentional tort, you would set out each element of that tort, focusing your answer on the elements at issue. If one or more elements are clearly established, you could indicate quite briefly why that is so. For example, if one element of a battery is a contact, and the question specifically says that A touched B's arm, you could simply note that the contact element is fulfilled because A touched B, and therefore uncontroversial, and then move on to more difficult issues.

If the problem involves a statute, organize your answer by the statute's requirements that are relevant to the question. One important point concerning questions based on statutes will help to save words: Do not repeat all the language of the statute. Focus on the language at issue and analyze how that language applies. Then identify the analytical classifications that courts have used to interpret the statute. For example, under Uniform Commercial Code § 2–302, a court may refuse to enforce an unconscionable contract. Courts usually analyze contracts attacked as unconscionable in terms of procedural and substantive unconscionability. Thus, you would organize your answer into each of these two categories. Then you would analyze the facts of the hypothetical according to the factors the courts have used to determine whether a contract is procedurally or substantively unconscionable.

Answering Specific Questions Specifically and Providing Discussion

The traditional law school exam consists of a series of hypothetical questions. The professor will ask you to apply to those questions, in some fashion, the analytical framework you have developed in the course. Some of these questions will invite extended discussion, perhaps even upwards of an hour, while some questions may require much less time.

Besides in some way asking for discussion of a question of law, many exam problems will also pose a concrete legal issue, sometimes one that is procedurally focused. One example of such an issue would be, "Should the court grant the motion to dismiss?" At some point in your answer, and if possible at the beginning, answer the specific question.

Giving that answer, to be sure, is only one part of your task. The question about how to rule on the motion to dismiss is not a yes or no question. As we have said, but can't emphasize enough, exam answers do not stop with a single word or phrase, unless they are multiple choice. In fact, most exam problems call for discussion. Therefore, you should engage in discussion. A stark question like whether a court should grant a particular motion usually implies, "Discuss," or "Analyze," or "Explain." Often the professor will use words like that. Yet, be sure to answer the bare question, too. One advantage of compelling yourself to do that is that it will force you to analyze the problem, an analysis that should lead you into a discussion that exhibits your applied knowledge of the subject. Ultimately, for most professors, that analysis is more important than the answer yes or no, although you certainly should specify that answer.

Do Not Repeat, or Invent, Facts

Helpful preliminary advice for exam writing is, do not simply repeat the facts that are given to you in the problem as you would in a facts section of a memorandum. The professor knows the facts; she wrote them. You would just be wasting time to repeat them. What you should do with the facts is use them for analysis, as we'll emphasize later on.

Most exam problems will include sufficient facts to stimulate discussion. The professor will have spent some time thinking about those facts in order to test your ability to pull out relevant ideas from the course and apply them. Thus, a good general rule is, do not invent facts; use what is there. As an example, assume an exam problem that says that a man suffered great agony from a disease caused by a virus that escaped from a research facility, and clearly indicates that there was no negligence on the part of the owner of the facility. In analyzing this problem, you should concentrate on the question of whether there should be liability without fault in such a situation, and surely should not pause to discuss whether the owner of the facility was negligent unless you refer to that point in a transitional sentence or clause ("Since the facts make it clear that the company was not negligent ...,"). The facts of the problem do directly present the issue of liability without fault, which is quite worthy of discussion ("... I focus on the question of strict liability"). Moreover, although the virus caused great agony to the afflicted man, do not invent a family for him—a family not mentioned in the problem—and discuss whether they should be compensated for having to watch his pain. That would be inventing your own question, and your own issue, rather than those the professor presented.

There is at least one qualification to our warning against inventing facts. If the exam problem truly seems to lack an important fact, make an assumption and identify it as an assumption. This will show the professor that you are not trying to construct a better question than he or she did by making up facts, but also that, as a good lawyer should be able to do, you are able to state your premises. You can also state the assumption that the exam contains a mistake, for example, using the wrong person's name. In that case, you could say, "Assuming that you meant Charles and not David. . . ."

Be Relevant

Be relevant. If there is a single piece of advice we would offer for writing exams—or for just about any lawyerly activity—that is it. This advice is easier preached than practiced. But it lies behind everything we have said to this point, and it applies as well to everything we say in the rest of the chapter. For common law claims, relevance means identifying and analyzing each element or factor of the claim. For statutory claims, relevance requires you to identify and analyze the particular statutory language at issue. In all cases, relevance requires that you identify the facts on which your analysis turns.

For example:

• Suppose that in your contracts class, the professor presented four major ways for a person to impose liability on someone who has reneged on a promise or failed to live up to something analogous to a promise: a conventional offer-and-acceptance contract, promissory estoppel, moral obligation, and the theory of quasi-contract. Your contracts exam includes a problem that clearly, and only, presents the question of whether someone has accepted an offer. Because that seems a little too simple, you mentally review all the theories of contract formation that you have studied. Although you decide that none of these really applies, you provide your instructor a learned little essay not only on offer and acceptance, but also on promissory estoppel, moral obligation and quasi-contract. At some point, your professor's eyes will glaze as she realizes that you are just listing things you have memorized and not applying them to the problem at hand.

Certainly, if the facts had raised any or all of the other three theories as plausible grounds for recovery, discussion of those methods would be relevant. Indeed, if the facts gave you an opportunity to discuss all four of those methods, even if to explain briefly why one or more don't apply, then you would discuss all four; that would be the difference between a good answer and a below average one. But when the facts do not fairly present an opportunity to discuss a particular rule or principle, you should not continue on in a way that does not address the exam problem.

Look at the matter from the professor's point of view. She has given a problem that focuses on one issue and you have written an essay that includes three other issues. If you were she, would you think the part of your answer concerning the other issues was relevant? Would your discussion of them get any credit on your exam grade?

• Exam questions may involve more than one element or subsection of a statute or document, and may involve a combination of documents. Again, it is important to focus on the key language in each statute or document as it relates to particular texts. For example, § 2–207(2) of the Uniform Commercial Code provides that new terms in an acceptance of a contract become part of that contract unless

(a) the offer expressly limits acceptance to the terms of the offer;

(b) they [the new terms] materially alter the offer; or

(c) notification of objection to them [by the offeror] has already been given or is given within a reasonable time after notice of the new terms is received.

Now assume an exam question that takes place in a state that has adopted § 2–207(2). The question includes facts about a party's acceptance made on a form, and about the language of the offer and of the acceptance, in which the accepting party introduced new terms. The offer form does not include language that limits the offer to its terms. You would identify the issue as whether new language in the acceptance will become part of the contract. Your answer should then address each element of § 2–207(2), which is the rule in that state. You would observe quickly from the facts given that the offer was not expressly limited to its terms, so that the next issues are whether the new language in the acceptance materially altered the offer, and whether the offeror notified the accepting party of its objection in a reasonable time. Your answer would then discuss what you know about those two issues, applying the rules of subparts (b) and (c) of the statute to the facts given in the problem, and making analogies and distinctions from the case law you have read and your other reading, and from what you learned in class.

Some students think that they need only identify an issue—for example, in the UCC question we have just been discussing, that they need only say that if the new language materially alters the offer, the new terms are not part of the contract. To analyze an issue, however, we repeat, you must go beyond identifying it. You should discuss whether the new terms of the contract presented in the hypothetical do or do not materially alter the offer and *why.* In giving such a question on an exam, most professors will include facts that can be used to show why the new terms alter the offer, and also facts that can be used to show why the new terms do not alter the offer. Given such a question, you should weigh the competing sets of facts and arrive at the conclusion that seems most reasonable.

What we have been saying about relevance has strong practical application. Good lawyers can pick out the facts on which a question turns and apply what they know in ways that pertain to the question—that are relevant to the facts of that problem. We do not mean to suggest that there will not be times when there is a genuine issue as to relevance itself. Moreover, the presentation of an interesting angle on an issue that really is in an exam problem may earn you points, both for providing reasons to support your answers and for creativity. But we would not bank on credit for irrelevant discussions. Perhaps our principal single piece of negative advice about exam technique is that you should not throw the whole garbage can of your outline at every problem. Be selective about the law you apply and the facts that you analyze; that is the essence of relevance.

Get To the Point

Remember that time is precious when you are writing an exam, so you must get to the point. Ordinarily one should not begin answers to problems that focus on fact-based legal issues with essays about the background of the subject or about the great conflicting social interests it represents. That type of introduction may be appropriate if the question asks you only to discuss a particular policy or policies relevant to the course. But when answering a more traditional exam question, one should move directly into the *analysis* of the particular factual problem, and weave the relevant background about competing social interests into your analysis.

An illustration of how you might achieve a blend between the facts of a problem and its social background, in one sentence, is this: "The argument against the defense of assumption of risk in workplace cases is that this defense was better suited to the days of its origin, when courts used it to protect infant industries." That way you have identified the issue—the applicability of the assumption of risk defense in cases involving worker injuries—but you also have set that issue in a framework of history and social policy. You have thus showed the professor your ability to engage in relevant analysis, rather than offering an exercise in casual essay writing.

Some Pitfalls to Avoid

Many teachers grade exams by assigning points to each issue in a question. The better you analyze an individual issue, the more points you get, up to a maximum number. This means that your exam-taking strategy should be to use your time in ways that will add points to your answer, including an effort to apportion your time efficiently among multiple issues, and surely to answer each question. Of course, the best way to maximize your score is by the quality of your answer, which is what much of this chapter has been about. However, you should also be aware of some ill-advised practices that take time and get you no points. For example:

- Don't repeat. Repetition will not add to your score. So, do not summarize your point in an introduction, then do a full analysis, and then repeat the introduction as a conclusion. You will be saying the same thing three times and getting points only once.

- Don't restate the facts. Of course, you should *use* the facts and analyze them. However, you need not begin your answer with a statement of facts as you would for a memorandum.

- Don't announce to the professor your situation concerning time. You need not explain at the end of your answer that your time is up or that the registrar is taking your paper. Your teacher will know that the end of your writing means that the time for the exam is over. Instead, use that extra sentence to write one last point analyzing the exam question or a short outline of an answer you didn't have time for.

Summing Up

Here are a few things that may impress professors when they grade examinations:

- Clear organization
- Identification of the issue
- Analysis of issues, using the important facts that give rise to those issues
- Applying relevant legal rules and analogies to the specific facts of problems
- Applying broad policy ideas to concrete situations
- Identifying the arguments for and against a particular result and arguing persuasively to a conclusion
- Clear writing
- Concision

* * *

In conclusion, we first offer some advice about how to function after an exam, particularly if there are other exams to come. The gist of the lesson is, do not reflect on an exam after it is over. This may be an anti-intellectual suggestion, but for most students, it will be useful to preserve sanity.

If possible, avoid talking about the exam with other students. If you do, someone may ask about something you did not discuss—something like, "What did you do with the promissory estoppel issue in the case involving the uncle?" Reacting, horrified, "Oh my gosh, I never even saw a promissory estoppel issue," you will believe that your contracts grade is ruined. There are at least three reasons not to brood this way: 1) There may have been no promissory estoppel issue; your classmate may have been wrong; 2) If there was such an issue, the professor may not give it as much weight as your classmate thought it deserved; 3) One way or the other, you cannot do anything about it, and brooding about either uncertainty or perceived certainty of failure will make you unnecessarily miserable until the grades come out.

So move on. Go to a movie, or start studying for the next exam, if there is one. Get some sleep. This is almost compulsory advice if there is a next exam. Even if you have finished with a set of exams, we still suggest that you do not re-play the exam week in your mind. You cannot do anything about it. Enjoy whatever break time you have. If you have been lucky enough to get a summer job, concentrate on that.

Our final advice is to play your game as well as you can during the whole period of exams. By playing your game, we mean that you write up to the limits of your ability and knowledge, as well as the pressure of the moment allows. In addition, without being overconfident, you should trust your instincts.

You will miss some issues and not discuss some others as fully as you would like. But even great basketball players miss free throws at crucial moments, great golfers miss short putts late in the tournament, and great hitters strike out with the bases loaded. The key is consistency. Thus, shrug off what you perceive as mistakes and keep taking your free throws and hitting your putts. If you play your game, you will come out on your average, which is all any of us can ask.

SAMPLE EXAM QUESTION AND ANSWER

PROBLEM

For this question, you need to know that there are two types of gifts: a gift causa mortis (in contemplation of death) and an inter vivos gift (a lifetime gift). You also have to know that oral wills are not valid.

Just prior to going to the operating room for an operation Ms. Betty Jones wrote the following note to her husband, from whom she was separated.

"My Dear John:

"In the kitchen, in the bottom of the cabinet, under the wine bottle, there is one hundred dollars. Alongside the bed in my bedroom, in the bottom drawer of the small table you will see about seventy-five dollars. Where the coats are in the closet, in a round tin box, on the floor, where the shoes are, there is two hundred dollars. This is for you to give to Diane. Please put it in the bank for her. This is for her schooling. And my old desk is for her too.

"The savings passbook is yours, and also the money that is here in the hospital in my night table drawer and the key to my dresser drawer at home.

"Give Margaret my sewing machine.

Pray for my recovery, Betty"

Ms. Jones placed the note in the drawer of a table beside her hospital bed, at the same time asking an old friend, Wendy Carver, who was also confined in the hospital, to tell her husband or daughter about it. That afternoon, while Ms. Jones was in the operating room unconscious under the effects of anesthetic, her husband came to the hospital and was told about the note by Ms. Carver. He took the note from the drawer beside his wife's bed, went home, found the cash, the savings account passbook, and the other items mentioned in the note, and has retained possession of them since that time.

Ms. Jones did not recover from the operation and died two days later.

Did Ms. Jones make valid gifts to her daughter Diane, and to Mr. Jones?

A SAMPLE ANSWER

(This answer is abbreviated in most parts, for example, comparisons to precedent cases and analysis as an inter vivos gift.)

The items mentioned in Ms. Jones' letter to her husband could be gifts causa mortis or intervivos (lifetime) gifts. A gift causa mortis is a gift made in contemplation of immediate death. If the donor does not die, the gift is recoverable.

Introduction with definitions

Both types of gifts require that the donor must intend to give the gift and must deliver the gift, and the donee (the recipient) must accept. Courts tend to enforce delivery requirements more strictly for gifts causa mortis because without delivery of the gift item, a gift causa mortis is like an oral will, which is not enforceable as a will.

Requirements for a gift

Ms. Jones' letter shows that she intended to give the listed items as gifts. She identified them and used language of giving, i.e., "This is for you to give to Diane," "my old desk is for her too," and "the savings passbook is yours." Mr. Jones accepted the gifts because he retrieved the items.

First two requirements summarized quickly

The issue is whether Ms. Jones delivered the items. Gift law usually requires manual delivery, that is, the donor must physically hand over the items to the donee. The reasons for this requirement are that delivery provides evidence of the gift and prevents fraudulent claims. However, most courts also recognize both constructive delivery and symbolic delivery when manual delivery is not possible—where, for example, the items are too large to manually deliver or the donor is not able to hand them over immediately. [Here, you would explain the types of items mentioned in cases in your casebook on these topics, for example, a piano or sofa.]

Identifying key requirement at issue and policy behind requirement

Ms. Jones may have construct- *First*
ively delivered some of these items. *alternative*
A constructive delivery gives the donee
the access to and control of items *Explanation*
that he would not have had otherwise.
Examples are the case of <u>A v. B</u>, in
which the donor drew a map showing *Examples from*
where he had buried his treasures, *relevant cases*
and <u>C v. D</u>, in which the donor gave
the donee the key to his safety
deposit box. Ms. Jones' letter was
like the map; it revealed hiding
places of some of her "treasures" *Application*
for Mr. Jones to find. Some of the *to facts*
items, however, were at the hospital.
The money for her husband and
the key to her dresser drawer were
in the table next to her bed. They
were not hidden or incapable of *Counterarguments*
being retrieved and were capable of
hand delivery. Also, in the cases
just mentioned, the donor had manually
given the donee the means of access
to the gifts, for example, the map.
Ms. Jones, by contrast, left the note
in her bedside table and did not give
it to Mr. Jones. She could have given
Mr. Jones the note at an earlier time,
before she was taken for surgery. To
be sure, she had no control over the
time her husband arrived at the
hospital or the time that she was
taken for surgery. However, I believe *Conclusion*
a court would be likely to conclude
that, as a woman facing surgery, she
did all she was able to do before her
operation to provide the information
her husband required for access to the
items.

If Ms. Jones didn't *Second*
Constructively deliver *Alternative*
the gifts, she may have
symbolically delivered them. Courts
sometimes allow symbolic delivery, *Definition*
which requires that the donor give
to the donee something symbolic of the
intended gift, usually by referring
to the items in a signed writing where
the items could not feasibly be
manually delivered.

A strong case may be made   *Counterarguments*
against symbolic delivery in this
case. Ms. Jones didn't give the
letter directly to Mr. Jones, and
she could have retrieved the note
if she came back to her hospital
room before he arrived; moreover,
some of the items at issue were
capable of manual delivery. Courts
surely will impose more difficult
delivery requirements on gifts
causa mortis than on intervivos
gifts, but the facts
mentioned above might incline a court
to conclude that there was no inter
vivos gift. [Here, explain this
conclusion.]

Moreover, the delivery issue   *New Issue:*
aside, there is some ambiguity as   *Ambiguity as*
to what gifts Ms. Jones intended to   *to intent*
make. For example, what did she mean
by "the key to my dresser drawer"?
She may have intended to just give
John the key as a gift, which is
what she wrote. However, it is
more likely that she intended
to give him the items in the
dresser drawer, which she
knew was locked. Decisions
involving gifts of a key have   *Application to*
focused on the key as providing   *facts: The key*
access to the locked-up intended gift
items. [Here, analyze the precedents].
Keys have been symbols of ownership
and dominion. A court would probably
conclude that Ms. Jones intended to
give the items in her dresser drawer,
and not just the key itself.

Beyond that, it is not clear   *Application*
whether Ms. Jones intended the gift   *to Facts:*
for Diane to include all the items   *Language of*
listed prior to "this is for you to   *identification*
give to Diane," or whether the "this"
referred only to the $200. However,
because no other recipients are
mentioned in the first paragraph of
the note, and Ms. Jones was careful
to otherwise identify the different
recipients, she most likely intended
Diane to receive all the items
mentioned in that paragraph.

I conclude that Mr. Jones and *Overall* Diane can make out a good case for *Conclusion* constructive delivery of the items in Ms. Jones' home, but probably not for the items in the table by her hospital bed.

*

16

It's a Mind Game: Psychological Tips for the Study of Law

Law study puts mind, body, and emotions to the test.

This book principally aims to provide the most basic tool kit for the mind, but you should not neglect your physical and emotional well-being. The best one-word advice for dealing with the physical demands of law study is: exercise. How you specifically should act on this advice will depend in large part on your prior habits and life style. We do *not* suggest that if you have always been a couch potato, you should begin your first week of law school by running fast miles. We do think that even those whose main commitment to physical activity has been channel surfing will benefit from at least regular walking, built up by increments, as often as you have time to do it. If you are used to exercise, strenuous or otherwise, it is quite as important that you do not put away that part of your life, even if you do not continue to push yourself at your pre-law school level. The basic point is that you get some regular exercise, at what is a reasonable level for you, unless there is a medical reason not to do so. Your body and your mind will thank you for it.

There is a corollary concise suggestion: rest. Apart from defined exercise, get some rest and relaxation. Besides imposing a heavy workload, law school is stressful, and the combination of a lot of work and stress is fatiguing. This point requires emphasis for people whose prior lives have tended to ignore the need for relaxation as well as for sleep. No matter how important it may seem to do the extra half hour's work, consider listening to a favorite recording without a law book in front of your nose, or observing the squirrels, or chatting with friends about something other than law, or even watching a lawyer show on television.

Building on our lengthy advice for the mind throughout the book, and our brief advice for the body just above, this chapter presents some ideas to help you overcome common psychological hurdles on the way to a law degree. We have culled these ideas from listening to and observing many students. To see what some successful lawyers say about what they took from their law school experiences, look at the appendix following this chapter.

There Is Pressure in Law School

There is no denying that there is pressure in law school, particularly in the first year. If you have some significant experience in employment, you should be no stranger to some degree of pressure. Hard undergraduate or graduate work or demanding extracurricular activities may also have given you some toughening. However, even many people with work experience find that law school is especially taxing. Almost everything you encounter is new, much of it is confusing, and everything takes more time. Therefore, as a friend who is a clinical psychologist remarked, "You should feel that you have permission to feel overwhelmed."

There has been a lot of discussion over the years about whether law school needs to be as unpleasant as it is for many students. Derek Bok, a law professor who became dean of Harvard Law School and president of Harvard University, reflected on the question of whether the first year could be "done without the fear, without the doubts and the gnawing sense of inadequacy that often accompanies" that period of law study. He answered doubtfully, rationalizing that "one of the unpleasant but enduring truths in life is that most of our greatest personal advances, our most creative leaps, the times when we really move forward in our self-understanding and our self-awareness come from unhappy, stressful, and unpleasant experiences."[1]

Although we have mixed feelings ourselves about some of the harsher aspects of law school life, we think it appropriate to say that whatever your previous range of experiences, if you want to be a lawyer, you might as well get to used to pressure. A lawyer we know told us that when he interviews a student for a job, he is trying to project an image of her fifteen years ahead, to a time when she is a full-fledged lawyer. He pictures this person in the following situation: A client walks in, on the verge of tears, and tells the lawyer that the company he has built for twenty years is about to go down the drain because of its legal problems. He asks for her help, quickly. Now, that is pressure. When you find it useful to put the pressures of law school in perspective, you should consider that law school generally, and most professors, are less emotionally demanding than professional life.

A different perspective on the subject appears in a letter from a lawyer to a university alumni magazine. This letter writer was responding to an article in which a law graduate complained bitterly about his law school experiences. In his response, the letter writer noted that he had come to law school immediately after finishing his service as a company commander in Vietnam. He declared that he was "profoundly grateful during every single day of my three years at [Harvard Law School] that (a) it was conducted indoors; (b) I had the luxury of devoting my time wholly to reading, writing, discussion and other purely intellectual activities; and (c) no one was trying to kill me."[2]

If you have led a relatively sheltered life, the pressures of law school may be more daunting than they were to this combat veteran. However, there are ways to cope with those pressures. We have already suggested the two simplest and most practical, to get rest and exercise. Another coping strategy is this: keep up your relationships with family and friends. In fact, make new friends, just as you have all your life. Some of the friends you make in law school may even turn out to be professional assets, but make friends for whatever reasons you have always made them.

Keep in mind, finally, that it is not a mark of weakness to seek help when you need help. All law schools have personnel

---

1. Derek Bok, Derek Bok IL, Harvard Law Bulletin, Fall 1995, 35 at 36.

2. David C. Carrad, Letter, in Harvard Magazine, May–June 1995, at 7.

designated to help you over personal and family crises and to guide you to counselors or therapists if you begin to feel that you cannot cope. Professors, even if they are not therapeutically trained, can usually offer some help and can at least put you on the track to the right people. If you think that your feelings of inadequacy or anxiety are really beyond normal limits, do not hold back. Let someone know about your problems.

Preserving Your Humanity

Despite the ferocious image of competition in law school conveyed by the media, fiction, and general rumor around campus, we think that law students are decent folks. Moreover, even if there are a few piranhas, you can exert a lot of influence on who you choose to deal with—as friends, acquaintances, or study group members. However, you do want to stay alert to the challenge that the competitive aspect of law school poses to your humanity.

Since law students learn early that hours and even quarter hours are precious, part of the challenge to your good instincts has to do with how you spend your time. A heartening example is one talented student in both of our first-year classes who put in a considerable amount of time helping another student, whose first language was not English, practice for an oral argument. The same student also spent a significant amount of time psychologically buoying up another classmate who had been diagnosed with a serious disease. P.S. The altruistic student did pretty well his first year and went on to become editor-in-chief of the Law Review.

It is true that difficult problems of choice will arise, presenting local versions of age-old moral conflicts. Here is a hypothetical drawn from more than one real-life situation. Sam is a third-year student who is a member of the Law Review. As a help to its members, many of whom skip a lot of classes to do their work for the publication, the Review maintains a bank of outlines for upper-year courses. This batch of outlines has been developed over the years, and has no identifiable authors. These outlines are thus not like study group outlines, primarily written by one person or by a very small group for the group. Still, it is the custom of the Review that the outlines are meant only for Review members.

Martha, Sam's wife, is a second-year student who is taking a course covered by one of the outlines. Should Sam share a Law Review outline with Martha, who is not a Review member? Do you find it amazing that this issue even poses a problem? We can only put the question, noting that it comes from a real-life situation a student described to us. When law school challenges one morality with another, you will have to make choices about your personal priorities.

Having left that question with you, we will underline some previous advice. On some days of law school, even in some weeks, the pressure of work will pretty much cause you to lose touch with your family and your friends. Try not to let that become a habit. The reason is not only that it is doing the right thing to make time for those to whom you are closest. It is that they want to help you, and can do so only if they understand the process you are living through. A disposition to talk about that process will benefit both you and them. They will feel more a part of your life, and you will be able to unburden yourself more easily.

Echoes of the Paper Chase: The Socratic Method And Feeling Put Down by the Professor

There aren't many professors left, if there ever were very many, like Professor Kingsfield, the tyrannical Contracts teacher of the movie and TV show *The Paper Chase*. But that does not change the fact that the atmosphere of some law classrooms is intimidating to many students, and may manifest itself in student psychology in the feeling that the professor has delivered a put-down.

To deal with this kind of reaction, you have to understand that a lot of law is about argument. That is evident when you think about the litigation side of the law. Even in nonlitigation branches of the profession, however, you sometimes will have to do some arguing—if only with yourself—in order to serve your client. For example, if you are preparing the legal end of a business deal, you must keep posing "What if" questions to yourself in order to consider the implications of a proposed course of action and to protect your client. People who engage in legal and business planning often benefit by challenging their own initial analyses. In that sense, testing out your ideas against yourself—or having a partner argue with you to make sure that you have considered all the angles—is part of being a lawyer.

We hope that your professors will employ this technique in *true* Socratic style, putting questions that inspire you to think through the implications of your position. Thus, when the professor asks what may seem to you a put-down question, you should view the question as a way to make you think. That is really all most professors are trying to do when they use a questioning style of instruction—make you think. We understand that sometimes the method comes across as a professor's self-satisfied triumph. However, if you learn what the teacher wants you to learn, the triumph will be yours.

Most importantly, you should understand that this form of argument is not personal. In the Socratic classroom situation, the student who must personally respond to the instructor's questions is just a representative of his or her colleagues, one through whom the professor develops ideas that are important to the class.

Of course, in a class of one hundred and twenty, or even twenty, it will seem embarrassing if you give the "wrong" answer. But remember that the professor is concentrating on developing the lesson, and, a day later, probably will not even recall what you said. Even if she does, she may think your "wrong" response was more acute than you gave it credit for. In general, the only answers professors tend to associate with particular students are the brilliant ones. Remember also that if you are confused about a class, or want to test out your understanding of a subject, or just want to get a better sense of your professor, you can always go to her office and talk about the material. Conversations like that may also give the professor a better sense of who you are, which may be useful if you later ask her to serve as a reference.

If you are concerned about what other students may have thought of an alleged little "mistake," consider that your remarks in class are subject to a lot of competition in your classmates' own minds. They may be struggling with the material so hard they barely hear you. They may be concocting fabulous answers of their own. They may be thinking about their sick spouse or child. So understand, for your own mental health, that your "wrong" answer was not as much the center of the universe as you thought.

What Does the Professor Want?

When you are not thinking that the professor is putting you down, you may be saying to yourself, "What does he want?" Sometimes a student will say that right out in class: "I don't know if this is what you're after." Well, sometimes the professor is not entirely clear himself. He probably does have a goal in mind—an idea that he wants to work around to. But, particularly if he is learning the subject himself—or rethinking it—he may not have a firm idea of "the answer."

Whatever is in the professor's mind, our advice is to relax a little. If you are the subject of the teacher's questioning, bend with the questions. Let the discussion sift itself out. At any point in the dialogue, all you can do is try to answer the one question on the floor. If you are not clear, ordinarily the professor will rephrase. Eventually, there probably will be progress. At worst, most class hours are only 50 minutes long. If you are not the subject of the professor's questions, take notes on them. Some of your most valuable notes may be those questions, rather than answers.

The Professor Can Be Wrong

You may think you sustained bruises when a professor "put you down." But the professor can be wrong. Different professors will react in different ways, mostly according to their personalities, to the question of how subversive this statement is.

However subversive, it is true. Naturally, though, you will have to gauge your professor in deciding how much you want to argue about ideas he has expounded that seem clearly mistaken. People call that prudence.

To place the matter at a particularly crucial juncture, when you are writing exams, you will have to make judgments about how hospitable individual professors are likely to be to arguments that do not agree with their basic premises. That is *certainly* prudence. Frankly, there are a few professors who have a view of their subject that is so set in concrete that they honestly cannot see a fair argument on the other side, or even another way to define the problem. Humor them. Or at least, humor them on the exam, at least to the point of viewing the problem as they would view it. Understand, however, that you do not have to give up your private assessment of a legal problem, which may include a judgment that the professor is wrong.

Remember that a successful legal education should prepare you to assess ideas on their merits. As a lawyer, you will have to do that all the time, and sometimes entirely on your own. Thus, do not view the professor with a different viewpoint as a capricious roadblock to understanding. View her as a way to challenge your own ideas, to discard those that are not as good as hers, and at least privately to validate those ideas of yours that you believe—after reflection—are better ones. More generally, view her as a vehicle for helping you to enhance your own intellectual independence.

The Awesome Other Student

Sometimes the responses of other students in class will sound like Holmes, Brandeis, and Cardozo all rolled into one. We will offer some explanations for the psychology of this phenomenon.

Often students who speak in class—at least volunteers—are speaking because they have thought about a problem, or perhaps have done a little extra reading on it, and because they think they have something special to contribute. Thus, students who speak up are self-selected; they are giving out what they at least consider the cream of their thought on a subject.

The responses of several of these students may tend to blend in your mind into one Awesome Other Student. You may put together in your own mind the best responses that six or eight students can give, and associate all those answers with the hypothetical person of one enormously talented individual. If your anxiety level rises, you may get to thinking that every other student in the class is the Awesome Other Student—everyone but you is capable of distilling in his or her mind the greatest wisdom possessed by the best prepared and most aggressive group of students in the class on any one occasion.

This perception is false. Even if it were true, there would be nothing you could do about it. You should not make yourself feel inferior to the Awesome Other Student, because that student does not exist. He or she is a composite of the strongest intellects in the class. So just play your game and think through things as well as *you* can; that is all you can ask of yourself in any event.

Yet, we should add that playing the game does include listening to what other students have to say. Sometimes their remarks will be sensible and even penetrating; often they will at least make you think. Moreover, now and then, there will be a genuinely talented person in the class whose answers make sense, time after time. Do not be envious, and do not be daunted. Learn from that person. Even if this genius happens to be arrogant about his or her talent, recognize it for what it is: a gift. One of the authors was in several classes with a very bright and verbal student, and took notes on everything he said. We would add that you should not judge talent prematurely. What may seem an incomparably fine mind in September may appear less scintillating by April—and the other way around.

Resentment and Alienation

Sometimes law school breeds resentments and alienation. There is, in fact, a scholarly literature that has developed about these phenomena. But in part, they are an outgrowth of some very positive developments. For example, a generation ago, few people expressed concern that women and minorities felt alienated from a law school culture that was overwhelmingly white and male. The reason there was little concern was that there were few women or minorities in law schools. One of us cannot recall a single African-American, and can remember only a few Latinos, in a large law school when he began teaching in 1965. When the other was a member of a law review in 1975, every one of the dozen top editors was male and she was one of only eight women out of a total of 76 members of the Review.

It is not surprising that as groups previously excluded from the process of legal education have moved into law school, new tensions have arisen. Some women complain about what they regard as male domination of both the content of legal rules and the perspective of the classroom. Some minority students view themselves as marginalized by a lack of attention to the experiences that have shaped their lives. And some white males themselves resent what they perceive as employment preferences given to females and minorities.

The strife extends even to pronouns, as uses of "he" and "she" become occasions for criticism. Male students may get tired of professors, both women and men, who seem to hypothesize only female judges, just as female students have thought that too many of their professors talk only about males. Backlashes and overreactions abound.

These diverging views in law schools are certainly not unique, and they reflect changes in society as a whole. We could say that everyone should celebrate diversity and leave it at that. Instead, we will indicate that one of the best things law school can do for you is to teach you to judge people, as well as ideas, on their merits, and to see that their merits may be diverse ones.

A Conclusion

We conclude with some ideas what law school should do, what it does do, and how generally to cope with the process of legal education. Law school should make you better—intellectually richer, mentally sharper, psychologically more sensitive to a variety of viewpoints, more practiced and more secure in dealing with situations involving conflict.

It actually will do all of these things. However, there are likely to be times when the process will get you down. Sometimes a particular trigger will be your belief that you gave a foolish answer in class. Or it may be the heavily edited paper that comes back to you on your first legal writing assignment—especially a shock because your prior teachers assured you all through high school and college that you write like a dream. Or it may be a disappointing set of examination grades. To Derek Bok, the Harvard Law School student who became dean of that school and then president of the university, it was his grades on midyear practice exams: "I was sure I would flunk out."

You will have to work your way through episodes like these as best as your psychological resources permit. You can be assured that at some time or another, a majority of your classmates will share these feelings of inadequacy or vexation. Surely, you should not forget how your own resilience has carried you through past difficulties.

Having presented several practical therapeutic suggestions in this chapter, we offer a few parting comments and exhortations.

- Maintain your own values and goals.

- Life tends to reward effort.

- In any event, effort produces its own intrinsic reward.

- Grades are not your measure as a human being.

- Humor provides both perspective and relief.

- You can do only your best, and only you can decide what your best is.

- Life is a marathon, and early leaders are not always winners.

- Only you can decide what "winning" is—that is, only you can determine the measure of your own success.

We hope you have a rewarding, and even enjoyable, three years.

*

17

Lawyers Reflect on Law School

What do successful lawyers remember as the lessons they learned in law school that have proved most useful in practice? We offer here a collection of comments by a group of lawyers who we have known as students, alumni, and co-workers in professional activities.

General Advice on Law School

Law school taught me to read, think and reason in a new and disciplined way. I quickly learned that resolving a legal problem by a superficial—or even a careful—reading of a statute or a case probably will just not work. The case or statute must be read in context of other cases. Are some of the cases conflicting? The differences between the case facts and those involving your problem must be considered. How do you fill in the blanks in the law? That is, what are the arguments you can make to create new precedent to resolve the problem when the law is not settled? How would you counter the argument of an opponent in this situation?

I methodically applied this type of legal analysis in law school. And I still use it regularly in my professional (and non-professional) life.

— Judge Marvin E. Aspen, United States District Court, Northern District of Illinois.

Most law students–and many young lawyers–entertain a paralyzing fear that anything that they write or say is likely to make them look foolish because of gaps in their knowledge. They realize that vast amounts of material on any given assignment remain to be discovered no matter how much time and effort they devote to mastering the subject. . . .

It is true, of course, that there is always more to read and more to learn, regardless of one's expertise and experience. . . . While there are obvious limits to the depth of understanding one can achieve quickly, it was a revelation to me that a significant degree of mastery could be achieved. What became clear to me as a law student, and remains true today after three decades of lawyering, is that the very indeterminacy that seems so frustrating to the law student wanting to know the "right answer" accounts for one of the strengths of the law, yielding a capacity for growth and change that enables new perspectives and creativity to devise new answers, previously unimagined. . . . Rather than worry about a failure to consider certain doctrines or cases, the incipient lawyer can assemble the law and facts in new and intriguing ways that exemplifies the real work of the profession.

— Robert S. Peck, President, Center for Constitutional Litigation.

As much as lawyers like to sit around complaining that law school is not "practical" enough and bears little relation to the practice of law, I think it plays a critical role in preparing you for practice. One of my partners . . . summed it up best for me: You leave law school like an athlete who has spent 3 years in training, getting into the best physical condition you can. You just have no idea what sport you will be playing until you start practicing.

— Mary V. Carroll, Akerman Senterfitt, Miami, Florida, practice in mergers and acquisitions, private equity and venture capital.

The moral of the story is this: talk in class. Raise your hand. Engage. Don't be afraid of being labeled a "Gunner." Sure, you can sit in the back and try not to be noticed and do well enough to graduate with a J.D., but if you do that you will have missed out on the most valuable training law school has to offer.

— Elizabeth Olson, Assistant United States Attorney, District of Nevada.

My law school education included an analysis and overview of numerous major areas of law, which illuminated the fundamental principles, values and ideals of our legal system, which have been invaluable, as well as inspirational in my legal career.

And, I should never forget that this wonderful education was presented to me by law professors whose personalities, knowledge and wisdom have contributed immeasurably to my life and my career.

— Gerald Wetherington, Wetherington, Klein & Hubbart, Miami Florida; Formerly Chief Judge, 11th Judicial Circuit of Florida.

A Critical Perspective

The short answer is that law school (as it was in the 60's) has provided very little, if anything, that has been of use to me in my day-to-day trial practice. Indeed, it took me a long time to recover from the obstacles to effective trial practice that law school put in my path. Law school tends to punish creativity and interpersonal skills. It rewards argumentativeness and aggression. It squeezes whatever poetry you may have had out of you. It has a profound dehumanizing effect.

I suppose the only useful thing I learned in school was that law is not an immutable science, governed by fixed principles, and that cases and statutes can be made to "mean" pretty much whatever one wants them to. A corollary to this is that there are at least two—and usually more—sides to every controversy. I guess I also learned that if you can't explain it using simple terminology in a simple sentence or two, you don't know it, and are not ready to talk about it publicly.

— Alex Bell, trial practice, Lynchburg, Virginia

Use of Socratic Method

I learned a lot about being able to respond to the give and take of the Socratic method in most of my first-year courses and those skills really have held up over 125 plus oral arguments in federal appellate arguments. The processes are not that dissimilar and the rigor of the law school approach was extremely valuable.

— Carter Phillips, Managing partner, Washington D.C. office of Sidley Austin

The "Socratic Method" in law school, while often uncomfortable in the moment, is invaluable training for lawyers. When you are engaging with a professor and have made your argument on a legal issue, the professor throws curve balls at you, for example by suggesting unintended consequences of your position, and requiring you to either explain why the professor's prediction is wrong (or why it isn't as dire as the professor supposes), or to adjust your thinking and refine your argument to accommodate the new concern. When you are in practice, whether as a transactional attorney negotiating a contract, a trial lawyer cross-examining a witness, or (as in my case) an appellate lawyer writing briefs and arguing in the court of appeals, you will need this skill more than you will need any particular bit of substantive law you learned in law school.

— Elizabeth Olson

If I had to identify one thing that I learned in law school that has been the most useful to me in the practice of law, it would be that there are no shortcuts for being prepared. I didn't like the "Socratic method" but one thing that it drilled into me was the importance of preparation and that has paid many dividends over the years. Preparation of course is not just identifying the issue and the proper outcome but consideration of the counter arguments and the reasons why they are wrong (in the final analysis). It was embarrassing in law school when called upon and I didn't have the answer or, worse, I thought I had the answer only to find out that there was something that I had failed to take into account. Of course the consequences in law school were nowhere comparable to the consequences of being unprepared in real life.

— Larry Stewart, Stewart, Tilghman, Fox & Bianchi, Miami, Florida, practice in personal injury, former President of Association of Trial Lawyers of America.

Legal Reasoning

The most important parts of [law school] training were adopting the basic mode of legal thinking and learning a complex set of legal rules in a variety of subject areas. The discipline of legal reasoning, a specific mode of logical, critical thinking by which any issue is broken into component facts, assumptions and conclusions, analyzed and then argued, was drilled into us in law school. That discipline has been at the core of a wide variety of legal work over the course of my career; it has been less appreciated at home.

— Thomas McCandlish, Chair of McCandlish Holton, Richmond, Va., practice in health law, international trade, and government regulation.

Law school teaches you how to approach a legal problem, attack it, research it, and solve it, to the extent solvable. This is the groundwork for whatever type of law you intend to practice. As a corporate lawyer, I am not engaged in a typical practice, yet I still use daily the principles and approaches I learned in law school.... The purpose of law school in my mind is to understand the process of legal reasoning so you can apply it to whatever legal problem you need to solve.

— Mary V. Carroll

Quite unlike high school trigonometry, whose formulas I painstakingly memorized but have yet to use in my adult life, it is not for nothing that law school requires us to spend hours reading cases whose facts are similar, but not quite the same, to discern the outer limits of a legal precept....

— Kelly Begg Lawrence, Assistant United States Attorney, Boston.

Law school taught me a totally new way of thinking, which was centered on extrapolating legal principles, rules and theories from issues arising in actual cases involving conflicts between real people or legal entities in discrete factual situations. This method of legal analysis and reasoning principally employed Socratic questioning designed to distill the rational and just principles and rules of law, which should govern the proper resolution of the disputes involved.

— **Gerald Wetherington**

Argument

I learned to make an argument, defend that argument "on my feet," and respond directly both to challenges to my argument and to counter-arguments. In practice, you cannot make a convincing legal argument without fully understanding, and directly confronting, the strongest counter-arguments.

— **Elizabeth Olson**

[P]erhaps more than anything else I learned in law school, I found that one could grasp the significance and even the previously unrealized interplay of extraordinarily complex rules, statutory language, legal doctrine, and judicial and scholarly gloss in relatively short compass—at least sufficiently well to assemble it into a thoughtful, coherent argument.

— **Robert Peck**

Defining the Issue/Maintaining a Sense of Relevancy

The most useful thing I gained from law school was the ability ... to define the issue ... I mean the ability to distill what is at stake, to ignore the irrelevant, and to articulate to one's self or to one's audience the pertinent terms of the debate.

— **Matthew Burke, Assistant United States Attorney, Chicago.**

Law school taught me the importance of not having one's mouth in gear before the brain has been engaged, a lesson that I have tried to remember over the years. It has always amazed me how many people feel compelled to speak when they really do not have a cogent thought to offer. I think the key to effective advocacy is knowing what you need to say and then limiting your comments to the point at issue. People tend to think that those who speak the longest will win the point and they forget (or perhaps they never knew) that the most effective speeches in history have been very short—"Four score and seven years ago....."; "I have a dream..."; "Ask not what you can do for your country...."

— **Larry Stewart**

I came to law school from the studying and teaching of Philosophy wherein I was tested, orally and by written examination, to dilate upon a philosopher's or philosophical school's ideas or doctrines—to evidence my understanding thereof and ability to formulate arguments for and against their validity or reasonableness. My law school study oriented me to attune myself more narrowly to ascertained "facts" and the relationship of those "facts" to applicable law in the resolution of what purported to be the problem(s) before me.

— **Stephen Slepin, Slepin & Slepin, Tallahassee, Florida, practice in workers' compensation, worker safety, manpower issues, and appellate work.**

In trial practice, one quickly learns that—contrary to the lessons in law school—one ignores Occam's razor at one's peril, and mastery of the facts in any dispute almost always trumps mastery of the law. And it really is better to be lucky than to be good.

— **Alex Bell**

Professional Traits

The law school classroom is one to which students will, famously, bring quite varying degrees of preparation. "I am not prepared ..." But from the beginning, this is the standard by which successful law practice is defined—not brilliance, not facility with words or feats of textual recall, but preparation.

Trial lawyers will demonstrate it by immersion in a record, appellate lawyers by obsessive attention to the uses and misuses of cited case law, and all lawyers by the close reading of texts, the hard work of repeated re-writing and, yes, diligent proof-reading. Here, in just plain, committed endeavor and thoroughness, emerges the difference between excellence in practice and routine, passing-grade application of learned craft. It is immediately obvious which of these alternatives a client has received in return for the fee paid.

The lasting beneficial effect of good law school education is the drilling of habits of preparation. The truly fine lawyer is the one who spares nothing in preparation. Successful law practice is defined by preparation.

And, while not necessarily advertised in these terms, preparation is what really entitles lawyers to go by the name of "professional." Professionalism is, at heart, the way that a certain training is used, the way that a craft is practiced: it is manifested in the quality of preparation.

It may not seem so in those years of classes, when the unprepared student is passed over and the better prepared colleague answers in his place. But to admit "I am not prepared . . ."—to slight preparation—is unthinkable in first-rate law practice, and it means, also, that your client is in trouble or ill-served. If law school education should leave students with any lesson for the length of a career, it is this.

— **Robert Bauer, chair, Political Law Group, partner, Perkins Coie, Washington, D.C.**

Every sentence and every word you use professionally have to mean something, and you have to be prepared to back them up . . . There is no room for woolly thinking. Precision is critical both in reading the underlying materials and in expression.

— **D. Brock Hornby, Chief Judge, United States District Court, District of Maine**

I learned many things in law school, but one lesson in particular remains relevant to my day-to-day practice: pay attention to detail. In law school, barely perceptible differences in a fact pattern can tarnish an exam answer, and a misplaced comma can mar an otherwise perfect footnote citation, but neither outcome is catastrophic, even for a law student. But in professional practice, failure to attend to details, such as getting the facts exactly right and submitting error-free papers to the court, can result in lost credibility, or worse, lost cases.

— **Kelly Begg Lawrence**

Personal Growth

[L]aw school taught me the importance of focus, energy, commitment, judgment (often, merely the application of common sense) and character (in no particular order of importance) in pursuing my professional career (indeed, in pursuing my life).

These latter traits were taught by example—mostly through interaction with professors (often outside the classroom) who exhibited these characteristics in their lives (both professional and personal). I am eternally grateful for those lessons. They were critical to both my career as a litigator and to my efforts in firm leadership and management.

— Duane C. Quaini, former chairman, Sonnenschein Nath & Rosenthal.

The most useful lessons I learned in law school are ... Manage anxiety, or it will manage you ... A lawyer's job is to make the unforeseeable seeable ... Identify your assumptions and the other side's assumptions.

— Deborah Heilizer, Sutherland Asbill & Brennan, practice in securities regulation.

One can learn much collaboratively from colleagues, learning that goes far beyond the texts and the professor ... Friendships with colleagues matter, are rewarding personally and professionally, and can be lifelong.

— D. Brock Hornby

*

Glossary

The definitions in this glossary are often simplified. We intend them to be helpful guides to understanding terms that we have found are among the most puzzling to first-year students.

Affidavit: A written statement of facts relevant to an issue in a lawsuit, sworn to by the person preparing it, who is known as the affiant.

Alternative dispute resolution (ADR): Methods of solving legal disputes without going to court for a trial. ADR typically uses hearings conducted by agreed-upon third parties. Two frequently used means of ADR are arbitration and mediation.

Answer: A reply to allegations leveled against someone in a complaint. In litigation, an answer is a "responsive pleading." A person who has been sued files with the court an answer to the complaint that initiated the lawsuit.

Appeal: In litigation, the process of a review by a higher court of the decision of a lower court.

Appellant: A party to litigation who brings an appeal. An appellant challenges the decision of one court by appealing to a higher court.

Appellate court: A court of appeals, that is, a court where a party to litigation seeks review of, or appeals, the decision of a lower court.

Appellee: The party to litigation against whom the appellant brings an appeal. The appellee won in the lower court.

Arbitration: A formal process of resolving a dispute without going to court. The parties bring the dispute to a third party trained as an arbitrator, or to a panel of arbitrators. The arbitrator has the authority to make a decision that binds the disputing parties.

Arguendo: Literally, "in the course of an argument." A statement assumed to be true, but only for the sake of argument. Often used in this way: "Assuming arguendo that . . ."

Bench trial: A trial held before a judge without a jury.

Binding precedent: In case law, a case that provides a rule or rules that other courts, for example, lower courts in that jurisdiction, must follow. An often-used expression is that a rule is binding on the court.

Blackletter law: A specific legal rule, usually a fundamental rule.

Brief:

  a) A case brief: a summary of a case that law students write to prepare for class.

  b) Appellate brief: a document that each party to an appeal files with the court. The brief explains the case and offers arguments to persuade the court to decide for the party whose brief it is.

  c) Trial brief: a persuasive document that each party may submit to a trial court at different stages of a trial.

Casebook: A coursebook for your law classes. Casebooks are edited collections of cases relevant to the particular subject matter of a class.

Citations: Precise references, like those used in footnotes, to the sources of authority that support statements, like statements of law, and quotations. Citations tell readers where to find the source.

Civil law:

  a) The branch of law that deals with private rights, that is, the rights that private individuals claim that others have violated. Civil law in this sense contrasts with criminal law, which deals with alleged wrongs prosecuted on behalf of the public.

  b) A country's legal system in which all law is based on comprehensive codes enacted by a legislature and the courts function to interpret the codes. Modern civil law systems are historically based on the Napoleonic Codes, with more ancient antecedents in the codes of ancient Rome.

Code: A collection of statutes that is organized by specific topics, for example, a criminal code.

Common law:

a) Law that initially comes from court decisions, that is, judge-made law.

b) Common law system: By contrast with a civil law system, in a common law system law comes from court decisions as well as from a legislature.

c) Historically: The system of law that arose from the English common law courts.

A common law action is litigation brought under the common law rather than under a statute.

Concurring opinion: An opinion written by a judge who agrees with the majority decision but does so for reasons different from the majority's.

Coursebooks: Books used as the basis for law school classes, often also called "casebooks." The term "coursebook" is more inclusive, because it encompasses teaching materials that are different from cases.

Defendant: A party who is sued in a civil suit by another party or prosecuted by the state in a criminal action.

Deposition: An oral examination of a party to litigation or a potential witness that an attorney conducts out of court and before a trial, used to acquire information about the case.

Dicta: Statements that a court makes in its opinion that are not legally binding because they are not essential to the decision in that case.

Dictum: Singular of dicta.

Discovery: Procedures by which parties to a lawsuit gather information and learn about evidence before the trial. Frequently used discovery methods are depositions and interrogatories.

Dissenting opinion: An opinion written by a judge that disagrees with the outcome of the majority's decision.

Diversity jurisdiction: The constitutional authority of federal courts to hear cases involving state law if the parties to the litigation are from different states ("diverse citizenship").

Equity:

    a) Generally: Fairness

    b) Equitable remedies: A type of remedy that does not involve money damages but instead involves a court order to a defendant to do or to stop doing a particular act or acts. An often-used equitable remedy is an injunction.

    c) Historically: A system of law developed by the English chancery courts, which arose to give relief where no relief was available from the common law courts. In this meaning, equity was distinguished from law.

Federal Rules of Civil Procedure: A body of rules that govern the procedures used in the federal courts in civil suits.

Floodgates: As used in the law, the expression "open the flood-gates" means that a particular decision will lead to an undesirable volume of litigation that will clog the courts.

Holding: The authoritative part of a court's opinion deciding the issue or issues in a case.

Hornbook: A text written for law students that summarizes and explains a particular area of law.

Hypothetical: Often used in law classes, a made-up factual situation devised to explore how a particular rule of law applies.

Infra: Latin for below or under. In legal text, often used to mean that a topic will be discussed later in the text, as in "see discussion of possession, infra at page 10."

Injunction: A court's order that a defendant do something or stop doing something. An equitable remedy.

Instant case: A phrase that refers to the case at issue, rather than prior or precedent cases. "In the instant case, however, the defendant acted intentionally."

Inter alia: Latin for "among other things": "This case is about, inter alia, the parties' property settlement."

Interrogatories: Written questions by which one party to litigation elicits information from the other party. Interrogatories are a pre-trial discovery procedure.

Jurisdiction: The authority of a court to decide cases, sometimes determined by the subject matter of a case and sometimes by the geographical area over which the court has authority, and sometimes by both.

Jurisprudence:

a) The philosophy of law.

b) A body of law, e.g., "New Jersey jurisprudence," or "this state's jurisprudence on the subject of contracts."

Law review: A scholarly journal about law. Most law reviews are published by law schools, and usually are edited by law students. Law reviews consist of articles of various lengths, usually designated as articles, notes, or comments, written by faculty, practicing attorneys, and students.

Litigant: A person who is a party to a lawsuit.

Mediation: A typically informal process for resolving disputes; often not binding on the parties.

Overruling:

a) A court's decision that it will no longer follow its rule from a prior case.

b) A trial judge's ruling that rejects an attorney's objections in court.

Petitioner: A party who originates a lawsuit or an appeal by means of a petition. In an appellate proceeding, a petitioner is usually the appellant.

Plaintiff: A party that initiates a lawsuit by filing a complaint with a court.

Pleading: A fundamental litigation document that a party files with a court, such as a complaint or an answer.

Precedent: A prior decision that becomes an authority that binds courts in later similar cases.

Punitive damages: Extra damages awarded to the plaintiff in a lawsuit, usually for the purpose of punishing the defendant's especially culpable conduct.

Respondent: The party defending a suit against a petitioner. In an appellate proceeding, a respondent is usually the appellee.

Restatement of the Law: A compilation of rules and comments concerning an area of law published by the American Law Institute, a private body of lawyers. Examples are the Restatement of Contracts and the Restatement of Torts.

Reversal: An appellate court decision to set aside the decision of a lower court because the lower court wrongly decided the case.

Settlement: A resolution of a lawsuit by the parties that avoids a trial, or, if a trial has begun, terminates it before a final judgment.

Slippery slope: Lawyers use this term to identify a line of argument designed to show that an apparently reasonable legal principle is open to a progressive series of applications that become undesirable and perhaps horrendous.

Socratic method: In law school, a technique used mainly to teach first-year classes, principally involving questions and hypotheticals rather than lecture.

Stare decisis: Latin for "to abide by decided cases," meaning that courts must follow the holdings of prior cases in that jurisdiction, and decide similar cases in the same way as the prior decisions.

Statute: A law enacted by a legislature, for example, by Congress.

Supra: Latin for above. Used in legal text to mean that a topic was discussed earlier, as in "see discussion of possession, supra at page 10."

Tort: A civil wrong, distinguished from breaches of contract in civil litigation and also distinguished from crimes.

Uniform Laws: Codes of statutes in particular areas of law that are prepared by a private body, the National Conference of Commissioners on Uniform State Laws. A state legislature must enact a uniform law for it to gain any legal effect. A particularly important uniform law in first-year law study is the Uniform Commercial Code.

†